WILLIAM WILBUR MILLER BARBOUR

William Wilbur Miller Barbour

A Faith Full Witness for Human Rights

JEAN-PAUL BENOWITZ

First Printing, 2026
ISBN: 979-8-9948938-2-1
All proceeds from the sale of this book support the Elizabethtown College
Summer Enrichment Grants offered by the Office of Prestigious Scholarships
and Fellowships. These grants help students pursue meaningful summer opportunities such as faculty-mentored research, internships, conference participation, specialized training programs, or study-related travel. Through these
experiences, recipients enrich their academic development and strengthen
their preparation for nationally competitive scholarships and fellowships,
empowering them to pursue their calling, vocation, and purposeful life's
work while drawing inspiration from the life and legacy of W. Miller Barbour.

Printed in the United States of America

A Companion Documentary Film
The Prospect for Freedom: W. Miller Barbour's Human Rights Journey (2025)
Produced, Directed, Written, Edited, and Designed by Jean-Paul Benowitz
Screened publicly at multiple venues, 2025–2026
Sponsored and hosted by: Governor's Advisory Commission on African
American Affairs, Office of Governor Josh Shapiro; Greater Harrisburg Area
NAACP; Popel Shaw Center for Race and Ethnicity, Dickinson College; Penn-
sylvania Chautauqua
Official Selection, Hollywood International Indie Film Festival (December
2026)

Santos Books is committed to the sacredness of every person's story and to
supporting authors in discovering and telling those stories with honesty and
care. This volume embodies the Santos Books mission in a particular and personal way: the author's story and his subject's story are inseparable. In recovering a forgotten civil rights leader, the author discovered how he and
Barbour were formed by the same Anabaptist institutional tradition, separated by nearly a century, and the convergence gives this biography an intimacy no purely scholarly distance could produce.

CONTENTS

Dedicated to the memory of

Albert N. Keim (1935–2008)
Professor of History and Academic Dean Emeritus
Eastern Mennonite University

For other foundation can no man lay than which is laid,
which is Jesus Christ.

1 Corinthians 3:11

Preface

For years, a photograph hung on the wall of the Jay's Nest, named for the college's Blue Jay mascot, the snack shop tucked inside the Baugher Student Center at Elizabethtown College where generations of students and their faculty mentors gathered between classes for coffee and conversation. The picture showed the Brutal Thirteen, the college's clandestine 1928 football squad, posed in the informal arrangement of students who knew they were doing something their institution had not officially sanctioned. The image was unremarkable in most respects: a small group of athletes squinting into the autumn light of a Lancaster County afternoon.

Yet look closer, and the photograph begins to tell a richer story. There they stood, earnest and full of purpose, arranged with deliberate care speaking volumes about who they were and what they believed. A row of them upright, shoulders squared, staring into the camera with the quiet, unself-conscious dignity people of this era so naturally possessed. And in front of them, a second row, kneeling, as though in some informal ceremony of sport and fellowship no administration decree could quite extinguish.

Their uniforms, such as they were, had been assembled more from determination than from any athletic budget. Makeshift, hastily conceived, yet worn with unmistakable conviction. These were not the polished, well-outfitted squads of the great eastern universities. These were students who had made do, and in the making do, had made something rather remarkable.

And there, rising just behind them against the Lancaster County sky, was the roofline of Alpha Hall, a building representing, in this moment, something of a profound contradiction. For it was from within those very walls the administration had issued its proclamation, duly sanctioned by the board of trustees, forbidding the very thing these students had gathered to celebrate. The goalpost, primitive, hastily erected, leaning ever so slightly as if uncertain of its own legitimacy, stood as their quiet, defiant answer.

But one detail made it quietly extraordinary. Among the players stood a single African American student, his presence on the squad was as much a breach of the prevailing athletic color lines of Lancaster County as any event in the college's early history.

It was, in its way, a thoroughly American standoff. And yet, looked at another way, it was something older and more deeply rooted than any American tradition of rebellion. The Anabaptist founders of Elizabethtown had always understood themselves as a separate and intentional community, neither conformed to the world nor entirely of it. To stand apart, to live by a different set of convictions, to build something meaningful outside the boundaries others had drawn, this was not defiance for its own sake. It was, in the oldest sense of the college's heritage, a faithful expression of its founding spirit. These students, in their makeshift uniforms beside their improbable goalpost, were perhaps more faithful to the spirit of their institution than the board of trustees sitting in judgment of them ever quite realized. And someone, on the autumn afternoon of 1928, had the presence of mind to take a picture.

Peter DePuydt passed this photograph nearly every day. DePuydt was the college's librarian and archivist, the keeper of the institutional memory housed in the Brethren Heritage Room of the High Library, a man who had spent decades in the patient work of assembling and preserving the documentary record of Elizabethtown College's more than a century of existence. He knew the photograph. He knew its approximate date. He knew the team's informal designation and its single season of play. What he did not know, and what he found himself wondering each time he passed the image, was the identity of the lone African American player in the frame. The question would not leave him. Who was this young man? Where had he come from? What had his presence on the playing field meant, in a county and a period when such presence was rare enough to be historically significant? And what had become of him?

The answer to those questions, pursued through the college's archival holdings, its yearbook collections, its student newspaper runs, and the documentary databases connecting Elizabethtown's records to the broader world of twentieth-century American civil rights history, led to a name: William Wilbur Miller Barbour, Class of 1932.

When the archival record DePuydt had so carefully assembled was placed before me, I recognized immediately what it represented and what it demanded. More than three decades of teaching history within these same walls, of living with the institution and the region whose history I had made my life's work, had prepared me for precisely this kind of pursuit. I could not walk away from it.

What followed was several years of deepening research, and what the research revealed was a life of genuine historical significance which had been allowed to disappear from the record with a thoroughness Barbour's contributions did not justify and his communities did not deserve. The trail led from a Lancaster County college campus outward into the broader currents of twentieth-century American civil rights history, and the further it led, the clearer it became how much had been lost and how much remained to be recovered. This book is the result of the pursuit. It began with a photograph on a snack shop wall and DePuydt's persistent question, and it ends with the recovery of William Wilbur Miller Barbour, a civil rights leader whose story illuminates dimensions of the American freedom struggle which the standard accounts have left in shadow.

What began as a question about a face in a photograph became, in time, one of the most important questions a biographer can ask about the past: not merely who was this person, but what did his life cost him, what did it build, and what does it ask of us? William Wilbur Miller Barbour left no autobiography, no collection of private letters, no public monument with his name on it. He left instead the harder thing: a career of twenty-five years spent in the spaces between the law's promise and American life's reality, doing the work the law could not do, building the conditions for genuine human community in cities where the word community was used to describe what racial exclusion had produced and preserved. He died at forty-nine, in Los Angeles, in March 1957. He had been working all week. He was still working when his heart gave out. The movement he had been building toward since his graduation from Elizabethtown College in 1932 would culminate, in the Civil Rights Act of 1964, the Voting Rights Act of 1965, and the Fair Housing Act of 1968, in legislation he did not live to see signed. He was a builder of foundations. He never saw the structure rise.

In 2026, the United States marks two hundred and fifty years since the Declaration of Independence. The celebrations will be grand and the flags will be numerous. But there is another story worth telling alongside the familiar one, a quieter story, rooted in the same Lancaster County soil, among people who were present at the founding and who understood, from the deepest reserves of their tradition, what it meant to labor for something larger than oneself and never live to see it finished.

In the years just before the Revolution, as tensions between the colonies and the Crown were building toward the inevitable, the Mennonite communities of Lancaster County found themselves in a familiar and uncomfortable position. They had been here before, in a manner of speaking. Their ancestors had faced the armies and the magistrates of Europe for two centuries, and they had developed, out of long and costly experience, a settled conviction about violence and the state. They would not fight. They would not take up arms. And they needed their children to understand why.

It was to address precisely this need, in 1745, Mennonite leaders in Pennsylvania wrote to their counterparts in Amsterdam requesting help translating and printing a complete German edition of the *Martyrs Mirror*. The book had first appeared in Dutch in 1660, compiled by the Mennonite elder Thieleman van Braght from the testimonies of Christian martyrs across the sixteenth century, men and women executed for insisting on adult baptism, on the authority of scripture over the authority of the state, and on the incompatibility of the Kingdom of God with the kingdoms of the world. It ran to 1,512 pages. It contained 104 copper etchings by the artist Jan Luyken, depicting with graphic precision the persecution and execution of martyred apostles and Anabaptists. It was not easy reading. It was not meant to be.

The Mennonites in Pennsylvania needed their members, and especially their young people, to read these stories in a language they could actually understand. The Dutch editions brought over from Europe in the late 1600s were of limited use to a community now speaking German and Pennsylvania German in their homes and meetinghouses. The French and Indian War had made the urgency concrete. The Pennsylvania Colonial Assembly had refused Anabaptist appeals for military exemption on religious grounds. The next war, everyone could sense, was coming. The community needed to be ready.

The Amsterdam Mennonites advised the Pennsylvania community to undertake the project on their own. Mennonite leaders turned to Conrad Beissel at the Ephrata Cloister, on the banks of the Cocalico Creek, twelve miles north of what would one day become Elizabethtown. The Ephrata Cloister and the Church of the Brethren were not the same community, but they were kin. Both grew from the same early eighteenth century German Pietist and Anabaptist revival, sharing common roots in conviction, practice, and heritage. Beissel had broken away from the early Brethren movement in 1728 to establish his own Seventh Day community at Ephrata, but the two branches remained part of the same larger theological family, the very family whose descendants would one day build Elizabethtown College.

The Mennonites could not have chosen a better partner for the work. Beissel accepted. Peter Miller, a German Pietist of extraordinary gifts trained at the University of Heidelberg, took up the work of translation. It consumed three years of his life. When the translation was finished, Beissel assigned fifteen men to produce the book, nine in the print shop and six in the paper mill. They worked from 1748 to 1749, and when they were done, they had created the largest book ever published in colonial America.

On the title page of this American edition appeared the same image readers of the 1660 Dutch edition would have recognized. A divine arm extends a laurel wreath from the heavens toward a man digging in the ground outside a village. Above the image, in Latin: "Fac et Spera." "Do and Hope." The phrase drawn from the thirty-seventh Psalm: "Trust in the Lord and do good; so you will dwell in the land, and enjoy security." At Ephrata, the translators did not leave the Latin on the page. They rendered it into the vernacular of their own community: "Arbeite und Hoffe." "Work and Hope."

Then the Revolution came. And soldiers confiscated copies of the *Martyrs Mirror* and used its pages for musket wadding. The book the Anabaptist community had produced as a testimony against violence was being literally consumed by the violence it had documented. Some soldiers, fearing divine punishment for desecrating a religious text, hid copies and returned them to the Ephrata Cloister. The irony was not lost on the conscientious objectors of Lancaster County. If anything, it confirmed what the book had been trying to say all along. The kingdoms of the world devour. The Kingdom of God endures. "Work and Hope."

Those two words proved to have a long life. They moved through the Anabaptist communities of Lancaster County across the following two centuries like a current running beneath the surface of daily life, surfacing in unexpected places, each time in a different voice but always in the same key. The Amish preserved the conviction in a nineteenth century song: "Schaffet, schaffet, Menschenkinder / Schaffet eure Seligkeit," meaning "Work, work, children of men / work for your salvation." The musicologist Joseph W. Yoder, who had grown up Amish and been educated at colleges established by the Church of the Brethren, gave it voice again in his poem Noch Denke: "Mir misse all angeh un schaffe / Und hoffe fur en gutes Gluck," meaning "We must all go on and work / and hope for the best of luck."

"Work and Hope" was not, in the Anabaptist understanding, a counsel of passive resignation. It was a theology of vocation. It described the life of a person who understood the relationship between faith and labor, who knew the work was real and the vindication was real, but who also knew the vindication almost certainly would not arrive on any schedule the worker could predict or control. You worked because the work was right. You hoped because the outcome belonged to God. The evidence of the relationship was not found in the privacy of one's devotional life but in the public work of justice and community, in what one actually did, in the world as it actually was, for the people who actually needed it.

Barbour learned, in ways no classroom could teach, what it meant to labor against odds for something larger than oneself. He built foundations. He laid groundwork. He worked in the soil of human rights and human dignity at a moment when the harvest was nowhere in sight, when the arc of history showed no visible signs of bending in the direction anyone who cared about justice might have wished. He did not live to see what rose from what he planted.

But he worked. And he hoped. And in the Anabaptist grammar of Lancaster County, in the theological vocabulary forged in the print shop of the Ephrata Cloister and carried forward across two and a half centuries of witness, there is no better way to describe a life well lived than exactly those two words.

This biography is published in the year the United States marks its Semiquincentennial, the 250th anniversary of the Declaration of Independence. All men are created equal. Endowed by their Creator with certain inalienable rights. Americans have been arguing about what those words mean, and who they include, for two and a half centuries. Barbour did not argue. He worked.

He brought to the work a dual formation few men of his generation could claim. The Anabaptist and Pietist tradition of the Church of the Brethren had pressed into him, during his years as a student at Elizabethtown College, a mandate both institutional and theological. The prophetic tradition of the African Methodist Episcopal

Church had formed him from childhood in a conviction equally deep and equally demanding: racial hierarchy was incompatible with the Gospel. These two traditions arose from entirely different histories and wholly distinct experiences of American life. In Barbour they converged on a single claim. The Declaration meant what it said. The Gospel demanded its fulfillment. The gap between democratic promise and democratic practice was not a fact to be accommodated but a civic failure to be opposed, by specific, costly, theologically grounded work, in specific cities, in institutional settings, for as long as it took.

He spent twenty-five years opposing it. At the Semiquincentennial, it remains opposed. His story belongs to this moment.

Barbour himself named what he was doing, in phrases drawn from different vocabularies, each of which turns out to be the same claim. His college gave him a motto, "Make Jesus King," not as a sentiment but as an institutional program, a mandate to build into the social arrangements of the world the values of the Kingdom of God. The Anabaptist tradition behind the motto had crystallized the same claim, two centuries earlier, into two German words on the title page of the *Martyrs Mirror*. The thread running from Ephrata's press to Elizabethtown's campus was not incidental. It was the whole fabric. "Work and Hope." "Make Jesus King."

This biography's own title names what those two phrases together produced in a single life: a faith full witness. Not merely faithful in the sense of diligence or reliability, though Barbour was both, but full of faith in the older and deeper sense, a life ordered and animated from its very center by the conviction of human dignity the Kingdom of God demands. He worked because he believed. He hoped persistently when the work produced no visible harvest. And he bore witness publicly, at considerable personal cost, to a vision of American life his country had not yet found the courage to realize. Three phrases. One conviction. One life.

There is one further distinction worth pausing on. In more than two decades of speeches, reports, correspondence, and public testimony, Barbour never once used the words civil rights. Not once. The phrase does not appear in his writing. What appears instead, consistently and deliberately, is another phrase entirely: human rights. The distinction was not semantic. It was theological, philosophical, and strategic. Civil rights, in the vocabulary of his time, described what the law owed American citizens. Human rights described what God owed every person born into the world. Barbour was not interested in the narrower claim when the larger one was available. He positioned himself, long before the international human rights framework acquired its present form, as a human rights activist, insisting the struggle was not a domestic legal argument but a universal moral one. This biography calls him a civil rights leader because history has built its categories around the movement he helped make possible. But the reader should know he would have chosen different words. He usually did.

Jean-Paul Benowitz
    Elizabethtown College
    Elizabethtown, Pennsylvania
    Thursday 19 March 2026

ACKNOWLEDGMENTS

This work would not exist without the generosity, wisdom, and encouragement of many remarkable people and institutions. To each of them, I owe a profound debt of gratitude.

I am deeply grateful to Ava Barton, Elizabethtown College Honors Stamps Scholar, Class of 2027; Amy L. Benowitz, Elizabethtown College Office Manager and International Recruitment Assistant in the Office of Admissions; Teresa Candori, National Urban League Senior Director of Media Relations; Peter DePuydt, Elizabethtown College Retired Librarian, High Library Brethren Heritage Room; Menika Dirkson, Morgan State University Associate Professor of History; Oya Dursun Ozkanca, College Professor of International Studies (Endowed Chair), Professor of Political Science, Director of the Honors Program, and Director of the International Studies Minor; Rachel Grove Rohrbaugh, Elizabethtown College High Library Archivist, Earl H. and Anita F. Hess Archives; 'Lois K. Herr, daughter of Ira Herr, Elizabethtown College Class of 1962, Retired Director of Marketing and Public Affairs; Susan Schlosser Hostetter, granddaughter of Ralph W. Schlosser, Juniata College Class of 1977; Gerald Huesken Jr., Elizabethtown Area High School Social Studies Teacher; Mechelle Johnson-Reeves, Elizabethtown College Honors Stamps Scholar, Class of 2028; Conrad Kanagy, Professor of Sociology Emeritus; J. Kenneth Kreider, Elizabethtown College Class of 1961, Professor of History Emeritus; Jodi Lancaster, Associate Provost for Student Learning and Dean of Faculty, Dean of the School of Sciences, and Professor of Biology; Luke D. Mackey, Elizabethtown College Class of 2017 and 2018, Assistant Director of the Honors Program; Deborah Neil, granddaughter of W. Miller Barbour; Paul Neil, great-grandson of W. Miller Barbour; Richard Newton, University of Alabama Associate Professor and Undergraduate Director of Religious Studies; Steven M. Nolt, Elizabethtown College Professor of History and Anabaptist Studies, Director of the Young Center for Anabaptist and Pietist Studies, and Senior Scholar at the Young Center, Elizabethtown College; Betty Rider, President of Elizabethtown College and Professor of Psychology; Eric J. Schubert, Elizabethtown College Class of 2023; Abigail B. Sholes, Elizabethtown College Honors Student, Class of 2023; Kevin Shorner-Johnson, Dean of the School of Arts and Humanities and Professor of Music; Louise Stevenson, Franklin and Marshall College Professor Emerita of History and American Studies; Carl J. Strikwerda, Elizabethtown College President, 2011–2019; Matthew Telleen, Provost and Vice President for Academic Affairs and Professor of Communication; Renee Whitby, granddaughter of W. Miller Barbour; and Jake K. Woodworth, Elizabethtown College Honors Student, Class of 2026.

The five scholars whose teaching most directly shaped this biography's interpretive frameworks are acknowledged in the Note on Sources and Method. Kenneth L. Kusmer, James W. Hilty, Richard H. Immerman, Albert N. Keim, and J. Kenneth Kreider gave me more than a bibliography; they gave me a way of standing before the past. Their influence is present in every chapter.

Sincere thanks also go to the Elizabethtown College High Library; the Elizabethtown College Earl H. and Anita F. Hess Archives; the Elizabethtown College Honors Program, sponsored by the Hershey Company; the Elizabethtown College Office of Prestigious Scholarships and Fellowships; the Elizabethtown College School of Arts and Humanities Public Heritage Studies Program; and the Elizabethtown College Summer Creative Arts and Research Program.

| 1 |

The Integrator

On May 17, 1954, William Wilbur Miller Barbour was driving east across the Mojave Desert when the radio bulletin broke through the static of the open road. Chief Justice Earl Warren had just delivered the Supreme Court's unanimous decision in Brown v. Board of Education of Topeka. Segregation in the public schools was unconstitutional. The legal death knell of the entire system of American apartheid had sounded across the frequencies of the California afternoon, and Barbour, who had spent twenty-two years working toward exactly this kind of legal transformation, could not contain what the moment demanded of him. "I don't mind confessing that for several moments I cried unashamedly," he wrote afterward. "As a Negro, and as a professional in race relations, I knew this decision was the death knell of the entire system of segregation. Although it applied to the public schools, its import was that segregation based on race as a way of institutional living was illegal. Then as an American citizen I was filled with pride, because this was truly one of our nation's finest hours."

He kept driving. The desert stretched in every direction, the hard blue sky of the Mojave arching over the flats as indifferent to history as it had been a thousand years before and would be a thousand years hence. And as Barbour drove, the spiritual glow the announcement had produced began, slowly, to give way to the harder question his entire professional life had been preparing him to ask. "What now?" he asked himself. "How could the changeover from segregation to mixed schools be made? Even the Supreme Court was hesitant and unsure."

He had watched, over two decades of human rights work in Philadelphia, Denver, Tucson, and Los Angeles, how law and human reality operated on different timetables and sometimes in entirely different directions. A court decision could abolish the legal structure of segregation. It could not, by itself, build the required human community integration. "Here was a delicate problem in human relations," he wrote. "The desegregator, a proper original role, seems definitely miscast in the new role of the integrator."

The integrator. Barbour had been developing this concept for years, and the Mojave Desert moment crystallized it into the sharpest formulation he had yet achieved. The integrator was not the lawyer, the judge, or the legislator who tore down the legal structure of segregation. The integrator was the person who came after, who moved into the demolished terrain and built something new: a harmonious whole out of separate parts, a community of genuine civic fellowship across the racial lines a society had spent centuries constructing and decades cementing. "For the sake of a working definition," he wrote in what would prove to be the last article he published, "I would define desegregation as the tearing down or the elimination of the legalized institutional structure of segregation. Integration is the ongoing process of creating a new harmonious whole out of the separate parts." Desegregation was a matter of policy. Integration was a matter of process. The process required something that policy could not supply: the patient, costly, morally grounded labor of the integrator, which was to say the labor of a person willing to spend a life in service of the Kingdom of God as it pressed its claims upon the social arrangements of mid-century America.

Barbour was forty-five years old when he crossed the Mojave with tears in his eyes. He had been working toward this moment for more than twenty years, since June 6, 1932, when he walked across the stage in Elizabethtown, Pennsylvania, and received his Bachelor of Arts degree from a small, church-related college whose motto had been pressed into him like a seal over four years of intellectual and spiritual formation: "Make Jesus King." He would live only three more years after the desert drive. In March 1957, nineteen days after chairing the Third Annual Winter League Ball in the Grand Ballroom of the Beverly Hilton Hotel in Beverly Hills, at which Dorothy Dandridge and Glenn Ford received the National Urban League's American Teamwork Award, Barbour died of a heart attack in Los Angeles at the age of forty-nine. His work was unfinished. His name was a stranger to most of the historians who would later construct the narrative of the movement he had served with the full force of his gifts and the whole energy of his theological conviction.

This biography recovers his life and argues for its significance. It does so at a moment when the argument is both overdue and urgent. Barbour belongs to the company of people who built the foundations of the American civil rights movement before the movement acquired its canonical shape in the mass action of the 1955 to 1965 decade. He belongs, in the precise historical and analytical sense developed by the historians who have most transformed our understanding of this era, to what Jacquelyn Dowd Hall named the Long Civil Rights Movement. In her landmark 2005 essay in the *Journal of American History*, Hall issued a challenge to the dominant narrative of the movement, the story beginning with Rosa Parks in Montgomery in December 1955 and ending, in the conventional account, with the Voting Rights Act of August 1965. This narrative, Hall argued, functioned as a "master narrative" serving contemporary political purposes rather than historical truth. It foreshortened the movement's timeline, narrowed its geography, and left out the vast majority of the people who had built it. The "classical" narrative, in Hall's formulation, "makes it hard to see, for example, how deeply the civil rights movement challenged not only racial segregation but also economic exploitation, and how much this challenge had to do with the movement's lasting power and ultimate defeat."

The movement did not begin in Montgomery in 1955. It stretched back, as Hall and the generation of historians building on her framework have demonstrated, at least to the New Deal era of the 1930s, to the labor organizing of A. Philip Randolph and the Brotherhood of Sleeping Car Porters, to the anti-lynching campaigns of Ida B. Wells and Jessie Daniel Ames, to the legal strategy being systematically developed by Charles Hamilton Houston at Howard University Law School, to the interracial peace church networks developing the nonviolent direct-action methods the movement would later deploy on a national scale. Patricia Sullivan, in *Days of Hope*, reconstructs the New Deal-era civil rights movement with comprehensiveness and scholarly richness, demonstrating how much organizing, coalition-building, and legal and political groundwork had been laid by unsung heroes. Glenda Gilmore, in *Defying Dixie*, recovers the radical roots of civil rights activism in the interwar years, tracing the networks of Black and white organizers, communists and socialists, and pacifists and Christians, building the movement's intellectual and organizational infrastructure in the years when the standard narrative imagines only quiescence.

Barbour moved through these very years, within these very networks, doing the same essential, foundational work. He began his human rights career in the 1930s, when organizing for racial equality meant confronting not only the Ku Klux Klan's violence and the New Deal's racial exclusions but also the theological silence of white Christianity on both. He carried the work forward through the Double V years of the 1940s, when the wartime paradox of fighting fascism abroad while practicing racial fascism at home was creating the political conditions for the mass movement of the following decade. He built the movement's institutional infrastructure in the postwar years in Denver and Los Angeles, using the tools of coalition politics, empirical research, and moral argument that the movement required. He died six months before Dwight David Eisenhower, a son of the Anabaptist tradition himself, raised in a family whose own roots reached into the same rivers of faith and conscience Barbour had navigated his entire life, sat down in the White House and signed the Civil Rights Act of 1957, the first such legislation the federal government had enacted in eighty-two years. Barbour had spent his career building the conditions making it possible. He did not live to see the pen touch the paper.

Barbour has been overlooked for reasons illuminating in themselves. He left no autobiography and no collected papers. His professional records are scattered across archives in Denver, Los Angeles, Philadelphia, and Elizabethtown, Pennsylvania. He worked for institutions generating records but rarely preserving personal correspondence: the National Urban League, the Mayor's Committee on Human Relations, the Colorado Committee for Civil Rights Legislation, and the World Affairs Institute. He died young, at forty-nine, before he could consolidate his legacy or attract the biographical attention age sometimes brings. Barbour worked in the interstitial spaces of the movement, the spaces between the great legal victories and the famous marches, doing the organizational, educational, and mediatory work without which the victories would have meant less and the marches would have been harder to sustain. His invisibility in the historical record is not evidence of his insignificance. It is evidence of how the record is made and what it leaves out.

Sullivan's argument about the importance of New Deal-era civil rights workers applies to Barbour with precision: he was an architect of foundations, a builder of the groundwork without which the more visible edifice could not have been constructed. Manning Marable, in *Race, Reform, and Rebellion*, analyzes the relationship between the Long Movement's earlier workers and the mass movement of the 1950s, demonstrating how the institutional, educational, and legal groundwork of the earlier decades made the later mass movement possible and shaped its character. Barbour belongs in the company of those earlier workers, alongside the labor organizers, the legal strategists, the local NAACP chapter secretaries, and the Urban League executives whose names rarely appear in the standard histories but without whom the history would not have unfolded as it did.

Two Traditions, One Life

What distinguishes Barbour's story, beyond its intrinsic human interest and its historical significance, is the theological architecture underlying his activism. He moved through the civil rights movement carrying a dual formation unusual among his contemporaries: shaped simultaneously by the Anabaptist-Pietist tradition of Elizabethtown College and the Church of the Brethren, and by the prophetic tradition of the African Methodist Episcopal Church. These two traditions arose from different historical moments, geographies, experiences of oppression, and theological emphases. Their convergence in a single human life, sustained across twenty-five years of human rights work in some of the most racially contested cities of mid-century America, is the central argument of this biography.

The years this biography covers were also the years in which the tradition-forming Barbour was being defined, argued over, and ultimately crystallized into a statement that would shape Anabaptist self-understanding for generations to come. The interwar period had pressed the Anabaptists into an uncomfortable and clarifying position. The First World War had tested their commitment to nonresistance and found it costly. The rise of National Socialism in Europe and the gathering storm of a second global conflict were testing it again, with greater urgency and higher stakes. It was precisely in this climate, on December 31, 1943, that Mennonite historian Harold S. Bender stood before the American Society of Church History at Columbia University and delivered an address that became the most influential single act of theological scholarship in the history of the Anabaptist tradition.

Bender was Dean of Goshen College, a Mennonite institution in Indiana, and one of the most consequential figures in the mid-twentieth-century recovery of Anabaptist identity. The historiography he had inherited was not kind to his tradition. Four centuries of Protestant and Catholic polemical writing had rendered the sixteenth-century Anabaptists as dangerous radicals, social revolutionaries, or marginal figures whose significance to the main currents of Reformation thought was negligible at best and sinister at worst. Bender set out to dismantle this interpretation and replace it with a systematic account of what the movement meant.

His argument rested on three affirmations, each of which cut against the received caricature with the precision of a scholar who had spent his career in the primary sources. The first was discipleship: for the original Anabaptists, the Christian life meant following Jesus in daily practice, not merely affirming correct doctrine or cultivating inner conviction. Faith required visible conformity to the teachings of Jesus, above all, the ethical teachings of the Sermon on the Mount. The second was the church as a voluntary community of believers: the Anabaptists had rejected the territorial church, in which membership was determined by birth and enforced by the state's sword, insisting that the church must consist of people who had consciously chosen to follow Jesus. This conviction expressed itself institutionally in adult baptism and in an uncompromising refusal of any alliance between church and state. The third was what Bender called the ethic of love and nonresistance: the early Anabaptists had rejected violence and warfare categorically, believing Christians were called to practice love, reconciliation, and peace in every dimension of life, personal, communal, and political, without exception and without qualification.

Bender's address, published the following year under the title *The Anabaptist Vision*, proved enormously influential. It gave the Anabaptists a coherent and dignified account of their own origins. This would have been the definition of Anabaptism that Barbour learned through his association with the Church of the Brethren, and for the purposes of this biography, it is the definition of Anabaptism used to tell Barbour's story.

The Church of the Brethren, known until the First World War as the German Baptist Brethren, traces its origins to 1708 in the German principality of Wittgenstein, where eight adult believers were baptized in the Eder River and organized a community of voluntary discipleship, nonresistance, and *radical inclusion* under the leadership of Alexander Mack, a miller's son turned reformer who had found in the New Testament the same blueprint the Mennonites had first drawn nearly two centuries earlier, in the Swiss cantons and the lowlands of the Netherlands, under the hands of former Dutch Catholic priest Menno Simons and the framers of the Schleitheim Confession.

The Brethren community combined two impulses in productive tension: the Pietist renewal movement insisting on the transformation of the entire person, head and heart and hand together, and the Anabaptist conviction of the Radical Reformation insisting on voluntary church membership, adult baptism as a covenantal act, the separation of church and state, and the nonresistant refusal of violence. The Brethren arriving in Pennsylvania in 1719 carried this double inheritance into a new world, maintaining their separation from both the established churches of Europe and the new democratic state of America while insisting, through the witness of their community life, that human social arrangements could be organized around the teachings of Jesus rather than the imperatives of power.

The African Methodist Episcopal Church traces its origins to 1792 in Philadelphia, where two African American clergy, Methodist minister Richard Allen and Episcopal priest Absalom Jones, walked out of St. George's Methodist Episcopal Church rather than submit to racial segregation at the communion rail. The precipitating incident was simple in its facts and profound in its implications: white church leaders moved to drag Black worshippers from their knees during prayer and direct them to the segregated gallery constructed to contain them. Rather than comply, Allen, Jones, and their companions walked out. The AME Church, formally organized in 1816, was born from this act of refusal: the refusal to accept the definition of one's humanity imposed by a system of racial domination, and the refusal to participate in a community of faith on terms that required submission to one's own degradation.

In their historical origins, cultural contexts, and social locations, these two traditions could hardly have been more different. The

Church of the Brethren was a community of German-speaking European immigrants, predominantly white and rural, formed by the theological debates of the Radical Reformation and by the persecutions of a state church exercising political power over religious communities. The AME Church was a community of African Americans, Black and increasingly urban, formed by the experience of enslavement and the theological demand for liberation from a racial hierarchy claiming Christian sanction. The Brethren had crossed an ocean to escape persecution. The AME's founders had, many of them, been forced across an ocean in chains.

The convergences between these two traditions run deeper than the differences and reach to the root of each. From their founding moments, each insisted authentic Christian faith is incompatible with structures of domination. Each organized itself as a voluntary community of the committed rather than as an established church embedded in the power of the state. Each read the Gospel of Jesus Christ as a mandate for public action rather than a comfort for private withdrawal. Each understood the gathered community of believers as bearing corporate responsibility for the shape of the society in which it was embedded. And each, in its own way, was formed by the experience of persecution: the Brethren by a state church willing to imprison and execute its members in the public squares of Germany for the crime of worshipping outside its authority; the AME by a racial hierarchy willing to drag believers from their knees at the communion rail for the crime of being Black.

In Barbour's life, these two traditions met at Elizabethtown College in the late 1920s and amplified each other across the subsequent two and a half decades. The Brethren tradition gave him a framework for discipleship as costly, embodied, and necessarily public; a conviction which made Jesus King mean making his values reign in the social and political arrangements of human civilization; and a relational network of interracial partnerships unusual in the segregated world of mid-century America. The AME tradition gave him a theology of prophetic confrontation, a model of the church as the institutional backbone of Black civic life, and a deep formation in the understanding that following Jesus in the context of American racial apartheid meant confronting white supremacy as both a theological error and a civic failure. Together, these traditions gave Barbour a vocabulary, a mandate, and a method for his human rights work, setting him apart from activists formed in only one theological tradition and making him, in a documentable sense, more effective and more theologically grounded than he could have been with either tradition alone.

The Motto As Mandate

In the quiet deliberations of a boardroom, where men of conviction gathered to reckon with the work they had set in motion, the numbers told a story no ledger could fully capture. It was 1913, and the trustees of the college looked out upon something remarkable. With humble gratitude, they reported what they had witnessed: "Scores of young people have been converted to the religion of Jesus Christ through the influence set in motion by the college."

Two years later, on a summer day in July, the twenty-ninth to be precise, those same trustees gathered once more. What had been lived out in practice, what had quietly shaped the rhythms and purposes of the institution, now needed to be spoken aloud. Formally. Officially. Permanently. They voted, and with quiet and unhesitating resolve, they gave the college its motto.

Three words. Just three. But three words carrying the full weight of everything they believed the college was meant to be and to do.

"Make Jesus King"

The motto of Elizabethtown College, "Make Jesus King," stands at the center of this biography not as a rhetorical device but as a historical reality. It was the three-word imperative pressed into Barbour during four years of intellectual and spiritual formation at a small Brethren college in south-central Pennsylvania, carried with him through twenty-five years of human rights work in Philadelphia and Denver and Tucson and Los Angeles, and finally embodied in his understanding of himself as the integrator: the person who moved into the spaces between legal change and human transformation and built, by patient, costly, theologically grounded work, the conditions for genuine community.

Elizabethtown College's motto was not, in the Brethren tradition from which it came, a platitude. It was a program. It expressed, in three words, the core theological conviction animating the College's founding and sustaining its institutional life across more than a century: the conviction: Jesus's Kingship was not a metaphor for private piety or ecclesiastical authority, but a mandate for the transformation of the specific, concrete, measurable conditions of human life in the specific, concrete, measurable communities where his followers lived and worked. To "Make Jesus King" was not to pray for God's Kingdom. It was to build it: to organize one's life, one's work, one's community, and one's civic engagement around the values the New Testament described as the values of this Kingdom. "Not everyone who says to me, Lord, Lord, will enter the kingdom of heaven," Jesus told his followers in the Sermon on the Mount, "but only the one who does the will of my Father who is in heaven." The College's motto took this seriously. It demanded action, not only aspiration.

For Barbour, the motto took shape at the intersection of his two theological traditions. In the Brethren register, making Jesus King meant building communities of *radical inclusion*, refusing the violence and exclusion of the surrounding social order, and enacting, in institutional life, the nonresistant love that the Anabaptist tradition described as the essence of Christian discipleship. In the AME register, making Jesus King meant confronting racial hierarchy as a theological error and a civic failure, refusing the definition of human dignity the social order imposed on Black Americans, and insisting on the full membership of every person in the community of the Kingdom. In both registers, the motto was an imperative pointing outward, toward the social arrangements of the world, rather than inward, toward the private life of the believer.

The motto appears in every chapter of this biography because it did in Barbour's life. This is not a rhetorical choice of the biographer. It is a historical claim about the man: the three-word imperative given to him at Elizabethtown College organized his understanding of his work across twenty-five years and in circumstances his college professors could not have anticipated. Making Jesus King in North Philadelphia in 1945 meant going to the police station with frightened teenagers and insisting on reciprocal accountability across the boundaries of gang and institution. Making Jesus King in Denver in 1949 meant organizing all Black ministers in the city to contact state legislators to support fair employment legislation. Making Jesus King in Los Angeles in 1956 meant recognizing the Beverly Hills entertainment industry as a site where the values of the Kingdom needed to take visible form in the everyday practices of a mass culture capable of shaping a nation's conscience. The motto was portable. It traveled with Barbour wherever his work took him and found fresh application in every new terrain.

The college was founded in 1899. Its motto came sixteen years later, in 1915, and the date was not incidental. The decision fell in the middle of the First World War, at the precise moment when the question of what loyalty to Jesus demanded of His followers was being posed with maximum urgency by the spectacle of European Christian nations slaughtering each other by the millions in the mud of France and Belgium. For a Church of the Brethren institution to declare, in this moment, the authority of Jesus as the ultimate criterion by which all other authorities, including the authority of the state, were to be judged, was something more than a pious gesture. It was a deliberate theological and political act.

The phrase itself reflected a broader theological emphasis circulating widely in Protestant circles during the early twentieth century, an emphasis on what theologians were calling the Social Kingship of Christ. This theological emphasis, developed most fully in the Social

Gospel tradition associated with Walter Rauschenbusch, the Baptist minister and theologian, whose 1917 Theology for the Social Gospel became the movement's defining text, understood discipleship not merely as a private spiritual disposition but as a public, political, and institutional commitment. For Rauschenbusch, whose work engaged the social conditions of industrial capitalism and urban poverty in America at the turn of the century, making Jesus King meant making His values reign over the economic arrangements of human society, addressing the structural conditions of poverty and exploitation that personal charity alone could not. Reformed American theologian H. Richard Niebuhr's *Christ and Culture*, which would provide the most systematic scholarly framework for this debate, had not yet been written in 1915, but the questions it addressed were already organizing the theological conversation from which Elizabethtown College's motto emerged.

For Barbour, who arrived at Elizabethtown College thirteen years after the motto's formal adoption, the phrase carried all of these layers of meaning simultaneously. He heard it in the institutional context of a Church of the Brethren college formed by the theological conviction: Jesus's authority was ultimate, and his teachings on peace, service, and the dignity of every person were not optional supplements to a Christianity otherwise organized around private piety and social accommodation. He heard it as a young Black man who had spent his entire life inside a social order organized around a very different set of ultimate authorities, authorities whose claim to legitimacy the motto implicitly and explicitly contested. He heard it as a person already formed by the AME Church's own version of this claim, the insistence that racial hierarchy was incompatible with the Kingdom of God, whose kingship the motto proclaimed. The convergence was not accidental. It was the specific form in which theological truth presented itself to him in the historical moment of his formation.

The institutional expression of the motto's racial justice implications within the broader Church of the Brethren reached its most formal denominational articulation in 1935, when the Annual Conference of the Church of the Brethren adopted a resolution titled "The Inter-Racial Problem." The language of the resolution was striking in its clarity and directness. The Conference called on members of the church to "condemn every form of unjust discrimination against people of other races' and insisted upon 'equal justice in our civil courts and equal opportunity in our systems of education, regardless of race, culture, or social status." The theological grounding of these demands was explicit and unambiguous: "Racial prejudice contradicts the teachings of Jesus."

This was not the language of political liberalism or progressive civic reform. It was the language of Anabaptist discipleship, a direct application of the conviction that the teachings of Jesus in the Sermon on the Mount were the authoritative guide for the conduct of the believing community in every dimension of life, including social and political life. When the Church of the Brethren declared in 1935 how racial prejudice contradicted the teachings of Jesus, it was making a claim whose implications extended to every institution, every law, every social practice, and every personal behavior through which racial hierarchy was maintained. The claim was sweeping in its logical extension, even when it fell short in its institutional consequences.

The 1935 resolution came three years after Barbour's graduation from Elizabethtown College, and he did not hear it debated in the campus community. But the theological conviction underlying it, the insistence: Jesus's authority demanded the dismantling of racial hierarchy as a condition of authentic discipleship, was present in the Elizabethtown community during his four years there in the form of institutional practices, faculty commitments, and the motto itself. The resolution formalized in denominational language what the campus had been imperfectly and partially embodying in institutional practice: the claim that making Jesus King was incompatible with the racial exclusions the surrounding society maintained and defended.

Donald F. Durnbaugh, the Church of the Brethren historian widely regarded as the dean of scholars on Anabaptist and Pietist history, in his *Fruit of the Vine* traces the development of the Church of the Brethren's racial justice commitments across the twentieth century, showing how the 1935 resolution was part of a longer and more contested process of denominational self-examination about the relationship between the Brethren theological tradition and the racial hierarchy of American society. The Brethren tradition's principled commitment to racial equality was real and documented; so was its frequent failure to translate that commitment into institutional practice consistent with it. This gap between commitment and practice was itself theologically significant: it revealed the distance between the Kingdom, the motto proclaimed, and the community the college and denomination embodied, and it made the motto's imperative a continuous challenge rather than a completed achievement.

The most concrete institutional expression of the Elizabethtown community's racial justice commitments during the interwar years was the Interracial Work Camp movement, which connected the college's peace church networks to one of the most innovative and significant experiments in interracial community-building produced by the Long Civil Rights Movement's organizational phase. The movement's origins lay in 1934, when Quaker leader Clarence Pickett, working with colleagues in the American Friends Service Committee and the Fellowship of Reconciliation, organized the first work camp in Westmoreland County, Pennsylvania, for unemployed college students during the Great Depression. The Brethren Service Committee, collaborating with the Fellowship of Reconciliation and the AFSC, rapidly developed this model into a broader program of racially integrated summer service.

The structure of the work camps was carefully designed to be simultaneously practical and pedagogical. Participants, recruited from diverse racial backgrounds, lived together in a community, worked with their hands on neighborhood improvement and community development projects in nearby towns and cities, and gathered regularly for structured conversations about poverty, war, and racism. Projects included repairing homes, improving community facilities, assisting poor rural communities, and supporting African American neighborhoods denied adequate public resources by racial segregation. The combination of shared manual labor and structured reflection was not accidental; it reflected the Brethren tradition's conviction that genuine transformation required the engagement of the whole person, head and heart and hand together, in the practices of community which authentic discipleship required.

The theological rationale for this model drew directly on the Anabaptist-Pietist conviction that barriers of race and class were incompatible with the community of believers envisioned in the New Testament, a community in which, in the Apostle Paul's formulation, "there is neither Jew nor Gentile, neither slave nor free, nor is there male and female, for you are all one in Christ Jesus." The organizers of the work camps believed, and their experience consistently confirmed, that something transformative could happen when people of different races worked side by side, shared meals, slept in the same quarters, and talked honestly about their experiences and convictions. Shared labor and shared life created conditions for genuine mutual recognition, not the superficial tolerance of liberal multiculturalism, but the deeper recognition of common humanity and mutual dignity which the Brethren theology of the image of God demanded.

Elizabethtown College students who participated in these camps were not merely doing charitable service; they were practicing, in embodied and relational form, the discipleship they had been formed in through the college's liberal arts interdisciplinary curriculum, the Brethren theological tradition, and the campus community of worship and debate. They were doing, in the institutional form the 1930s made available, exactly what the motto demanded: making Jesus king in the social arrangements of the communities they were serving, building the genuine interracial community which the integration process would require long before the legal structures of segregation had been sufficiently dismantled to make that community legally possible.

Mennonite historian Albert N. Keim and Mennonite sociologist Grant M. Stoltzfus's *Politics of Conscience* traces how this work-camp tradition fed directly into the Civilian Public Service program of the Second World War, providing both the organizational model and the trained personnel who sustained alternative service during the war years. Students who had lived and worked in racially integrated communities through the work camp program, who had confronted poverty and injustice directly, and who had developed habits of nonviolent engagement with conflict were far better prepared than their peers to navigate the moral and practical challenges of conscientious objection, alternative service, and the forms of civil rights work the postwar years would demand. The continuity between the work camps of the 1930s and the nonviolent direct action of the Congress of Racial Equality CORE in the 1940s was not accidental; it reflected a deliberate strategy of formation that understood service and witness as complementary expressions of the same theological commitment.

For Barbour, this network was part of his Elizabethtown inheritance, even if he did not participate in work camps during his college years. The institutional connections, relational networks, and organizational culture of the peace church service tradition were available to him through his college relationships, giving his subsequent human rights work an organizational dimension unusual among practitioners formed primarily in the Black church tradition. When he organized interracial coalitions in Denver, when he collaborated with the Anti-Defamation League, the CIO, and the Mayor's Committee, he was deploying the coalition-building habits of a tradition that had been practicing interracial community in the institutional form of work camps since the mid-1930s.

It was also in 1935. The Mennonites, the Brethren, and the Quakers came together to form the Historic Peace Churches. Three traditions, each with its own deep and separate roots, each shaped by its own history of suffering and conviction, now joined in a single coordinated witness. They brought together their shared commitments to nonviolence, conscientious objection, and international relief into one deliberate and unified voice. The roots ran back at least to the aftermath of the First World War, when Brethren and Mennonite volunteers had traveled into the wreckage of Europe to provide food, medical care, and rebuilding support to communities the armies had passed through and left broken. It was a direct and deliberate expression of a conviction reaching back to the Anabaptist origins of both traditions: the Christian response to war is not participation in its violence but service to its victims.

In 1939, with the storm gathering again over Europe, the Church of the Brethren moved to institutionalize what had previously been carried by individual conscience and informal networks. The Brethren Service Committee was established to coordinate the community's commitment to ethical witness and humanitarian service. The committee became the vehicle through which Elizabethtown students and alumni would channel their formation into concrete action when the war came.

The theological formation of students at Elizabethtown College in the late 1920s and early 1930s drew not only on the Anabaptist-Pietist tradition of the Church of the Brethren but on the broader theological ferment of the European interwar period, and above all on the work of German Lutheran theologian martyr, Dietrich Bonhoeffer, and Swiss Reformed theologian Karl Barth. These two theologians, working in the context of Germany's encounter with National Socialism, were developing arguments about the relationship between Christian discipleship and political power that gave the motto "Make Jesus King" its deepest and most urgent intellectual support.

Dietrich Bonhoeffer's *The Cost of Discipleship*, published in German in 1937 and read in Anglophone peace church circles within a few years of its publication, offered one of the most searching analyses of Christian discipleship produced in the twentieth century. Bonhoeffer's central argument, that following Jesus meant obeying Jesus in every part of life, including those parts that brought the disciple into direct conflict with the powers of the state, was both a theological and a political claim. He distinguished sharply between what he called "cheap grace," the gracious dispensation of forgiveness without the demand of obedience, and "costly grace," the grace calling the disciple to a life of unconditional obedience to the commands of Jesus. For Bonhoeffer, as for the Anabaptist tradition preceding him by four centuries, there could be no separation between faith and ethics, between belief and conduct, between the private disposition of the heart and the public pattern of life. Discipleship was total, or it was nothing.

For students at Elizabethtown College encountering Bonhoeffer's work in the context of a campus whose official motto was Make Jesus King, the resonance was immediate and profound. The motto was not, as Bonhoeffer's analysis made clear, a merely spiritual slogan. It was a political claim, a declaration: Jesus, and not any earthly ruler or ideology, was the ultimate authority to whom the believing community owed its loyalty. This conviction was expressed institutionally by the Confessing Church in Germany, whose formation Bonhoeffer was centrally involved in, and theologically by the Barmen Declaration of 1934, which Karl Barth had played the leading role in drafting.

The Barmen Declaration's central claim was simple and absolute: Jesus Christ, as attested in Holy Scripture, was the one Word of God which the church had to hear and trust and obey in life and in death. Against this affirmation, Barmen rejected the claim that the German Christian movement was advancing, which the church could recognize the events, powers, and truths of Nazi ideology as sources of its proclamation alongside God's revelation. The declaration belonged to the Reformed theological tradition rather than to Anabaptism, but its christological structure and its insistence on the absolute authority of Jesus Christ over the pretensions of the state were entirely consonant with Elizabethtown College's motto.

Together, Bonhoeffer and Barth helped the Elizabethtown community understand the motto in its fullest theological depth. "Make Jesus King" was not a call to theocracy or to the imposition of Christian doctrine on political institutions. It was a call to the kind of discipleship at the heart of the Anabaptist tradition: a discipleship active, relational, and courageous, caring for the oppressed, speaking truth to power, resisting unjust laws, and building communities guided by the ethics of Jesus. In the 1930s and 1940s, when Europe was under the shadow of totalitarian regimes making precisely the opposite demands of their subjects, this discipleship was not merely a spiritual ideal. It was a counter-politics, a way of organizing communal life bearing witness, by its very existence, to the possibility of a world ordered by justice and love rather than by violence and domination.

In 1935, the same year the Historic Peace Churches were forming, and the Confessing Church in Germany was drafting its Barmen Declaration, Joseph and Josephine Greenberg opened the Greenberg Garment Factory on West Bainbridge Street in Elizabethtown. They were among a small number of Jewish families who had made their lives in this quiet Pennsylvania town, and in the years following, others would join them, some by choice, some by necessity, some by the most desperate kind of urgency.

In 1938, a man named Max Hess arrived. He was a Jewish shirt manufacturer who had escaped. He had gotten out of Germany, out of what was happening there, and he had brought his sons, Werner and Gunther, and his nephew, Fred Stern, with him. Together they opened the Hestteco Manufacturing Company on West High Street, making women's dresses and children's clothing.

Also in 1938, Benjamin Weiman and his son-in-law, Milton S. Goldstein, established the Empire Shoe Company on West Washington Street, turning out 3,000 pairs of boys' shoes every day. The Weimans and Goldsteins did something else as well. They became the first employers in Elizabethtown to provide hospitalization for their workers, and they proposed child day care for working mothers. In a small Pennsylvania town, in the middle of the Depression, ordinary people were putting flesh on principles. In 1957, John B. Greenberg and his son Joel started J. B. Athletic Shoes, manufacturing ice skates and soccer and basketball shoes right there in Elizabethtown.

For the students and faculty at the college, and for the people of the town who lived alongside these families, the scholarship of Bonhoeffer and Barth was not something encountered only through the lens of newsreel footage and newspaper headlines. It had a face. It had a name. It lived on West Bainbridge Street, West Washington Street, and West High Street. It came to work every morning.

For Barbour, formed at Elizabethtown in the years immediately before this European theological crisis reached its full intensity, the college's motto bore the weight these interpretive traditions ascribed to it. Making Jesus King in America in the 1930s and 1940s, in a nation practicing racial apartheid while claiming democratic legitimacy, was an act in the same tradition as the Confessing Church's refusal of the German Christian movement's compromise with Nazi ideology. The forms of domination were different; the theological logic of resistance was the same. Barbour knew this. His entire human rights career was an expression of the knowing.

The Shape of the Argument

This biography advances four interlocking arguments, each corresponding to one of the thematic threads woven through every chapter. The first argument is: Barbour's human rights work arose from the center of two theologically serious communities whose understanding of Christian discipleship demanded public engagement with unjust social conditions. His was not secular activism wearing a religious costume. His activism was the direct fruit of a theology of discipleship absorbed over a lifetime in two communities insisting, from their founding moments, that authentic Christian faith is incompatible with structures of domination. Every act of his professional life, from the gang mediation in North Philadelphia to the FEPC campaigns in Denver to the direct-action test at the Denver swimming pools, grew from this theological root.

The second argument is: Elizabethtown College gave Barbour, at the precise moment of his maximum receptivity, the intellectual tools, the theological convictions, and the relational networks he needed for a lifetime of human rights work. The college motto "Make Jesus

King" was not incidental to his formation. It was central to it, and its centrality is documentable in the ways his mature human rights writing draws on the intellectual formation the College provided: the liberal arts interdisciplinary curriculum equipping him to argue from first principles across the full sweep of Western political philosophy; the debate training giving him the rhetorical tools for effective public advocacy; the Anabaptist theological tradition giving him a vocabulary for the costly, embodied, communal character of authentic discipleship.

The third argument is that the convergence of Church of the Brethren and African Methodist Episcopal theology in Barbour's life was not incidental or superficial. It reflected a deep structural compatibility between two traditions sharing a fundamental hermeneutical conviction: the Gospel of Jesus Christ is incompatible with structures of domination, and the community of faith bears corporate responsibility for enacting that incompatibility in the world. Understanding where these traditions converged, where they differed in emphasis, and how Barbour navigated the creative tension between them is essential to understanding what made him the kind of human rights leader he became.

The fourth argument is: Barbour belongs in the canon of American civil rights history, in the company of the Long Movement's builders, whose patient, foundational work made the mass movement of the 1955 to 1965 decade possible. His recovery from historical obscurity serves not only the cause of accurate historiography but also the cause of understanding the movement he served: its theological depth, its organizational sophistication, its institutional infrastructure, and the kind of person, formed in specific ways by particular communities and institutions, required to build it.

The chapters follow Barbour's life in chronological order. Chapter One establishes the biography's central argument and introduces Barbour as the integrator, the person who moved into the space between legal change and human transformation and built, by patient and theologically grounded work, the conditions for genuine community.

Chapter Two reconstructs his family background, the social geography of Middletown and Steelton, Pennsylvania, and the formative role of the AME Church in his childhood. Chapter Three follows him to Elizabethtown College, where the motto "Make Jesus King" became the organizing principle of his intellectual and spiritual formation. Chapter Four traces his first years after graduation as the Great Depression deepened and the early civil rights movement took shape. Chapter Five places him in the transformative decade of the 1940s, when World War II and the Double V campaign were reshaping the political possibilities of American race relations. Chapter Six narrates his postwar years in Denver, where he built a model of municipal civil rights work with national significance. Chapter Seven follows him to Los Angeles and the Mojave Desert moment in which his life's work crystallized into its fullest intellectual statement. Chapter Eight draws together the biography's four themes and makes the case for Barbour's place in the canon of American civil rights history.

His life also provides a model for the kind of interreligious and interracial collaboration the integration process requires. The convergence of Anabaptist-Pietist and AME theology in his formation was not accidental. It was the product of an institutional moment, the founding of Elizabethtown College as an institution genuinely committed to *radical inclusion,* and of a specific personal history, the Great Migration family, which landed in a community where the Black church and the plain church coexisted in the same landscape. These historical conditions are not replicable. But the theological conviction underlying the convergence, the insistence of both traditions that authentic Christian faith is incompatible with structures of domination, is portable. It can be carried from one historical context to another by people willing to let it cost them what it cost William Wilbur Miller Barbour.

He was forty-nine years old when he died, having spent twenty-five years in the integrator's work. He was, by any measure, too young. The movement needed him for at least another two decades. The work he was doing in San Bernardino and throughout the western region in the final weeks of his life suggests the energy and the engagement were still fully present. The heart gave out. The work did not. The legacy he left was not a completed project but a demonstrated possibility: one person, formed by two theological traditions in productive tension, equipped with the intellectual tools of a serious liberal arts education, trained in the professional methods of community organization, and sustained by the conviction making Jesus King was not a metaphor but a mandate, could spend twenty-five years building the foundations of genuine integration in the cities of mid-century America.

It was enough. It was more than enough. It was, and remains, an example.

| 2 |

The World of His Birth

The Philadelphia Lying-In Charity Hospital served the women of the city's working poor, the women whose labors sustained the households of Philadelphia's middle and upper classes, while receiving, in return, the wages that made charity hospitalization necessary. It was not a place of comfort or distinction. It was a place of survival. On September 20, 1908, within its walls, Minnie Gertrude Mumford Barbour gave birth to a son, the first child of a marriage between two Virginia migrants who had made the long journey northward in search of the safety and economic possibilities the South had refused them. The birth certificate recorded the child's name as William Henry Barber, after his father. In time, the son would refine the name, adding the middle names, which placed him in his own generational identity and signaled, in the way a man signals such things when he understands the weight of naming, both his connection to his family's history and his determination to make something new from its materials.

He would become William Wilbur Miller Barbour. The world would come to know him as W. Miller Barbour, human rights leader, social work executive, racial integrator. But on September 20, 1908, he was simply a newborn in a charity hospital in a northern city, the son of parents who had brought everything they owned and everything they hoped for to Pennsylvania because Virginia had offered too little of either. The world into which he was born was shaped by forces he would spend his entire adult life working to transform, and understanding those forces is essential to understanding the man who formed in response to them.

The World He Was Born Into

To understand William Wilbur Miller Barbour, one must first understand the America of his birth, a nation in which the legal, social, and theological architecture of racial apartheid was not merely present but comprehensive, not merely tolerated but celebrated by the most powerful institutions of civic life. Twelve years had passed since the Supreme Court's decision in Plessy v. Ferguson had endorsed the doctrine of separate but equal and provided the constitutional foundation for the entire structure of Jim Crow. The Court's 1896 ruling, delivered by a seven-to-one majority, had licensed a generation of state and local governments to codify racial separation in every sphere of public life: schools, transportation, restaurants, hotels, hospitals, parks, libraries, cemeteries, and courtrooms. In 1908, the United States was a legally segmented society in which a person's race determined, with near-total predictability, the quality of every service, institution, and public accommodation to which they could gain access.

In the South, from which Barbour's family had recently migrated, the regime was enforced by law, by custom, and by organized terror. Lynching was not an aberration but a social institution, a mechanism of racial control backed by the implicit or explicit approval of law enforcement, the courts, the churches, and the press. Between 1882 and 1951, according to records compiled by the Tuskegee Institute, white mobs murdered more than 3,400 Black Americans in the South, an average of nearly forty lynchings per year across seven decades. In 1908, the year of Barbour's birth, the tally reached at least eighty-nine documented murders. The federal government offered no legal protection. Congress had repeatedly debated and repeatedly failed to pass anti-lynching legislation, with southern Democrats successfully filibustering every attempt. The Supreme Court showed no interest in revisiting Plessy. Theodore Roosevelt, the Progressive president who had dined with Booker T. Washington in the White House and thereby provoked a national furor, had abandoned serious commitment to Black civil rights by the second year of his presidency.

The founding of the NAACP in 1909, just months after Barbour's birth, was a direct institutional response to this climate of organized terror. The Springfield, Illinois, race riot of August 1908, in which white mobs attacked Black neighborhoods in the hometown of Abraham Lincoln, had provided the galvanizing moment. The spectacle of racial violence in Lincoln's city, at the centennial of Lincoln's birth, prompted a group of prominent reformers, including Ida B. Wells, W.E.B. Du Bois, Oswald Garrison Villard, Mary Church Terrell, and the social settlement leader Mary White Ovington, to call a national conference on the condition of Black Americans. Out of this conference emerged the National Association for the Advancement of Colored People, organized around the twin commitments to legal challenge and public advocacy.

One year later, in 1910, the National Urban League emerged from a merger of three earlier organizations: the National League for the Protection of Colored Women, founded in 1905; the Committee for the Improvement of Industrial Conditions Among Negroes, established in 1906; and the Committee on Urban Conditions Among Negroes, founded in New York City in 1910. Where the NAACP focused primarily on legal strategy and political advocacy, the Urban League focused on economic opportunity and workforce development: job placement, professional development for graduates of historically Black colleges and universities, and the building of the institutional infrastructure through which Black Americans could participate in the economic life of the northern cities to which they were migrating in growing numbers. Together, the NAACP and the Urban League represented the two main institutional tracks of what would become the Long Civil Rights Movement, and William

Wilbur Miller Barbour would spend his career working within and alongside both.

The debate over the path to Black advancement had been sharpened, in the years before Barbour's birth, by the great intellectual contest between W.E.B. Du Bois and Booker T. Washington. Du Bois, whose 1899 study *The Philadelphia Negro* had pioneered the empirical sociology of Black urban life, argued education was the foundation of both individual dignity and collective advancement, and the systematic denial of quality education to Black Americans was the deliberate mechanism by which the racial hierarchy perpetuated itself. Washington argued instead for vocational education and economic self-sufficiency, accommodating the racial order in the short term in exchange for the economic foundations from which Black communities could later press their claims for full citizenship. This debate, between Du Bois's claim for the full liberal arts education of the Talented Tenth and Washington's Atlanta Compromise, shaped the educational landscape into which Barbour would eventually walk when he chose to attend Elizabethtown College rather than Lincoln University.

Barbour's family came from the tobacco country and small-farm landscape of Powhatan County, Virginia, one of the small counties of the central piedmont lying between Richmond and Charlottesville. The landscape was rolling red clay hills and second-growth timber, tobacco fields worked by tenant farmers on terms designed to reproduce the dependency of slavery through the mechanisms of the crop-lien system rather than through chattel ownership. The tenant farmer did not own the land he worked; he rented it from a white landowner on terms that required him to plant the cash crop the landowner designated, sell it through the landowner's marketing arrangements, and settle accounts at year's end, a process the landowner controlled. The crop-lien system, under which the tenant borrowed against the expected value of his crop to purchase the seed, tools, and supplies he needed for the year, created a debt structure that made it nearly impossible to accumulate the savings that would have allowed him to escape through land purchase or relocation.

The county's name preserved the memory of the Powhatan Confederacy, the Indigenous political organization whose territory this had been before European settlement dispossessed it. The plantations on whose former grounds the Mumford family farmed as tenants had been built by enslaved labor, the same labor whose descendants were now renting the land at rates designed to ensure they could never accumulate the capital to purchase it. The historical layers of dispossession, Indigenous and African, were embedded in the landscape in ways visible to anyone who knew how to read them, and Barbour was the descendant of people who had been living within those layers long enough to read them without being told.

His mother, Minnie Gertrude Mumford, had grown up in Macon, a small community in Powhatan County, where her parents and grandparents had labored as tenant farmers in the years after emancipation. Her father, Edward Mumford, died in 1876 at the age of twenty-four, leaving his widow Isabella and their children in circumstances of particular precarity. The post-Reconstruction decades, when the withdrawal of federal protection had left Black southerners exposed to the reimposition of coerced labor through the Black Codes and the sharecropping system's economic coercion, were years when a Black widow with children and no male labor to offer a white landowner had few options and all of them constrained. The strategies Isabella Mumford employed to sustain her family through these years are not preserved in the historical record, but the fact of her family's survival and eventual migration to Pennsylvania is evidence that she found them.

Leon Litwack's *Trouble in Mind*, the most comprehensive reconstruction of Black southern life in the age of Jim Crow, documents the texture of daily existence in the world the Mumford and Barbour families inhabited and eventually left. Litwack's synthesis of memoirs, oral histories, newspapers, and legal records creates a portrait of a social order organized around the continuous, comprehensive, and violent enforcement of racial hierarchy, a social order in which the forms of daily humiliation, the enforced deference, the restricted access to public space, the vulnerability to arbitrary violence, and the systematic denial of legal protection were not aberrations from a system otherwise committed to equal treatment but the system's normal and intended operations. To understand why the Barbour family left Virginia for Pennsylvania is to understand, through Litwack's reconstruction, what staying in Virginia meant.

His father, William Henry Barbour, known locally as "King" Barbour, was a native of Richmond, the former capital of the Confederacy, the son of Rufus Barbour. The elder William Henry had made his way north through Mississippi and Missouri, two states with their own traditions of racial terror, before arriving in Pennsylvania. He married Minnie Gertrude Mumford in 1907, and the couple had two sons: William Wilbur Miller, born September 20, 1908, and James Edward, born in 1910.

The Barbour and Mumford families' migration to Pennsylvania in the years around 1907 to 1910 placed them in the first wave of the Great Migration, the movement that between 1910 and 1930 brought approximately 1.6 million African Americans from the South to the North and West. Isabel Wilkerson's The Warmth of Other Suns, the defining account of this migration, frames the decision to leave the South not as a labor-market response but as an act of self-determination, a refusal by millions of individual men and women to accept indefinitely the terms of life that the South imposed. The Barbour family's migration belongs within this framework. "King" Barbour and Minnie Gertrude Mumford did not migrate because a labor recruiter came to their door. They migrated because the South had made them an offer they refused.

Minnie's migration to Pennsylvania was shaped by the economic opportunities and the personal networks of the Great Migration's first wave. She arrived in the Philadelphia area around 1907 to 1910, moving through the domestic service economy, in which Black women migrants from the South typically found their initial employment in the North. In Montgomery County, she worked as a household servant for a Pennsylvania politician, and it was in the

Harrisburg area she settled permanently, eventually making her home in Middletown, Dauphin County, the small industrial town on the east bank of the Susquehanna River where her son would spend his childhood.

Pennsylvania was a distinctive destination for Great Migration families from Virginia and the Carolinas. Its geographic proximity made it accessible to families making their first migration, and its industrial economy, centered on Pittsburgh's steel mills and Philadelphia's manufacturing and domestic service sectors, offered employment opportunities that the immediate postwar South did not. The Pennsylvania Railroad's recruiting agents, who traveled through the mid-Atlantic and upper South in the years around World War I, targeted exactly the communities from which the Barbour and Mumford families came. Joe William Trotter Jr.'s edited collection *The Great Migration in Historical Perspective* situates the Pennsylvania migration within this broader demographic transformation, showing how the south-central Pennsylvania corridor, running from Harrisburg through Lancaster to Philadelphia, was shaped by the domestic service economy more than by heavy industry, drawing migrants from the upper South who arrived in smaller towns and borough communities rather than in the massive urban centers of the Midwest.

The Barbour family's settlement in Middletown, rather than in a major urban center like Philadelphia, was consistent with this pattern. Middletown offered employment in domestic service and day labor, was accessible from Virginia by railroad, had a small but established Black community centered on the Ebenezer AME Church, and offered the kind of semi-rural stability which families making their first migration often preferred to the more overwhelming scale of major city life. Wilkerson insists, and the evidence of the Barbour family's experience supports her insistence, the migration was generational in scope: it was not only the migrants themselves whose lives were transformed but the children of migrants whose social and political horizons were fundamentally expanded by the decision their parents made. By moving to Middletown, the Barbour family gave their son access to a public school system better than anything available to Black children in Powhatan County, to the institutional life of an AME congregation with connections extending throughout the Philadelphia Conference, to the cultural life of Philadelphia's Black community, and ultimately to Elizabethtown College. None of this was available in Powhatan County. The migration made it possible.

Yet the move north was not an escape from racial hierarchy; it was a transition from one form of it to another. This disjuncture between the state's formal commitment to equal rights and the daily reality of racial exclusion shaped Barbour's political education in ways he would later articulate with unusual precision. He understood, from personal experience before he understood it theoretically, what later scholars would theorize: the distinction between de jure segregation, the legalized apartheid of the South encoded in statute and enforced by the state's coercive power, and de facto segregation, the informal architecture of racial exclusion operating in the North through custom, practice, real estate, and the thousand small mechanisms of social pressure. He grew up in the de facto version. He knew how it worked. He knew how it felt. He knew, above all, how resilient it was: how it persisted even when the legal structures explicitly prohibiting it were in place, how it adapted and survived the legal challenges directed against it, how it required something beyond legal strategy to address. The integrator, the concept he would spend his career developing, was his answer to the resilience of de facto segregation.

Founded in 1755 by British Anglo-Saxon Quakers on the eastern bank of the Susquehanna River, Middletown had developed over the following century and a half into a regional transportation and industrial hub. The 1828 completion of the Union Canal, linking the town to inland markets to the west, had catalyzed its early growth. The arrival of railroad connections reinforced its role as a transportation node. By the early twentieth century, Middletown was a modest industrial town of several thousand people, its economy shaped by the railroad repair shops and the industrial establishments of the Harrisburg-Lancaster corridor, its civic character marked by the Quaker reformist memory of its founders.

The Quaker memory had a civic valence in Middletown which shaped the town's self-understanding, even as it coexisted with the daily realities of racial exclusion. During the antebellum and post-bellum periods, African Americans had migrated to Middletown for work in iron manufacturing and formed the Five Points neighborhood along West Main Street. Five Points also functioned as a site of antislavery activity: Mary Brown, a formerly enslaved Virginian, had served as a conductor on the Underground Railroad alongside members of the Fisher family, descendants of the borough's Quaker founders, and in 1864, twelve African American families arriving through this clandestine network had settled nearby in Royalton. The town told itself a story of antislavery heritage and civic inclusion. The story was not false, but it was incomplete.

The physical evidence of this incompleteness was present on Iron Mine Road, where the Old Negro Burying Ground had long stood. Established as a segregated section of the Quaker Middletown Friends Meetinghouse burial ground, it predated the American Republic. Among the dead it held were veterans of the United States Colored Troops: Thomas Dossey of Company G, 6th USCT; EV George Shorter, Company E, 127th USCT Regiment, who had lived from 1843 to 1916; and Jacob Wilson of the 25th USCT Regiment, who had lived from 1825 to 1910. These men had served the Union in its most desperate years, had fought for a country that had enslaved their fathers and grandfathers, and had been buried in a segregated section of a Quaker meetinghouse graveyard. The Quakers who founded Middletown and who sheltered freedom seekers on the Underground Railroad had also, from the town's earliest institutional moment, set aside a separate section of earth for their Black neighbors' dead. In 1929, the Old Negro Burying Ground was formally renamed the East Middletown Cemetery. The new name carried no reference to race. Members of Barbour's own family, including his mother, Minnie, and his stepfather, Charles Henry Archer, rested there alongside those veterans. The community whose faith and formation had shaped him had buried its dead in segregated ground since before living memory. The name changed. The history it had accumulated did not. When Barbour himself died in March 1957, he was interred at Mount Lawn Cemetery, Lincoln Memorial Park in Sharon Hill, Delaware County, established in 1925 to provide burial space for African Americans excluded from white-owned cemeteries. The two cemeteries, one in Middletown and one in Sharon Hill, separated by sixty miles and the full arc of his life, were products of the same racial order. He was born into a world that consigned its Black dead to separate ground. He was buried in a world that still did.

Middletown operated, as James W. Loewen documents in his systematic study of American sundown towns, as a community where African Americans knew they were unwelcome after dark. The mechanisms of exclusion were informal rather than statutory: not an ordinance posted at the city limits, but a climate of intimidation, hostility, and potential violence that made the social geography of the town legible to anyone living within it. Pennsylvania law was formally egalitarian in ways distinguishing it from the states of the former Confederacy. The state had prohibited school segregation as early as 1881 following Allen v. Meadville, and subsequent statutes in 1887 and 1935 prohibited discrimination in public accommodations. Yet the persistence of racially homogeneous neighborhoods, informal school zoning practices, and exclusionary civic customs rendered these legal guarantees uneven in practice. Dauphin County Recorder of Deeds records from the 1920s and 1930s document the restrictive covenants encoding racial exclusion into property law in the communities surrounding Middletown.

Barbour's social world extended beyond Middletown to the neighboring town of Steelton, whose history illuminated in concentrated form the dynamics of racial labor exploitation accompanying the Great Migration. Steelton had been established in 1866 as a company town by the Pennsylvania Steel Company, purchased in 1916 by Bethlehem Steel, and organized around the production needs and social control ambitions of its industrial owner. By 1900, twelve hundred African Americans lived in Steelton, drawn by the availability of industrial employment in the steel mills. The historian John E. Bodnar, in his study of the Black community of Steelton, traces the complex dynamics of a Black industrial workforce navigating the racial hierarchy of a company town. Black workers in the Steelton mills found employment but encountered a system designed to confine them to the lowest-paid, most dangerous, least skilled positions while reserving the better jobs for white workers. The AFL unions, when they organized the steel industry at all, typically maintained segregated locals or otherwise prevented Black workers from accessing the full benefits of union membership. The Wagner Act of 1935, which Barbour would later cite as a major structural obstacle to Black economic advancement, explicitly protected workers' rights to organize but contained no prohibition against racial discrimination by labor unions, thereby allowing the AFL to maintain its racially exclusionary practices with the blessing of federal law.

The Federal Housing Administration, created in 1934, compounded the racial architecture of the labor market with the racial architecture of the housing market. The FHA's underwriting guidelines, developed in the 1930s and systematically applied through the postwar period, mandated racial segregation in federally supported housing development and established the practice of redlining: the designation of predominantly Black neighborhoods as high-risk investments, thereby denying their residents access to federally insured mortgages and confining them to the deteriorating housing stock of racially restricted neighborhoods. The combination of racially exclusionary labor practices and racially exclusionary housing policy created the structural conditions for the concentrated urban poverty Barbour would spend his career addressing: not the poverty of individuals lacking the motivation or skill to improve their circumstances, but the poverty of communities systematically denied access to the economic resources and the residential stability required for advancement.

William Henry Barbour died in Middletown in September 1917, while Minnie and the boys were still in Virginia, his death the event that finally set her migration north in motion. What the father had passed on to his son in nine short years was the knowledge, absorbed through a lifetime of navigation in a racially organized world, but dignity was not given. It was claimed, and claiming it cost something. Two years after her husband's death, Minnie remarried, wedding Charles Henry Archer, a widower from Maryland working as a chauffeur in Middletown. Archer's occupation gave the household a somewhat more stable income base than "King" Barbour's household servant and day laborer work had provided, a stability sufficient to support Barbour's continuation in school and ultimately his enrollment at Elizabethtown College.

At the center of Barbour's social world in Middletown stood the Ebenezer Methodist Episcopal Church. The church stood on Market Street, almost directly across from the Barbour family home, less a destination than a daily presence, the threshold between his family's door and the gathered life of his community so narrow it was nearly no threshold at all. The church was not merely the religious institution of his family's affiliation. It was, as the historians of Black religious life have documented across a wide range of communities and periods, the central institution of Black civic life: the place where mutual aid was organized, where leadership was formed, where political discourse was conducted under conditions of relative safety from white surveillance, where the community's connection to a larger network of Black institutional life was maintained, and where the theological conviction sustaining resistance to racial hierarchy was nurtured and transmitted across generations. C. Eric Lincoln and Lawrence H. Mamiya, in their comprehensive study *The Black Church in the African American Experience*, describe the Black church as serving simultaneously as a spiritual fortress, a community center, a political organization, and an economic base, providing in the absence of a responsive state the full range of social services and civic functions a community requires for its flourishing.

The African Methodist Episcopal Church itself embodied this theology in its institutional identity. Born from Richard Allen's founding act of refusal at St. George's Methodist Episcopal Church in Philadelphia in 1792, as described in Chapter One, the AME organized its entire institutional life around the conviction the Gospel of Jesus Christ was incompatible with racial hierarchy. James T. Campbell's *Songs of Zion*, the definitive comparative study of the AME Church, traces the denomination's development from its founding through the twentieth century, demonstrating how the AME's institutional growth from a single congregation in Philadelphia to a denomination with churches across the United States, Africa, and the Caribbean was itself a civil rights achievement: the building, over two centuries, of an institution large enough and stable enough to sustain the civic, educational, and political aspirations of Black communities denied access to the white-dominated institutions performing these functions for the majority population.

James H. Cone, the theologian who gave the most powerful contemporary voice to the tradition of Black liberation theology, argues in *The Spirituals and the Blues* the Black church's spiritual expression always carried within it the seeds of social and political resistance: the spirituals sung by enslaved people contained, encoded in their language of biblical deliverance, the claims of a people who refused to accept their degradation as the final word on their humanity. The theological tradition of the AME Church, building on this foundation, had always insisted the God worshipped in its congregations was the God of the Exodus, the God who took the side of the enslaved against the enslaver, the God whose Kingdom was incompatible with racial hierarchy, and the God whose followers were called, precisely by their faith, to confront which hierarchy with the full force of their moral and civic engagement.

The Philadelphia Conference of the AME, within which Ebenezer AME in Middletown operated, connected the congregation to a denominational network extending through the mid-Atlantic region and beyond. Dennis C. Dickerson's Religion, Race, and Region documents how the AME's organizational structure, from the local congregation through the annual conference to the general conference and the Council of Bishops, created a framework for civic leadership development that was unique among American civic institutions in its geographic scope and institutional depth. Black men and women who moved through the AME's organizational structure were being trained in the forms of democratic self-governance that the surrounding white civic world denied them access to. The AME was, in this sense, a school of democracy, preparing its members for the full civic participation that the surrounding society's racial order systematically prevented

For Barbour growing up in this environment, the combination of AME Church formation and sundown town constraint was not a contradiction but a formative tension: the church taught him what he was, a child of God of full dignity and unlimited potential, while the town taught him what the surrounding world thought he was, a member of a subordinate caste whose place in the social order was defined by the racial hierarchy the surrounding white community maintained and enforced. The resolution of this tension, the refusal to accept the town's definition against the church's teaching, was not a single dramatic moment but a daily practice, a daily choice to act from the church's understanding of his humanity rather than the town's. This daily practice was the foundation of the human rights career that Elizabethtown College's motto would eventually name and organize.

The Philadelphia weekends Barbour spent throughout his high school and college years deserve attention, because their significance for his formation was considerable, even if their content is not fully recoverable from the documentary record. Philadelphia was one of the great centers of African American civic and cultural life in the 1920s and early 1930s. The Black Philadelphia he visited on his weekend escapes from Middletown was a world of remarkable density and energy: the AME's denominational headquarters and its associated institutions; the Philadelphia Tribune, one of the oldest Black newspapers in the country; the NAACP's Philadelphia branch; the

Philadelphia Urban League; the literary societies, musical organizations, and theatrical clubs of a community engaged in the same project of cultural production Barbour would later contribute to; and the professional networks of teachers, doctors, lawyers, social workers, and businesspeople who formed the city's Black middle class. Matthew Countryman, in *Up South*, traces the development of Black Philadelphia's civil rights politics from the 1930s through the 1960s, showing how this dense institutional infrastructure provided the organizational base for a sustained campaign of civil rights advocacy. Barbour was being formed, in the Black Philadelphia of the late 1920s and early 1930s, by the same institutional world that would produce the civil rights leaders of the subsequent decades.

His nickname "Sunday," the wry acknowledgment of his habitual weekend departure, suggests a regularity of practice which went beyond casual socializing. He was deliberately and consistently building his Philadelphia network, cultivating relationships and institutional familiarity that would serve him professionally in his social work career and human rights advocacy. The young man who showed up in Philadelphia every weekend was not merely escaping the constraints of a sundown town, though he was certainly doing so. He was constructing the relational infrastructure of a professional future, building the human connections without which no amount of formal education or institutional positioning could produce the kind of human rights leadership his formation was preparing him for.

His early schooling in the Middletown public schools prepared him well enough to enter Middletown High School, where he distinguished himself in ways his high school yearbook editors recorded with evident surprise. His academic concentration was chemistry, and he arrived with aspirations toward medicine, the traditional path of Black professional ambition in a period when medicine offered both social status and genuine service to a community chronically underserved by the white-dominated healthcare system. The chemistry concentration placed him in the most demanding science curriculum the school offered, giving him a foundation in quantitative reasoning and systematic empirical investigation which would prove relevant, in unexpected ways, to the social scientific research methods he would later develop in his human rights work. But it was in debate his distinctive gifts emerged most clearly. The editors of his high school yearbook suggested he pursue a career as a lawyer because of his impressive debating skills, a judgment that anticipated, with some precision, the rhetorical and analytical powers he would later deploy in the legislative chambers and civic forums of Denver and Los Angeles.

The structural obstacles facing Black students in Middletown's public schools were not the product of statutory segregation, since Pennsylvania law formally prohibited school segregation. They were the product of the informal architecture of racial disadvantage which operated throughout the North: the tracking systems directing Black students away from college preparatory courses and toward vocational programs; the lower expectations of teachers whose own racial assumptions shaped their assessments of their students' capacity and potential; the absence of Black faculty and administrators who could serve as role models and advocates; and the economic pressures bearing on Black families, including the need for young people to contribute to family income through part-time work. Barbour navigated these obstacles with sufficient success to graduate with distinction and earn the confidence of his debating coach.

The year 1927 was the threshold between his formation years and the active phase of his life Elizabethtown College's four years would inaugurate. He graduated from Middletown High School as its first African American graduate, a biographical fact whose significance deserves the weight it carries. Graduating from a segregated-in-practice northern high school as its first Black graduate was not a small achievement; it was the product of sustained effort against structural obstacles that the school system had not been designed to remove and, for the most part, was not actively working to address.

In the same year, at the age of eighteen, he was elected secretary of the Young People's Conference of the First District of the Dauphin County Sunday School Association, African Methodist Episcopal

Church. The election was both a recognition of his gifts and a placement in the AME's organizational apprenticeship structure. The position required organizational skills, meeting management, record-keeping, correspondence, and the coordination of programs across multiple congregations, which civil rights leadership would demand at every stage. The combination of the academic achievement of becoming the first Black Middletown High School graduate and the civic achievement of being elected to the Young People's Conference leadership was exactly the preparation that Elizabethtown College's environment would require.

The Harrisburg Evening News reported on September 23, 1928, that Barbour's original intention was to enter Lincoln University in Oxford Township, Pennsylvania, one of the nation's oldest historically Black colleges and universities, and the alma mater of Langston Hughes and Thurgood Marshall. Lincoln would have placed him in the company of the Black intellectual and professional elite being formed at HBCUs across the country. The choice to attend Elizabethtown College instead, a predominantly white institution in the neighboring county, was a departure from the expected path, and its significance for his subsequent development cannot be overstated.

He did not go to Elizabethtown College alone. Two of his Middletown High School classmates, Robert Houser and Vance Rank, enrolled with him. The three were known on the Elizabethtown campus as "The Middletown Trio," a designation reflecting their shared hometown origin and the natural fellowship of students who had traveled the same road together. Barbour was the only African American among the three. Houser and Rank were white, both members of the Swatara Hill Church of the Brethren in Middletown, and the familiar company on that road was not simply classmates who shared a hometown but friends whose church was the very tradition Barbour was traveling toward.

The social support of commuting with familiar faces was not trivial. To enter a predominantly white institution in 1928 as a young Black man from a sundown town required not only academic preparation but a kind of moral and social courage: the capacity to inhabit spaces not designed for you, to carry yourself with dignity in an environment shaped by assumptions of white centrality, and to find within which environment the intellectual and relational resources for which you came. Barbour made that journey with two white classmates who knew him, which was its own form of grounding, familiar company on an unfamiliar road.

When Barbour arrived at Elizabethtown College in 1928 and encountered the college's motto for the first time, he was, in the deepest sense, already prepared for it. The three words, "Make Jesus King," expressed in the Brethren's Anabaptist-Pietist vocabulary what the AME had been teaching him since childhood in a different vocabulary. What Virginia had instilled as survival, and what Middletown had sharpened into understanding, Elizabethtown would give a name and a direction. The surprise was not the content of the imperative. The surprise was finding it embodied in the institutional life of a predominantly white college, finding it pressed into every dimension of an educational community shaped by a theological tradition different from his own but converging at precisely the points he cared about most. The convergence would shape everything.

| 3 |

The Formation of a Disciple

Middletown, Pennsylvania, was the world Barbour came from. Hard-edged, practical, ethnically mixed, its neighborhoods sorted by the economics of labor and the accidents of migration. It was a world that Barbour escaped every weekend by visiting Philadelphia.

As part of the Middletown Trio, commuting to college, he traveled the Harrisburg Pike south-southeast, eight miles across the county line from Dauphin into Lancaster. The road was the same road. The sky was the same sky. But when Barbour arrived in Elizabethtown, he had crossed into somewhere else entirely, not just another town, but another civilization.

Elizabethtown was Middletown's neighbor, but it was not Middletown's world. Where Middletown was defined by its railroads, its industries, and its diverse working-class population, Elizabethtown was defined by its churches. Elizabethtown was Anabaptist-Pietist from the ground up. The banks were directed by the Brethren and the Mennonites. The college was Brethren. The businesses lining Market Street, the civic life, all of them drawn from the same deep well of faith: the Church of the Brethren, the Mennonites, the United Brethren in Christ, the Brethren in Christ, the River Brethren, and the United Zion Church. The Brethren in Christ ran their publishing house and their mission outreach operations right in the middle of town, on Market Street, a few blocks from the Church of the Brethren's Elizabethtown College.

This was not a community where religion was one feature of civic life. Religion was civic life. The whole borough was organized around a theology, and the theology demanded something of everyone who lived inside it. When Barbour stepped off the road and onto the Elizabethtown College campus, he stepped into this world, and what happened next was a convergence: between the Black prophetic tradition of the AME Church forming him in Middletown and the Anabaptist-Pietist theology now surrounding him, between the world he had come from and the world that would send him out. It would mark him for the rest of his life.

Long before Penn's surveyors walked this ground, the French were in Elizabethtown. The Conoy and the Susquehanna became arteries of a commercial network connecting the Allegheny, the Ohio, the Mississippi, and the Missouri rivers, tying together an empire of trade from Quebec to Louisiana. Between 1612 and 1632, the explorer Etienne Brule reached Pequea Creek, a tributary of the Susquehanna, where the French traded with the Shawanese. Chartier, Bezaillion, and Le Tort followed, working the Conestoga River, building relationships and accumulating land.

Peter Bezaillion was among the most consequential of them. In 1708, he laid out Old Peter's Road, connecting Pequea Creek to the Conestoga and following the Susquehanna north from Conestoga, later Lancaster, the county seat, to Paxtang, later Harrisburg, the state capital. A portion of the road still bears his name. By 1719 Bezaillion owned seven hundred acres at Conoy Town, some of which eventually became part of Elizabethtown.

In 1681, King Charles II granted William Penn nearly forty-eight thousand square miles of American land. Penn welcomed everyone. And everyone came. The Piscataway, an Algonquian people of the Chesapeake region converted to Christianity by the French Jesuit Andrew White, built their village at the confluence of the creeks in 1701 and lived there for four decades before the council of the Six Nations moved them north to Shamokin. French Huguenot refugees Ferrees, LeFevres, Dubois settled Lancaster. Catholic priests from the Jesuit mission served Elizabethtown from 1741. The Scotch-Irish Buchanans put down roots and eventually sent a president to Washington.

The Swiss Mennonites arrived in the 1720s, purchasing land from Martin Chartier along Conoy Creek. In 1709 Melchoir Brenneman, a Mennonite refugee from the German Palatinate, made his way from Philadelphia to the Conestoga valley, eventually purchasing nine hundred and fifty acres in the region. His grandson, Melchoir Brenneman III, carried that inheritance into what would become Elizabethtown. He built gristmills, sawmills, and distilleries along the creek. He operated a ferry across the Susquehanna at Conoy Town for westward travelers. And he established what became the second oldest Mennonite congregation in Elizabethtown, the congregation now known as Good's Mennonite Church, with origins of 1785. The oldest Mennonite congregation in Elizabethtown, Risser Mennonite Church, traces its origins to 1739.

But it was the German Baptist Brethren who would transform Elizabethtown most completely. In 1868 they migrated from the Weiseichenland settlement on Chiques Creek near Manheim, drawn by the railroad, the canal, and the turnpike. They founded the banks. They established Elizabethtown College. They developed College Heights, the residential subdivision surrounding the campus, attracted the Grand Lodge of Pennsylvania to build the Masonic Village, and persuaded the Commonwealth to locate the State Hospital for Crippled Children in Elizabethtown in 1925. Together with the Mennonites, the United Brethren in Christ, the Brethren in Christ, the River Brethren, and the United Zion Church, the constellation of Historic Peace Churches makes Elizabethtown unlike almost any other American small town. The Historic Peace Churches of Elizabethtown, the Brethren, the Mennonites, the Brethren in Christ, the River Brethren, and the United Zion Church, acting in coordinated witness, twice blocked the federal government from building major military-industrial bases in their midst, in 1942 and again in 1951. They were pacifists, and they meant it.

In most American towns, what you wore announced your income. In Elizabethtown, it announced your baptism. The plain people, the Mennonites, the Brethren in Christ, the Old Order congregations scattered across the limestone farmland of Lancaster County, dressed according to conviction. Elizabethtown was the place you came to buy it. In March of 1895, a young Brethren in Christ man named David H. Martin opened a grocery store on the northwest corner of the Square at 2 North Market Street. He was the great-great-great-grandson of a Swiss Mennonite immigrant named David Martin, who had come from Zurich to Philadelphia in 1727 and settled in East Earl. The family had been in Lancaster County for a century and a half, moving through the Mennonite and Brethren in Christ congregations, intermarrying with the Heiseys and the Engels, their roots threaded through every plain community in the region. David H. Martin knew his customers. He was his customers.

By 1905, he had added a line of clothing to the groceries, and by 1906, he had expanded across Market Street to the southeast corner of the Square. The store grew and grew again, remodeled, extended, and expanded into neighboring properties in 1967 and 1970. His brothers Ezra, Amos, Aaron, and Irwin worked alongside him. His sons, Walter and Harold, joined the business in time. Over the course of decades, it became the largest plain dress retailer in Lancaster County, perhaps in the country. By 1977, D. H. Martin's Store was selling four hundred plain suits a year. Plain people came from all over central Pennsylvania to shop there. The inventory of prayer coverings alone was unmatched anywhere: every style required by every plain church, from the most conservative Old Order Mennonite to the more progressive Brethren in Christ, each congregation with its own precise specifications about the shape and fabric of the covering a woman was to wear.

The store's advertisement said it plainly: "The Store for Plain Folks." In a town organized around Anabaptist-Pietist faith, this was not a niche market. It was the whole market.

The Martin family did not simply sell plain clothes. They lived plain. David H. Martin's brother Aaron was an ordained Brethren in Christ minister and cashier at the First National Bank of Elizabethtown, a man whose days moved between the sanctuary and the vault with no apparent sense of contradiction, because in Elizabethtown, there was none. In 1910, the two brothers helped establish the Elizabethtown Brethren in Christ congregation, building a meetinghouse on the corner of Arch and South Hanover Streets, where horse-and-buggy members parked in long sheds along the property line, while the more progressive members, some of them already driving automobiles, came in from the other direction. The congregation was plain but not rigid. It allowed Sunday schools. It embraced missionary work. It moved, carefully, with the times.

This spirit of engaged, outward-looking faith animated the family for generations. David Martin's daughter Dorothy became a missionary in Rhodesia. His son Walter served as a missionary in Jordan. His son Harold was a conscientious objector in the Second World War, serving in Civilian Public Service camps in Florida and Mississippi rather than bearing arms. Harold's wife Grace, Elizabethtown College class of 1940, served alongside him.

In 1942, David H. Martin partnered with the Reverend Paul McBeth to bring the Brethren in Christ Evangelical Visitor Publishing House to Elizabethtown, with offices and retail space at 24 East High Street. A year later, they renamed it the Christian Light Bookstore. By 1962, the corporate headquarters for the Christian Light Bookstore, the Brethren in Christ Mission Board, and the denominational administrative offices for the Church of the Brethren had all converged at 48 South Market Street, right in the center of town, a few blocks from Elizabethtown College. The Anabaptist-Pietist world had its commercial heart, its educational institution, its publishing house, and its denominational offices all within walking distance of each other on the same street.

Elizabethtown was, by every visible measure, a white community. James Loewen's study of American sundown towns identified it among the places where African Americans knew they were un-welcome after dark. The tension this created with the plain church tradition was real but rarely acknowledged. The Anabaptist vision demanded *radical inclusion* within the gathered community of faith, a conviction the Church of the Brethren made explicit in its 1935 Annual Conference resolution on "The Inter-Racial Problem," which denounced racism as incompatible with Christian discipleship and called its members to active opposition. Yet the same tradition that insisted on separation from the world's values also, in practice, main-tained a separation from the world's problems. The Brethren, who refused military service, refused fashionable dress, and refused the so-cial hierarchies of the surrounding culture did not, for the most part, refuse the sundown town. *Radical inclusion* within the sanctuary co-existed with racial exclusion beyond it, not as a contradiction anyone was compelled to resolve, but as the ordinary condition of a society whose ideals and practices had never quite caught up with each other, and which had long since stopped noticing the gap.

The Arrival

Barbour arrived in the fall of 1928 with Robert Houser and Vance Rank, the "Middletown Trio" commuting together from their shared hometown to the institution known throughout the community as College Hill, the place that would change all three of their lives. He was twenty years old. He had behind him the formation of Ebenezer AME Church, the discipline of Middletown High School, the Philadelphia weekends broadening his sense of what Black profes-sional and civic life could look like, and the nine years of growing up in a sundown town, which had given him both the wounds and the resourcefulness such an upbringing produced. He came to the College in the pre-med program, aspiring toward medicine, carrying with him the debating skills his high school yearbook editors had praised.

What he found at Elizabethtown College was not what he had been told to expect of a predominantly white institution. He found an institution genuinely shaped by a theological tradition insisting on *radical inclusion* as a condition of faithful discipleship. He found a president and a faculty taking seriously their responsibility to form the whole person: moral, intellectual, and cultural, as President Schlosser's formulation put it. He found a debate program offering him a stage on which his most distinctive gifts could develop under serious coaching. And he found, pressed into every dimension of institutional life in three words on the College motto, the imperative which would organize the next twenty-five years of his working life: Make Jesus King.

Founding The College

The founding of Elizabethtown College in 1899 cannot be understood apart from the legal and social context that produced it. The Pennsylvania Garb Law of 1895 had prohibited public school teachers from wearing any dress, mark, emblem, or insignia indicating membership in a religious order, sect, or denomination. The legislature had aimed primarily at Catholic sisters in public schools, but the law swept in every plain-dressed Anabaptist teacher in the Commonwealth. It ended careers. It closed doors. And it forced a community that had not been planning to build a college to build one.

To understand what the garb law attacked, a reader must first understand what plain dress is and why it is worn. Plain dress is not a costume or a cultural habit. It is a theological statement made with the body, a confession of faith worn into the world every day. Donald B. Kraybill, Distinguished Professor Emeritus at Elizabethtown College and the nation's preeminent scholar of Anabaptist plain communities, describes the theological root of plain dress in the concept of Gelassenheit: yieldedness, the surrender of individual will, including the individual's will to self-expression through dress, to the community of faith and to the will of God. To dress plain is to yield the self. To dress fashionably is to assert it.

The forms plain dress takes are precise and meaningful. For men, a dark suit with the lapels removed, lapels being a military and aristocratic convention and their removal being itself a declaration, replaced by a standing collar, the plain coat, sometimes accompanied by broad-fall trousers. Men wore a felt or straw hat, and the width of the brim could indicate their leadership role in the congregation. No neckties. No ornamentation. For women, the cape dress worn over the dress itself, often with an apron worn not only in the kitchen but as a daily statement, a visible symbol of the servant life discipleship demanded. Women grew their hair long, wore it pinned up, and covered it with a prayer covering, sometimes topped with a bonnet. No cosmetics. No jewelry. The body presented to the world as a servant and as a member rather than as an individual seeking status. George Fox described the practice as a form of preaching: "Be patterns, be examples," he told Friends in 1656, "that your carriage and life may preach among all sorts of people." The Quaker abolitionist John Woolman took the witness further still, wearing undyed cloth as a testimony against slavery, because the dyes used to color fabric were produced by enslaved labor. Plain dress, in his understanding, was not merely a spiritual discipline. It was a political act whose implications extended to every arrangement of the world organized around human exploitation.

This is why plain dress and racial justice are connected by more than analogy in this biography. The theological tradition asserting the world's arrangements of rank, status, and exclusion must be refused, and the refusal must be made visible, worn on the body, carried into every room, is the same tradition that produced the Elizabethtown College campus Barbour entered in 1928. The plain-dressed students and faculty he encountered on College Hill were not merely wearing old-fashioned clothes. They were enacting, in the language their tradition had developed over three centuries of persecution, the same claim Barbour's own AME formation had given him in a different register: the kingdoms of the world are not the Kingdom of God, and those who belong to the Kingdom are not obligated to honor the world's hierarchies of rank and dignity. The garb law's purpose was to remove this witness from public institutional life. The Elizabethtown founders' refusal to accept this purpose was the institutional expression of the same conviction Barbour's human rights career would express in the language of constitutional law and urban coalition politics. Both said: the world's arrangements of exclusion are not final.

The story of how it worked in practice is the story of Elizabeth Myer, born in Bareville, Lancaster County, on June 7, 1863, the fifth of twelve children in a farm family, a member of the Conestoga Church of the Brethren, a congregation founded in 1724. In September 1885 she enrolled at the Millersville State Normal School and walked through its doors in her plain dress. She was the only student on campus dressed that way. She considered leaving. The principal, Benjamin Franklin Shaub, born in 1841, came from a Mennonite background and understood from the inside what plain dress meant and why it was worn. He promised her she would be respected for her convictions. It was a promise that cost him something: student and faculty opposition to his support of Elizabeth Myer forced Shaub to resign as principal in 1887. He paid for his integrity with his position. But Elizabeth Myer stayed. In 1887, the same year Shaub resigned, she graduated and delivered the salutatorian address. She then taught in the public schools of Lancaster County for fourteen years. Her persistence sent a signal through the plain church communities of the region. It was possible. A plain-dressed woman could earn the highest academic honors a normal school offered, and other Anabaptists from the plain sects took courage from her example.

Then the state changed the rules. The Pennsylvania legislature passed the Garb Law in 1895, and Elizabeth Myer's fourteen years in the public school classroom were over. She came to Elizabethtown College in 1900 as its first faculty member, teacher of mathematics, elocution, and English, because the College offered a teaching home from which the law could not reach her. The statement the hiring made could not have been clearer if it had been carved in stone above the door. This institution existed, in part, because the state had tried to silence a form of witness. The college's response was to place the woman who embodied that witness at the center of its academic life.

Myer's presence in the institution for twenty-four years, until her death on May 19, 1924, four years before Barbour arrived on College Hill, meant she did not live to teach him directly. But the institution he arrived at in the fall of 1928 bore her mark in ways both literal and deep. The chapel talks she had given for two decades, whose humor and practical wisdom made "necessary and important lessons palatable and believable," her flexible wit, her infinite store of curious anecdotes, had shaped the institutional culture Barbour inherited. The *Our College Times* memorial tribute, published June 1, 1924, offered the students' own honest assessment: "Her very eccentricities endeared her to us." On May 22, 1924, three days after her death, the College suspended classes for the day. At the morning chapel service, Ralph W. Schlosser, the man who would mentor Barbour four years later, rose to speak, emphasizing the Christian ideals for which Myer had stood. The Faculty Quartet sang "Lead Kindly Light" and "In a Far Away Land." She was buried in the Myer Cemetery near Bareville, the family farm where the plain church tradition she had carried to Millersville had first formed her. Her epitaph was from Shakespeare: "After life's fitful fever she sleeps well."

The author's peer-reviewed study with Steven M. Nolt, "Plain Dress in the Docket," published in *Pennsylvania History in 2021*, reconstructs in archival detail the next chapter of this story: the 1908 to 1910 case of Lillian Herr Risser, born in 1887, a Mennonite alumna of Elizabethtown College who became the subject of the first legal challenge to the garb law when she was hired by the Board of School Directors of Mount Joy Township to teach in the public schools. She dressed plain, as her faith required. In 1909 the board was brought under investigation for violating the Garb Law. The case came before Charles Israel Landis, born in 1856, President Judge of the Courts of Lancaster County, an Episcopalian descended from Swiss Mennonites from Paradise Township, Pennsylvania. Judge Landis ruled the Act of 1895 unconstitutional. The opposition organized quickly. The Junior Order of United American Mechanics, founded in 1844 and strongly anti-Catholic, held their annual convention in Lancaster and appropriated one thousand dollars toward the expenses of appealing the ruling to the Supreme Court of Pennsylvania. Elizabeth Myer, now editor of the college newspaper *Our College Times*, published a call to raise no less than five hundred dollars to defend the case through the courts. The Reverend George Bucher, born in 1845, one of the founders of Elizabethtown College and chair of its first Board of Trustees, wrote a series of articles in the *Daily New Era* defending plain dress, later printed as a pamphlet: The Garb Law: An Argument on the Pennsylvania Garb Law in Relation to Public School Teachers. The college rallied. Money was raised. Legal counsel was engaged. In 1910, the Supreme Court of Pennsylvania heard the matter under the title Commonwealth v. Amos R. Herr. The justices upheld the Garb Law and found the school directors of Mount Joy Township in violation of it. Lillian Risser could not teach in her plain dress in a Pennsylvania public school.

But Lillian Risser did not disappear. She went to work managing the plain dress department at Hager's Department Store at 25 West King Street in Lancaster, the premier dry goods and clothing establishment serving Lancaster County's plain church communities. The woman the Pennsylvania Supreme Court had ruled could not be seen in plain dress in a public school classroom became the person the Mennonites and Brethren of Lancaster County went to when they needed to buy plain clothes. The state had tried to make her invisible. The market made her indispensable. The college that had fought for her had lost the lawsuit. But it had embedded in its institutional character a habit of choosing a side when choosing cost something, a habit that would prove more durable than any legal brief. The Garb Law of 1895 was absorbed into the Public School Act in 1949 as Section 1112, its language nearly unchanged. On November 6, 2023, Governor Josh Shapiro signed legislation eliminating Section 1112 from the Public School Code, repealing a law that had stood for one hundred and twenty-eight years. The repeal came eighteen months after the publication of the Benowitz and Nolt study documenting its history and constitutional significance. All of this had happened before Barbour arrived. The institution he was about to enter had already been tested, had already chosen its side, had already paid a price for its convictions. He could feel the institutional character those choices had shaped the moment he climbed College Hill.

The founding charter of the College had declared it "open to all such as desire to avail themselves of its privileges," and a statement crafted by faculty and students published in Our College Times in 1904 affirmed the doors were "open to everybody, regardless of creed." These were not rhetorical gestures. They reflected the Anabaptist theology of *radical inclusion*, the conviction that the gathered community of voluntary believers could not be organized around the exclusions of the surrounding social order without betraying its theological identity. Steven M. Nolt, in his authoritative institutional history, The Brethren Heritage of Elizabethtown College, traces the development of this founding commitment across the College's first century, showing how the tension between the institution's Brethren character and its stated openness to all was navigated across successive generations of leaders and students. The tension was never fully resolved, as tensions between institutional identity and genuine inclusion rarely are. But the commitment was real, and it shaped the environment Barbour encountered when he arrived in 1928 in ways distinguishing Elizabethtown from many other educational institutions of the period. He was not admitted grudgingly. He was admitted as the fulfillment of a founding commitment.

To understand what Elizabethtown College gave Barbour, one must understand the theological tradition from which the institution emerged. The Church of the Brethren carried two impulses in productive tension. The first was Pietism, the late seventeenth-century renewal movement associated with Philip Jacob Spener and August Hermann Francke, which charged the magisterial Reformation with having changed doctrine while leaving the heart untouched. Pietist teaching insisted on the necessity of personal transformation, the integration of head and heart and hand in a comprehensive renewal of the whole person, and the expression of that renewal in both private devotion and public life. The Pietist emphasis on practical holiness, charitable service, and the transformation of social conditions was not a departure from the Reformation's theological commitments; it was, in the Pietist argument, their necessary fulfillment.

The second impulse was Anabaptism, the radical wing of the sixteenth-century Reformation, which insisted on voluntary church membership, adult baptism as a conscious covenantal act, the complete separation of church and state, and the nonresistant refusal of violence in all human relationships. The Anabaptists had been persecuted by both Catholics and Protestants during the sixteenth century, drowned, burned, and executed for their refusal to accept the established church's authority over the gathered community of voluntary believers. Their persecution had pressed into their theological tradition a deep understanding of what it meant for the state to use its power against communities of conscience, and a deep commitment to the freedom of the gathered community to organize its life according to its own theological convictions rather than the imperatives of the surrounding society.

Harold S. Bender, the Mennonite historian whose 1944 presidential address to the American Society of Church History gave the Anabaptist tradition its most celebrated twentieth-century scholarly articulation, organized the Anabaptist Vision around three interlocking emphases: the transformation of the entire way of life according to the teachings and example of Christ; the church as a voluntary community of the disciplined and committed; and Christian love and nonresistance applied to all human relationships. The Brethren who founded Elizabethtown College in 1899 were operating within precisely this theological inheritance, working out its implications for the education of a new generation before Bender gave it its landmark scholarly expression.

This theological inheritance bore directly on Barbour's formation in several ways. It gave him a framework for understanding discipleship as necessarily costly and necessarily public: following Jesus was not a private spiritual achievement but a communal practice, sustained in the gathered community of the committed and expressed in the total orientation of one's life toward the values of the Kingdom of God. It gave him a vocabulary for understanding the relationship between the church and the state as fundamentally one of witness rather than accommodation. And it gave him a model of *radical inclusion* as a theological commitment rather than a political concession: the gathered community was open to all willing to commit to its disciplines, not because inclusion was politically convenient but because exclusion was theologically incoherent.

The Mentor

For sixty-three years, from 1907 to 1970, the Reverend Dr. Ralph W. Schlosser gave himself wholly to Elizabethtown College, weaving himself so completely into the life of the community, the college and the man became, in some essential way, inseparable.

The presiding intelligence of Elizabethtown College during Barbour's years there was President Schlosser, and no single figure did more to shape what those four years produced. A member of the Class of 1907, Schlosser had devoted his entire adult life to the institution, serving successively as professor of English, vice president, dean, and president. He knew what the College had cost to build because he had helped build it, spending a year and a half soliciting funds across Lancaster County before he could teach a single class. When he assumed the presidency on January 1, 1928, the very year Barbour arrived, he was not merely an administrator. He was the institution's most invested memory. He was Barbour's English professor, his academic advisor, his debate coach, his theatrical director, and his faculty advisor and student employment supervisor on the yearbook staff. He was, in the fullest sense, his intellectual mentor.

Schlosser articulated the College's educational philosophy in a 1928 letter in precise terms: "The primary purposes of this college are moral, intellectual, and cultural." The formulation was theologically dense. Moral signaled an education oriented toward the formation of character, rooted in the Pietist conviction that authentic transformation encompassed the whole person and expressed itself in the concrete practices of civic life. Intellectual affirmed the dignity of rigorous inquiry, the belief that the mind's capacity for critical judgment was a gift to be cultivated rather than a threat to be managed. Cultural implied the formation of whole persons capable of participating in and contributing to the common life of civilization, persons who understood themselves as inheritors and responsible stewards of accumulated human wisdom. These were not three separate goals. They were three dimensions of one.

The curriculum through which Schlosser pursued this vision engaged students directly with the foundational texts of Western civilization across the full range of human inquiry. The syllabus was comprehensive and demanding: Homer's *Iliad* and *Odyssey*, Plato's *Republic* and *Symposium*, Aristotle's *Ethics, Politics, and Metaphysics, Virgil* and *Plutarch*, Augustine's *Confessions* and *City of God*, Aquinas's *Summa Theologica*, Dante's *Divine Comedy*, Chaucer's *Canterbury Tales*, Machiavelli's *Prince*, Erasmus's *In Praise of Folly*, Shakespeare's complete works, Milton's *Paradise Lost*, Locke's *Essay Concerning Human Understanding* and *Two Treatises of Government*, Rousseau's *Social Contract*, the *Declaration of Independence*, the Federalist Papers, and forward into the nineteenth and twentieth centuries. Students did not read about these texts. They read them, argued about them, and wrote on them.

This was intellectual formation with a purpose: the cultivation of what the Aristotelian tradition calls phronesis, practical wisdom, the capacity for independent moral judgment in complex circumstances rather than the mechanical application of rules. The faculty appointments supporting this curriculum expressed the same philosophy. Harry Hess Nye held the professorship of American History and Philosophy, a deliberate pairing that refused to separate empirical inquiry from moral reflection. Forrest L. Weller was Professor of History and Sociology, integrating the study of the past with the analysis of present social structures. These were not administrative conveniences. They were expressions of a curricular vision insisting that the boundaries between disciplines were sites of productive inquiry rather than barriers to be maintained.

What did these texts do to a young Black man from a Pennsylvania sundown town who would spend his life arguing for racial justice in city halls and legislative chambers? They gave him the deepest possible grounding for the arguments he would need to make. Plato's *Republic* posed the question 'What is justice?' with a directness no subsequent treatment has superseded. That question was not, for Barbour reading it in Schlosser's classroom, a theoretical exercise. It was the question his entire life was organized around answering. The Republic's argument that justice is a condition of the whole community, that injustice distorts the entire social order rather than merely the individuals it most directly harms, mapped precisely onto the structural analysis of racial discrimination his human rights career would develop. When he later argued before Denver's city council that racial discrimination imposed costs on all taxpayers through the social consequences of enforced poverty, he was making a Platonic argument dressed in the language of municipal budgeting.

Aristotle's *Politics and Ethics* raised questions about the relationship between the individual and the community, between the virtues of the good citizen and the virtues of the good person, that bore directly on his understanding of what an integrator must be. Aristotle's phronesis described precisely the skill Barbour was developing: the ability to read situations accurately, to deploy the right method in the right context, and to hold the long-term goal of genuine community while navigating the short-term constraints of political possibility. Locke's Second Treatise provided the philosophical architecture for the civil rights movement's most fundamental claims, and Barbour knew the architecture from the inside. When he traced the lineage of human dignity from the Magna Carta through the Declaration of Independence to the Universal Declaration of Human Rights, he was not invoking names for rhetorical effect. He had read the primary texts. He could deploy them in argument with the authority of someone who had actually worked through them.

The biblical texts that moved through the curriculum alongside these philosophical works provided a different but complementary layer. The Sermon on the Mount's radical ethics of love, the prophets' denunciations of injustice, the Exodus narrative of liberation from bondage: these operated in Barbour's formation not as doctrinal impositions but as the literary and theological resources of a tradition insisting that human society could and should be organized around values beyond those the powerful preferred to maintain. When he later wrote about humanity's inexorable drive toward a society in which dignity and brotherhood become realities in social living, he was drawing on both philosophical and biblical traditions, synthesized in the way that only an education rooted in both could produce.

The students who passed through Schlosser's classroom did not leave neutral about the experience. They recognized they had encountered something uncommon. The Class of 1949 identified a passage from Schlosser's own History of Elizabethtown College as the essential Schlosser, the distilled mandate of everything he had pressed into his students: "Put your life on the side of those striving to consummate a constructive program for humanity. Dare to do right at any cost. Never flinch when duty calls." Three sentences, brief and absolute. They named with precision what Barbour's subsequent career demonstrated he had absorbed. The willingness to put his life on the side of those striving for humanity, to dare to do right at any cost, and to refuse to flinch when duty called organized every significant decision of his twenty-five-year career, from the Philadelphia police station in October 1945 to the Denver swimming pools in 1951 to the Mojave Desert drive of May 1954.

Schlosser himself articulated what he sought in the teaching relationship simply: "no greater reward can come to a teacher than his acquaintance with young people who have left the college and are now leaders in various vocations and professions." The remark was not vanity. It was a theological statement about the nature of formative education. The teacher's purpose was not the transmission of information but the formation of persons capable of leadership in the world the College was preparing them to serve. He found the deepest satisfaction of his teaching life in sharing what he called his philosophy of life, voiced in lines from Robert Browning: "A man's reach should exceed his grasp, what I aspired to be and was not comforts me." The lines were not a confession of failure. They were an affirmation of vocation: the conviction that the aspiring, the reaching, the persistent effort toward an ideal not yet achieved was itself the substance of a meaningful life. For the student who absorbed this philosophy across four years of formation in the late 1920s and early 1930s, the student who would spend twenty-five years working toward an integration he could define more clearly than he could fully achieve, they named the deepest truth of his own life as well. They named, in Browning's vocabulary, what the Anabaptist tradition had pressed into two German words on the title page of the Martyrs Mirror: Arbeite und Hoffe. Work and Hope. The aspiring was the substance. The harvest belonged to God.

There is one detail in Schlosser's account of his teaching that gives the relationship a human texture. In his 1970 letter explaining his retirement after sixty-three years of service, he cited among his reasons a hearing deficiency compelling him to use the lecture method, which was, he wrote, contrary to his own method of presenting materials to his classes. The hearing loss had forced him to abandon the practice he believed in most: discussion, the exchange of ideas in which the teacher learned from the student as much as the student learned from the teacher. Even so, at the very end, he asked to teach one more Shakespeare course, offered during the summer term when smaller enrollment made intimate discussion possible, because the small classes allowed him to use the discussion method without interference. He had been compensating for years, adapting his pedagogy to preserve what mattered most. Barbour's years at the College, 1928 to 1932, fell within this period. The debate coaching and the theatrical direction, both contexts where Schlosser could hear directly and adapt in real time, were precisely the settings in which his preferred method was most viable. The forms of mentorship Schlosser gave Barbour were not accidental. They were the forms his hearing allowed. In 1932, the year Barbour graduated, Schlosser completed a translation of the court scene from The Merchant of Venice into Pennsylvania German, rendering Shylock's bond and Portia's mercy speech into the vernacular of the Pennsylvania Dutch farms surrounding the campus. He noted that in discussions with students he learned much in keeping himself open to the ideas of youth. This was not a pedagogical method. It was a theological conviction: the exchange of ideas across the table, the teacher formed by the encounter as surely as the student.

The Word

The biblical dimension of this formation found its most sustained institutional expression in the work of Associate Professor Martha Martin, who taught Bible at the College from 1924 to 1949. Her contribution extended well beyond the classroom. Through the annual Bible Terms and Bible Institutes, gatherings drawing hundreds and at times more than a thousand participants from both the student body and the surrounding community, she built a culture of biblical literacy that was simultaneously intellectual and devotional, campus-based and communally grounded. Her work exemplified the Brethren synthesis of academic formation and congregational life that characterized Elizabethtown College at its best.

Martin's presence during Barbour's years placed him in direct contact with the most intensive institutional expression of biblical formation the tradition could offer. The Bible was not, at Elizabethtown, a text studied primarily for its literary or historical interest, though Schlosser's curriculum accorded it the same close textual attention it gave to Homer and Plato and Augustine. It was a text of formation: the primary record of the revelation from which the Brethren tradition derived its commitments to nonresistance, community accountability, *radical inclusion*, and costly discipleship. To read the Bible in Martin's classes was to encounter the theological roots of the institutional commitments the college's motto expressed.

The students who sat in Martin's classroom left a record of what the experience was like. The editors of the 1953 *Conestogan* dedicated the yearbook to her in these words: "With her radiant smile and cheerful countenance, she guides us in learning truths from God's word. From the opening prayer to the final assignment, her classes in Bible study impart scriptural knowledge and inspiration to students of all faiths. Over a period of twenty-five years as instructor in Bible, her consecrated life has challenged thousands of men and women to devote themselves to God's will." The phrase 'students of all faiths' is not incidental. It names precisely the context in which Barbour, formed by the AME tradition, sat in Martin's classroom and read the Bible through the lens of a tradition not his own but deeply consonant with it. She was, at her death, the only living charter member of the Elizabethtown Church of the Brethren, the congregation that had founded the college. The church preceded the institution, and it was from the gathered community's vision of what Christian education should be that the college had been called into existence. In Martin, that founding impulse was still present, still teaching. She had been there from the beginning. Barbour was one of the thousands whose lives her teaching tried to shape.

For Barbour, already formed by the AME Church's understanding of Scripture as a text of prophetic witness, Martin's Brethren hermeneutic offered a complementary lens: the reading of biblical texts through the disciplines of Anabaptist nonresistance, voluntary community, and radical inclusion. The two traditions read the same Bible toward the same horizon. The AME pressed its members toward prophetic confrontation with racial hierarchy. The Brethren pressed theirs toward the patient construction of the alternative community as a form of witness. Barbour needed both. His human rights career would require both.

The Argument

Schlosser understood that the capacity for clear argument, disciplined by evidence and constrained by logical form, was not merely a professional skill in the Anabaptist-Pietist tradition. It was a form of witness. The community of voluntary believers, organized not by the coercive power of the state but by the persuasion of truth, depended on its members' ability to make their convictions legible to their neighbors. Nonresistance did not mean passivity. It meant the rejection of coercive force in favor of the persuasive power of argument, testimony, and example. Debate was, in this tradition, a form of discipleship.

Between 1930 and 1938, Elizabethtown's intercollegiate debating program compiled approximately 150 contests and a formidable winning record. The Forensic Arts Club institutionalized instruction in oratory, extemporaneous speaking, interpretive reading, and parliamentary procedure. Schlosser coached the teams himself, bringing to the work the same theological seriousness and intellectual rigor he brought to his literature courses.

Barbour joined the debate team in his first year and was voted onto the squad. The 1932 Etonian records the judgment of his classmates: 'His logical and clever thinking, combined with his wit, made him successful.' The assessment is borne out by the subsequent career. The Barbour who argued for fair employment practices before the Colorado state senate in 1949, who presented the case for racial integration in housing before the Denver Mayor's Committee on Human Relations, who addressed civic audiences in Los Angeles and Tucson on the gap between democratic profession and democratic performance, was deploying exactly the skills developed under Schlosser's coaching. Preparing for competition required the research to understand a policy question in depth, the analytical capacity to identify the strongest arguments on both sides, the rhetorical skill to present those arguments clearly to a general audience, and the strategic intelligence to anticipate and respond to opposition in real time. These were precisely the skills his human rights career would demand. He was developing them in the community that would give him his theological mandate.

The literary and dramatic culture of the College reinforced what debate was building. Schlosser's commitment to serious theatrical work reflected his conviction that aesthetic cultivation was an essential dimension of moral and intellectual formation. Students who performed Shakespeare were developing empathetic imagination, the capacity to inhabit perspectives not their own and give them convincing expression, which the work of racial reconciliation would require.

The senior class production of *Othello* offered a concentrated instance of the racial dynamics Barbour navigated throughout his college years. Shakespeare's play is structured around an explicitly racialized protagonist, a Moorish general whose genius is acknowledged even as his racial identity marks him as threatening in ways the Venetian social order cannot fully contain. The production gave Barbour a role identified in the program as 'Julio,' a figure absent from Shakespeare's original text. The designation points to a localized modification, an addition or renaming designed to expand participation in a drama whose racial politics were too obvious to ignore. The choice to give Barbour a role, even one requiring textual modification, was a choice for inclusion over exclusion, consistent with the College's foundational commitment. The choice not to cast him as Othello was shaped by the racial assumptions of the period, assumptions the College shared even as it worked against their most obvious expressions. The gap between the College's theological commitment to *radical inclusion* and its imperfect institutional realization is itself part of the story. What Barbour made of the role is not recoverable from the surviving record. But the skills he brought to it, public performance, giving credible voice to a character not entirely his own, inhabiting a scene with conviction and clarity, were skills his human rights career would demand. The human rights leader who could walk into a room of white businessmen or white legislators and speak to them on their own ground, who could argue for racial justice in language calculated to persuade rather than alienate, was drawing on exactly the capacities debate and theater had developed.

He also served on the yearbook staff, and this too was formation. Writing about his classmates, crafting the language through which a community recorded itself, learning to observe people with precision and describe them with fairness: these were the skills of the advocate, the organizer, the writer who would spend a career making the case for integration in the language his audiences could hear. The 1932 *Etonian*'s portrait of him, warm and specific and slightly surprised by its own admiration, is evidence he had already begun to develop that capacity in others.

The Field As Classroom

For thirty-three years, from 1928 to 1961, Ira Herr walked the sidelines at Elizabethtown College, shaping young athletes season after season until his presence became not merely a fixture of the college, but the very heartbeat of its athletic soul. Herr came to the role with a formation the college could not have designed better had it tried. He came from an Anabaptist family whose heritage gave him the same theological commitments the college's motto expressed, and before earning his degree at Franklin and Marshall College he had been a student in Elizabethtown's own college preparatory academy, walking the same campus as a high school student that he would later walk as a coach. When Schlosser's letter arrived in 1928 outlining what the college expected of its athletic program, Herr did not need to be persuaded. He already knew.

Barbour's participation in the College's unofficial football squad, known affectionately as The Brutal Thirteen, extended his formation into the domain of physical discipline and team accountability, as did his place on the track team, where individual effort and collective purpose found a different but equally demanding expression, and on the basketball team, where the rapid interplay of competition and cooperation tested a different register of the same disciplined formation. Schlosser had been direct with athletic director Ira Herr at his appointment: the College's primary purposes were moral, intellectual, and cultural, and athletics existed in service of these goals rather than apart from them. Victory achieved at the cost of honor was to be regarded as defeat. Special treatment for athletes, whether through subsidies, scholarships, or academic concessions based on athletic skill alone, was prohibited. In this framework, the athletic field was not separate from the classroom. It was another site where the same formation was pursued by different means.

Herr understood and honored this framework. His coaching earned him recognition across Lancaster County not for winning records alone but for what his athletes became, praised for outstanding sportsmanship, Christian bearing, and the lasting influence he exerted upon coaches and players. That phrase, Christian bearing, named precisely what Schlosser's letter had required: the subordination of victory to character, the institutional expression of the College's theological commitment in the arena of competitive sport.

For Barbour, what the athletic field offered was the daily practice of discipline, fair play, and mutual accountability to teammates, and something more. Gerald Huesken Jr.'s careful reconstruction of The Brutal Thirteen demonstrates that Barbour's participation in 1928 may represent an earlier breach in Lancaster County's collegiate athletic color lines than any other documented case. At Franklin and Marshall College, the county's only other institution with a varsity football program, an African American varsity player does not appear in the record until 1958. Barbour's participation predated that by three decades. The explanation lies in the College's theological framework itself. When character is the measure of athletic participation rather than competitive utility, including a Black player is not a calculated risk. It is the fulfillment of the institution's founding commitment. The Anabaptist tradition of *radical inclusion,* pressed into the athletic field by Schlosser's framework, made possible what competitive logic alone would not have demanded.

The Mandate

The College motto "Make Jesus King" was not an abstract aspiration. It appeared on the College seal, was woven into official correspondence and college publications, and was understood by the faculty, administration, and students as the organizing principle of everything the institution was trying to do. In the Anabaptist-Pietist tradition from which it emerged, king did not mean sovereign political authority. It meant the Kingdom of God proclaimed by Jesus in the Gospels: the reign of God's values, the community organized around love, justice, nonresistance, and *radical inclusion.* To "Make Jesus King" was not to impose a theocratic order on the surrounding society, for the Brethren tradition of church-state separation explicitly rejected that. It was to organize one's own life and community around the values of the Kingdom, to refuse the competing claims of status, violence, exclusion, and domination, and to build in the institutions one inhabited a visible alternative to the social order organized around those claims.

Barbour arrived at Elizabethtown already carrying a version of this imperative from the AME tradition, where making Jesus King meant confronting racial hierarchy as both a theological error and a civic failure. The Brethren version added dimensions. The nonresistant refusal of violence. The emphasis on building alternative communities rather than only confronting existing ones. The conviction that persuasion and example, not coercion, were the instruments of the Kingdom. These were not contradictions to what the AME had given him. They were complements, adding to the prophetic confrontation of the AME the constructive institution-building of the Brethren and the rhetorical discipline of a tradition that insisted on argument rather than force. The formation was not conscious. He was a college student, studying literature and history, competing in debate, performing on stage, playing football, running track, and competing on the basketball court. But the motto was being pressed into him through four years of living in a community organized around it, and it would prove to be the most durable thing his education gave him.

What He Carried Out

The 1932 *Etonian* recorded the community's assessment of Barbour with warmth and specificity: 'In the trio from Middletown, we think Barbour the leader. Ever since our first year, his drollness, his alert mind, his tolerance, and his affableness have made him liked on College Hill. In his Freshman year he went out for debating and was voted a member of the team. His logical and clever thinking, combined with his wit, made him successful. In his Sophomore year, we think English Literature was his main vocation or avocation. We have even known him to compose verses on Lord Byron. He claims to have read every piece of literature in the history of English Literature, or at least it seemed that amount. Let into a conversation on literature sometime with Barbour and see how long it will last.' The editors concluded: 'Whatever he may do we are certain his personality will bring him hosts of friends. He will be a success, such is our wish.'

The portrait is true as far as it goes. The drollness and the affableness were real, and they would serve him in coalition work where the ability to find common ground across vast differences of race, class, and political conviction was not a social grace but a professional necessity. The alert mind and the logical thinking were real, and they would equip him for the empirical research, the policy analysis, and the public argument his human rights work required. The tolerance was real, the fruit of a formation in two theological traditions both insisting, from their founding moments, that authentic faith opened rather than closed the circle of community. What the editors could not yet see was the depth of the theological conviction that organized all of these gifts and gave them direction. They were seeing a college student. They were not yet seeing the human rights leader he was becoming.

On June 6, 1932, William Wilbur Miller Barbour walked across the commencement stage and received his Bachelor of Arts degree in English Literature. He was twenty-three years old, graduating from a college whose motto had given him a mandate and whose formation had given him the tools to begin fulfilling it. Four days later, more than one hundred guests gathered at Fisherman's Hall on South Lawrence Street in Middletown to mark the occasion. The reception was the local world's answer to the College Hill ceremony: one of the first African Americans from Middletown to graduate from college had done so with distinction, and his community knew it. He had crossed one stage. He was about to cross a wider one.

James Anderson, in The Education of Blacks in the South, documents how the liberal arts education Barbour received at Elizabethtown was systematically denied to most Black students of the period, channeled instead toward vocational training designed to produce compliant workers rather than critical citizens. Adam Fairclough, in *A Class of Their Own*, shows how Black educators and their white allies navigated these pressures, using the resources available to cultivate the intellectual and civic capacities their students needed for a life of freedom. Barbour's experience placed him in the small minority of Black college graduates of his generation equipped with the full intellectual resources for the kind of human rights leadership his career would demand.

He left Elizabethtown carrying the formation, the relationships, and the mandate. Schlosser would remain a presence in his life, tracking his career through the College's alumni communications. The peace church networks his formation had connected him to would continue to provide the interracial organizational infrastructure his human rights work would draw on. He had been given, in four years on College Hill, an education in history, literature, and biblical thought that equipped him to argue for justice from the deepest foundations of the Western moral tradition. He had been given a public voice, shaped by debate and theater and the discipline of writing for and about his community. He had been given an experience of genuine theological inclusion, imperfect but real, that taught him what interracial partnership could look like when it was grounded in conviction rather than convenience. And he had been given three words that would organize his professional life for the next twenty-five years, pressed into him not through lectures but through the daily practice of an institution that was, however imperfectly, attempting to live by them.

The Great Depression awaiting him was not the world he had been educated for. It was the world he had been educated to transform. He was ready to begin.

| 4 |

The Disciple Goes to Work

The summer of 1932 in Philadelphia arrived with the particular cruelty of heat layered over despair. The breadlines on South Street and Market Street stretched around corners and doubled back on themselves, their populations patient in the way people become patient when there is nowhere else to go. The relief offices, overwhelmed and understaffed, processed their applicants with the mixture of bureaucratic efficiency and studied indifference that institutions adopt when demand permanently exceeds capacity. Along the Schuylkill River, encampments of men had been growing since 1930, men who had worked in the Baldwin Locomotive Works and the Navy Yard and the textile mills of Kensington until the Depression swept those jobs away and left them in the river bottoms. By June 1932, the third year of the economic collapse, Philadelphia had spent most of its relief funds, was borrowing against anticipated revenues, and was contemplating austerity measures that, for the people at the bottom of the economic order, translated into hunger.

For Black Philadelphia, the Depression was not a new emergency but an intensification of conditions that had never been far from emergency. The racial hierarchy of the labor market had always confined Black workers to the most precarious, lowest-paid, most easily replaced positions, the positions that evaporated first when any employer faced pressure to reduce costs. Now, in the third year of a collapse which had reduced the entire economy, those positions were gone, and the positions which might have opened to Black workers in better times remained reserved for white workers whose own economic precarity gave them no interest in sharing whatever remained. The Urban League of Philadelphia estimated Black unemployment in the city at somewhere between 40 and 56 percent by 1932, figures representing not merely individual hardship but the systematic operation of a labor market organized to absorb white workers' losses before acknowledging Black workers had losses to absorb.

William Wilbur Miller Barbour stepped into this world on June 6, 1932, carrying the degree and the mandate described in the closing pages of Chapter Three. None of that formation changed the fact he was Black, in Philadelphia, in 1932, in the worst year of the worst economic crisis the country had experienced since the Civil War, and the mechanisms of racial exclusion operating in his city regarded his gifts as, at best, an interesting exception to a general rule and, at worst, an implicit challenge to a racial hierarchy which had survived far more explicit challenges than the mere existence of an educated Black man with a degree rooted in the classics.

The gap between his formation and his circumstances was the central fact of his early professional years. He had been trained, at Elizabethtown, to think rigorously and argue persuasively and understand the Western intellectual tradition from Plato to Locke; he had been formed, at Ebenezer AME, to understand discipleship as necessarily public and necessarily costly; and he had been given, through the intersection of these two traditions, the mandate "Make Jesus King" as the organizing principle of his professional life. Now he had to figure out what making Jesus king looked like in Depression-era Philadelphia, with limited financial resources, no institutional position, no professional network beyond his college friendships and his church connections, and a city in crisis providing inadequate services to everyone and particularly inadequate services to its Black citizens. The question was not whether to do the work. The motto did not permit this question. The question was how.

To understand what Barbour found when he returned to Philadelphia after graduation, it helps to understand the geography and institutional landscape of the city's Black community at the moment of his arrival. Philadelphia's Black population in 1932 was concentrated in a series of neighborhoods in North, West, and South Philadelphia, their boundaries defined not by statute but by the informal mechanisms of racial exclusion, restrictive real estate covenants, discriminatory lending practices by savings institutions and banks, and the social pressure of white neighborhood associations willing to use extralegal means to enforce the racial geography their legal instruments had established.

The neighborhoods themselves were dense, layered with the institutional life of three decades of Great Migration growth. The AME churches, Baptist churches, and smaller Black Protestant congregations anchored every significant block, their sanctuary buildings serving simultaneously as places of worship, community meeting halls, political organizing spaces, and social service centers. The fraternal lodges, the Prince Hall Masons, the Elks, the Knights of Pythias, provided the male civic networking which complemented the church's more comprehensive institutional role. The women's clubs, the Philadelphia chapter of the National Association of Colored Women, the local clubs affiliated with which organization, provided the political education and the civic advocacy which women's civic organizations had developed since the Progressive era. *The Philadelphia Tribune*, the NAACP branch, the Urban League, and a dozen smaller civic organizations completed the institutional landscape of a community which had built, out of the materials available to it, a civic infrastructure sufficient to sustain collective life in conditions designed to prevent it.

Matthew Countryman's *Up South* traces the development of this civic infrastructure from the Great Migration through the mass movement of the 1960s with the scholarly rigor and narrative accessibility of the best community history. Countryman demonstrates how the dense institutional network of Black Philadelphia, built in the decades before the Long Civil Rights Movement's organizational phase, provided the organizational base for civil rights campaigns that were locally distinctive even as they connected to national patterns. The organizations Barbour was encountering and engaging with in the early 1930s were not merely cultural institutions; they were the civil rights movement's local infrastructure, the organizations through which the political demands and the organizational capacity of the community were being developed and sustained in the years before those demands and that capacity were deployed in more visible campaigns.

The Philadelphia Tribune, under E. Washington Rhodes, was a civil rights institution as much as a journalistic one. *The Tribune* documented racial discrimination in Philadelphia's public and private institutions, advocated for legislative and legal remedies, provided the media platform through which civil rights organizations communicated with the community, and served as a vehicle of political education for a readership which needed, in the absence of civic institutions willing to serve them equally, to educate itself about the full range of its political rights and its political options. Barbour's later career as a writer and public advocate, his capacity to use the newspaper column and the magazine article and the public address as vehicles for civil rights argument, was shaped in part by his early observation of how the Black press functioned as a civil rights institution in its own right.

The Stage

Barbour organized the Cavaliers theatrical club in the months after his return to Philadelphia, and the character of the organization he created reflects both his Elizabethtown formation and his understanding of the institutional landscape he was entering. The Cavaliers was a club of African American college and university students, a deliberate choice reflecting the belief, shaped by the AME tradition's emphasis on educated leadership and the Elizabethtown tradition's formation rooted in the classics, that the Black community's most urgently needed civil rights advocates were its educated young people. By organizing a theatrical club specifically for this population, Barbour was creating an institution through which the gifts of college-educated Black Philadelphians could be directed toward the community's cultural and civic development.

The theatrical tradition from which the Cavaliers drew was itself politically charged in ways the academic history of theater sometimes obscures. African American theater in the 1920s and 1930s was engaged in the same project as the Harlem Renaissance's literary and visual art: the construction and assertion of a complex, fully human Black identity against a dominant culture insisting on Black people's simplicity and inferiority. The white theatrical tradition had produced, in its representation of Black characters, a gallery of stereotypes from the minstrel tradition which reduced Black humanity to caricature. Black theater's response was the production of dramatic representations of Black life in its full complexity, its dignity, its suffering, its humor, and its aspiration.

Barbour's 1933 one-act play, 'A Modern Version of the Assassination of Julius Caesar,' was his contribution to this tradition. The choice of subject matter was deliberate and sophisticated. Julius Caesar's assassination was not merely a historical event; in the theatrical tradition from which Shakespeare had drawn, it was a meditation on the tension between democratic legitimacy and the power of individual ambition, between the republic's institutions and the men claiming to serve them. To modernize this text in 1933, at the beginning of the New Deal, in the context of a Black community watching the democratic institutions of the United States systematically exclude them from the benefits of democratic governance, was to make a political argument through a literary vehicle which the white-dominated civic culture could not easily dismiss as merely political. Art had rhetorical access which politics often did not.

The contest among thirteen African American fraternities and sororities in which Barbour entered his play, and in which the play placed third, was itself evidence of the civic vitality of Black Philadelphia's educated community. Thirteen organizations of college-educated Black Philadelphians were producing, evaluating, and competing in cultural production as a form of civic engagement. The standard representing the field was evidently high enough placing third was a recognition of genuine merit rather than a consolation prize. Barbour was operating in a sophisticated civic ecosystem, contributing to a tradition of Black cultural production whose political dimensions were understood by its participants and its audiences even when they were not made explicit.

The musical drama "Fifty Years of Progress," Barbour directed at Haverford College and was performed multiple times for appreciative audiences, deserves attention as a specifically interracial production in a specifically Quaker institutional context. Haverford College, founded in 1833 by Quakers committed to the antislavery tradition, was an institution whose own institutional history had prepared it to host the kind of Black cultural production Barbour was offering. The Quaker connection, linking Haverford's antislavery heritage to the peace church networks Barbour's Elizabethtown formation had given him access to, was not incidental. It was an early instance of the interracial coalition-building characterizing his human rights work throughout the subsequent decades, and the institutional ground where it was conducted, the peace church world's genuine if imperfect commitment to racial justice, was ground he had learned to recognize and work with during his college years.

The Education

Barbour's employment with the Philadelphia Department of Public Assistance in the years after his graduation placed him at the operational interface between the formal institutions of the emerging welfare state and the communities those institutions were supposed to serve. This position provided the most intensive practical education of his professional formation, more demanding in its implications than any academic curriculum could have been, because it placed him daily in the situations where the gap between democratic profession and democratic performance was produced and maintained.

The Philadelphia Department of Public Assistance was, by 1932, overwhelmed. The Depression had converted what had been a modest city agency administering limited relief programs for the relatively small population of Philadelphia's chronic poor into a massive institution processing hundreds of thousands of applications from workers who had never previously needed public assistance and who brought to the relief office the combination of shame and anger economic catastrophe produces in people who have been taught to regard their economic situation as a reflection of their character. The caseworkers, themselves employed on terms frequently precarious and whose compensation was often paid late or not at all as the city's finances deteriorated, processed their caseloads under conditions of chronic institutional stress.

Within this stressed system, the racial dynamics were consistent. Black applicants encountered discrimination at every stage of the administrative process. At intake, they were more likely to be assigned to less experienced caseworkers, to wait longer for initial appointments, and to be required to provide more extensive documentation of their need than white applicants. In the determination of benefit levels, they were more likely to receive benefits calculated at the lower end of the allowable range, on assessments of need reflecting the caseworker's lower expectations about what constituted adequate provision for a Black family. In the assignment to programs, they were more likely to be directed toward the programs offering less: the work relief programs paying lower wages, the commodity distribution programs providing food and clothing in kind rather than cash, and the programs carrying the most administrative burden and the most social stigma.

These were not the results of overt racial animus, though overt racial animus was certainly present in some interactions. They were the results of the systematic exercise of administrative discretion by people whose racial assumptions shaped their professional judgments in ways neither they nor the formal rules could fully see or regulate. The caseworker who assigned a Black family to the lower benefit tier was not, in most cases, consciously deciding to discriminate. She was exercising the discretion the rules provided in a context shaped by assumptions about what Black families needed and deserved, were so thoroughly naturalized they registered as professional judgment rather than racial bias. This mechanism, the production of racially discriminatory outcomes through the exercise of nominally race-neutral discretion, was what Barbour was observing daily in his work with the Philadelphia Department of Public Assistance, and it would shape his human rights advocacy for the rest of his career.

Ira Katznelson's *When Affirmative Action Was White* provides the macro-level analysis of Barbour's daily observations were the micro-level experience. Katznelson demonstrates how the most significant social programs of the New Deal era were administered in ways producing racialized outcomes through exactly this mechanism: the exercise of discretion by state and local administrators whose racial assumptions systematically disadvantaged Black applicants even when the formal statutory language was race-neutral. The Social Security Act's exclusion of domestic workers and agricultural laborers from coverage was explicit, but the administration of the programs covering other workers was itself racially discriminatory in ways Katznelson documents with careful empirical precision. Barbour was living inside this system, seeing its operations from the caseworker's side of the desk.

The Agricultural Adjustment Administration, the first major New Deal program, paid landowners to reduce production in order to stabilize agricultural prices. The payments went to landowners, not to sharecroppers and tenant farmers, who were predominantly Black in the South and who bore the economic consequences of production reduction without receiving its financial benefits. When landowners reduced their acreage under AAA contracts, they typically did so by evicting their sharecroppers, converting cropland to pasture and thereby eliminating the labor agreements on which sharecroppers depended for their livelihoods. The AAA's administrators, drawn from the southern agricultural establishment and responsive to the political demands of southern congressional barons, made no serious effort to enforce the contractual rights of sharecroppers the formal program language nominally protected. The result was displacement and economic disaster for the South's Black rural population, produced by a program nominally designed to stabilize the agricultural economy.

The National Recovery Administration, establishing industry-wide wage codes for stabilizing employment and wages in the industrial economy, permitted regional wage differentials legally maintaining lower wages in the South, where Black workers were concentrated, than in the North. The differential was not explicitly racial, but its effect was racially specific: in an economy where Black workers were concentrated in the South and in the South's lowest-paying occupations, the regional wage differential allowed the racial wage hierarchy to persist within a formally race-neutral regulatory framework. Black workers and civil rights organizations recognized the mechanism immediately, dubbing the NRA the "Negro Run Around' and 'Negroes Ruined Again," names capturing the bitter recognition the program's formal neutrality was being used to perpetuate substantive inequality.

The Federal Housing Administration's racially discriminatory underwriting guidelines, established in 1934, were perhaps the most consequential of the New Deal's racial exclusions because they structured the postwar housing market in ways producing the residential racial segregation still visible in American cities. The guidelines directed appraisers to consider the racial composition of neighborhoods when determining property values, effectively defining racially mixed or Black neighborhoods as high-risk investments. This designation made it impossible for residents of those neighborhoods to obtain federally insured mortgages, denying them access to the primary vehicle of wealth accumulation available to white working-class families in the postwar suburban boom. Kenneth T. Jackson's Crabgrass Frontier provides the definitive account of how the FHA's racial guidelines structured the suburban development of postwar America along racial lines, creating the metropolitan geography of white suburbs and Black urban cores defining American cities through the remainder of the twentieth century.

Barbour's training at the Washington School of Psychiatry, he undertook during his years of social work practice, added a psychological dimension to the professional framework he was developing and reflected the intellectual climate of social work in the 1930s. The decade was a significant period in the development of psychiatric social work as a subspecialty, drawing on the psychoanalytic tradition Freud had established and the American adaptations of this tradition being developed at institutions including the Smith College School of Social Work and the psychiatric social work programs being developed in connection with medical institutions.

The training at Washington gave Barbour a framework for understanding the psychological dimensions of racial discrimination complementing and deepening his structural analysis. The experience of chronic racial subordination was not merely an economic condition or a political status; it was a psychological reality with documentable consequences for the individuals and communities experiencing it. Kenneth and Mamie Clark's doll experiments, conducted in the early 1940s and subsequently deployed in the legal arguments for Brown v. Board of Education of Topeka, would later provide scientific documentation of the psychological harm racial segregation inflicted on Black children. But the understanding of racial discrimination as a source of psychological injury was already present in the social work and psychiatric literature of the 1930s, and Barbour's training at the Washington School of Psychiatry gave him professional access to such understanding.

The probation work in Washington, D.C., complementing his psychiatric training extended his professional formation into the criminal justice system, providing direct experience of the domain where the racial disproportion was most extreme and the formal neutrality of the applicable law most thoroughly undermined by racially structured discretionary practice. The overrepresentation of Black Americans in the criminal justice system at every stage from arrest through conviction through sentencing, later scholars would document with systematic precision, was already visible to any practitioner working within the system in the 1930s. Barbour saw it from the inside, from the position of the probation officer who was simultaneously an agent of the system and an advocate for the people the system was processing with such disproportionate severity.

The combination of social work practice, psychiatric training, and probation experience gave Barbour, by the late 1930s, a professional formation of unusual breadth and depth. He understood the social conditions producing the problems his clients faced, through his social work training and his direct observation. He understood the psychological dimensions of those conditions, through his psychiatric training and his direct practice. He understood the institutional mechanisms through the formal justice system processing those conditions into legal outcomes reflecting and reinforcing racial hierarchy, through his probation work. And he understood, through all of it and through the theological formation underlying all of it, the problems he was observing were not the products of individual failure but of structural arrangements which could and should be changed. This understanding was the foundation of the integrator's method.

The Partnership

Barbour married Ruth Johnson in 1937, and the marriage transformed the architecture of his daily life in ways whose significance for his human rights career exceeded the merely personal. Ruth Johnson came from Arkansas, a state whose combination of rural Black poverty, cotton economy, and racial terror represented some of the South's most concentrated brutality. Her journey from Arkansas to Philadelphia was itself an act of determination and courage analogous to the determination and courage defining her husband's human rights career, though the historical record preserves it only in the most general outline.

What the family oral history, preserved in the recollections of Barbour's granddaughters and great-grandson, suggests about the marriage is a partnership of genuine mutual support and shared commitment. Ruth was not a passive observer of her husband's human rights career; she was a participant in the household and the community life making the career possible, managing the practical dimensions of a life organized around institutional service and frequent relocation leaving limited time and energy for the domestic logistics she necessarily absorbed. The couple's moves from Philadelphia to New York to Denver to Pasadena across two decades required from Ruth the combination of logistical intelligence and social adaptability sustaining a professional life organized around institutional service rather than residential stability.

The stroke Ruth suffered in the years before Barbour's death, stealing from her the ability to speak, is among the most moving and most underexamined facts of his biography. To lose a spouse's voice, the medium through which the conversation of a shared life is conducted, is a loss whose dimensions are not adequately captured by clinical description. Barbour's continuation of his human rights work at the same level of intensity through this period is evidence of the commitment the motto demanded, but it is also evidence about how something was being sustained without the conversation ordinarily sustaining it, a fact worth acknowledging even when the historical record does not permit its full emotional dimensions to be recovered.

Ruth's Arkansas formation gave her an understanding of what her husband's human rights work was for which no amount of northern education could have substituted. She had grown up inside the system his career was working to dismantle, had felt on her own person and in her own community the weight of a racial order regarding her humanity as conditional and her dignity as contingent. The family she came from had made the same determination her husband's Barbour family had made: the South was not survivable on the South's terms. The Johnson family migrated from Hope, Arkansas to Philadelphia in the mid-1920s, part of the same Great Migration whose consequences Barbour was spending his career documenting and addressing.

The civic world Ruth's family inhabited in Philadelphia was the world O'Dessa J. Shipley navigated with the same combination of determination and institutional intelligence her brother-in-law was deploying in Denver and Los Angeles. O'Dessa, described in her 1994 Philadelphia Inquirer obituary as a pioneering African American civic activist and advocate of public and private recreation, earned a bachelor's degree from the University of Denver, the same institution where Barbour taught sociology and social work night classes in the late 1940s. She became the first African American woman to manage a major recreation facility in Philadelphia, and the first Black woman executive director of the United Service Organization for the Niagara Frontier in Buffalo. She directed the first Girls Club for the Philadelphia Association for Youth in West Philadelphia, served as dean of women at Fisk University, and served as Equal Employment Opportunity Commission officer for Atlantic City Community College. Her career, parallel to her brother-in-law's in its commitment to institutional firsts and civic service, suggests something about the family formation Ruth Johnson Barbour brought to the partnership: the Johnsons of Hope, Arkansas by way of Philadelphia were people who worked at the intersection of race, dignity, and institutional change. This was the household Barbour married into. This was the formation his wife brought to the work.

While Barbour was developing his professional formation in Depression-era Philadelphia, the Long Civil Rights Movement was taking organizational shape at the national level in ways directly relevant to the work he would later do. Understanding this national context is essential to placing his local activities within their proper historical frame, because the civil rights movement was never primarily a story of isolated individual heroism. It was, from its early organizational phases through its mass movement culmination, a story of coordinated institutional action, of organizations building on each other's work and individuals drawing on networks extending far beyond their immediate geographic and professional circumstances.

Patricia Sullivan's *Days of Hope* provides the essential framework for this national context. Sullivan demonstrates the New Deal era was a period of intense civil rights organizing, coalition-building, and political mobilization, shaped by the convergence of several forces: the labor movement's dramatic growth through the CIO's industrial organizing, bringing Black and white workers into the same unions for the first time in industries including steel, auto, and meatpacking; the NAACP's systematic legal campaigns targeting the constitutional foundation of Jim Crow; the Southern Conference for Human Welfare's interracial coalition for New Deal reform in the South; and the growing awareness in the Roosevelt administration about how the racial exclusions of the New Deal were creating political liabilities as well as moral failures.

The Congress of Industrial Organizations, organized in 1935 under the leadership of John L. Lewis as a break from the AFL's craft unionism and racial exclusion, was the labor movement dimension of Sullivan's story most directly relevant to understanding the civil rights potential of the period. The CIO's commitment to organizing all workers in mass production industries, regardless of race, represented a fundamental departure from the AFL's practice, and its organizing drives in the steel industry, the auto industry, the meatpacking industry, and the electrical industry brought Black workers into industrial unions on terms of formal equality with their white coworkers for the first time in the history of the American labor movement. The CIO's civil rights commitments were imperfect and contested, and the gap between the formal commitment and the practice in locals and industries was often substantial. But the principle had been established, and its establishment created new organizational possibilities for the civil rights movement which the AFL's exclusionary traditions had foreclosed. Barbour, watching these developments from the casework desks of Depression-era Philadelphia, was absorbing the lessons that would shape his Denver coalitions: the labor movement could be an ally when its interests aligned with racial justice, an obstacle when they diverged, and the integrator had to be prepared to work with both versions.

Glenda Gilmore's *Defying Dixie* recovers the radical roots of civil rights activism in the interwar years with particular attention to the organizations and individuals operating at the movement's more radical edge. Gilmore traces the networks of Black and white organizers who were, in the 1930s, building the intellectual and organizational infrastructure of a civil rights movement more expansive and more radical than the standard narrative acknowledges: the Communist Party's organizing among Black workers in Birmingham and Harlem and the rural South, the International Labor Defense's legal advocacy for Black defendants in cases including the Scottsboro Boys, the National Negro Congress's attempt to build a broad coalition of Black organizations around a program of economic and political justice, and the Fellowship of Reconciliation's development of nonviolent direct action as a civil rights tool.

Barbour was not a Communist, and his theological formation made him deeply skeptical of any political framework reducing human liberation to economic categories alone while denying the transcendent sources of human dignity the AME and Brethren traditions affirmed. But he was embedded in the same organizational landscape as the people Gilmore traces, and his human rights work was shaped by the full range of political and organizational possibilities the period opened, including the tactical possibilities being developed in the peace church networks he had access to through his Elizabethtown formation. When CORE emerged in 1942 from the Fellowship of Reconciliation's interracial networks, bringing together Black and white civil rights activists who had been developing the principles of nonviolent direct action in the peace church tradition, it was formalizing a tactical possibility developing in Barbour's organizational orbit for a decade.

Barbour saw the consequences of these programmatic exclusions daily in his social work practice. The families he served in Philadelphia's Black neighborhoods were living in the housing the FHA's racial guidelines had confined them to, working in the occupations the NRA's wage differentials had designated as appropriate for Black labor, and trying to navigate a relief system whose administration reflected the racial assumptions of its administrators in ways the formal rules did not prohibit. This daily observation gave his human rights advocacy a specificity and a credibility which abstract analysis alone could not have provided. When he later argued in Denver about how racial discrimination in employment and housing was not merely a moral problem but an economic one, imposing measurable costs on the entire community through the social consequences of enforced poverty and confinement, he was drawing on fifteen years of direct professional observation of how those costs were produced.

By 1940, Barbour and Ruth were living in New York City, and the 1944 newspaper report connecting him to coaching for the New York Black Yankees of the Negro Leagues documents a dimension of his New York years the documentary record preserves only in this single reference. The significance of the connection lies not in the details of the coaching role but in what the Negro Leagues represented in the social and cultural landscape of Black America in the 1930s and early 1940s.

The Negro Leagues were, in the most literal sense, a Black institution: owned by Black entrepreneurs, managed by Black executives, played by Black athletes, and serving as a primary entertainment and civic institution for Black communities throughout the country. The men who built the Negro Leagues, from Rube Foster's founding of the Negro National League in 1920 through the brilliant careers of the subsequent decades, were doing in the domain of professional sports exactly what the AME Church and the Urban League and the NAACP were doing in their domains: building Black institutional capacity, creating Black economic opportunity, demonstrating Black excellence in a context designed to deny it, and providing Black communities with the institutional life the surrounding white-dominated world was unwilling to provide on terms of equality.

Donn Rogosin's *Invisible Men,* the definitive history of the Negro Leagues, traces the combination of athletic excellence, business enterprise, and civic significance the Leagues represented. The ballparks where Negro League games were played were civic spaces as well as athletic venues, sites where the Black community gathered not only to watch baseball but to conduct the social and political business of a community limiting access to the formal civic spaces of the surrounding white world. Barbour's connection to this world, however briefly documented, reflects the characteristic pattern of his Depression-era career: he was embedded in the full range of Black civic institutional life, contributing to its vitality and drawing on its organizational resources in ways building the network his subsequent career would deploy.

By the time Barbour and Ruth left New York for Philadelphia, where he would begin his graduate study at the University of Pennsylvania, the world was on the eve of a transformation whose civil rights dimensions were only beginning to become visible. The war in Europe, beginning with the German invasion of Poland in September 1939, was reshaping the international context of American politics. The antifascist argument, the argument about a nation fighting Hitler's racial ideology could not maintain its own racial premises at home, was gaining traction in the civil rights community and in some quarters of the Roosevelt administration. The contradiction was not new, but the war was making it newly visible and newly urgent.

Barbour at thirty-two was a different person from the twenty-three-year-old who had left Elizabethtown in June 1932. Eight years of professional practice in Depression-era Philadelphia and New York had given him a specific, granular knowledge of how racial inequality operated in the institutional contexts he was working within, knowledge his academic formation had prepared him to analyze and his theological formation had prepared him to confront. He had watched the New Deal's racially structured benefits reach the people they were supposed to serve with greater reliability and dignity than they reached the communities his professional practice had brought him into contact with. He had watched the labor movement's gains accrue primarily to white workers while Black workers remained in the precarious positions the racial labor market had always assigned them. He had watched the formal legal equality of the northern states coexist with the substantive racial inequality of their social and economic practices, and he had learned, from daily observation, the mechanisms through which this coexistence was maintained.

He had also accumulated, across these eight years, the professional relationships and institutional connections the civil rights career ahead would require. The Philadelphia Urban League knew him. The NAACP branch knew him. The AME Church connections he had built through his Young People's Conference work extended throughout the Philadelphia and New York regions. The Elizabethtown College peace church networks gave him access to the interracial organizational world of the Fellowship of Reconciliation and its affiliated organizations. The University of Pennsylvania social work program was adding the professional credentials and the scholarly network giving his advocacy institutional credibility in the professional world he was entering.

The formation, in other words, was nearly complete. Not complete in the sense of finished, because no human formation is finished while the person is still living and still being shaped by the world they move through. But complete in the sense of sufficient: sufficient for the next phase of the work, sufficient to walk into the institutional leadership role the Denver Urban League position would demand, and sufficient to do this work with the combination of theological conviction, intellectual rigor, professional skill, and relational capacity which making Jesus King in a western city required. The Depression decade had not been easy. It had been, in the most precise sense, formative: it had formed in him the person his subsequent career would need him to be.

The settlement house tradition from which the Wharton Centre emerged deserves more extended treatment than the main narrative has provided, because understanding the institutional character of the settlement house in its Black Philadelphia adaptation illuminates what Barbour was doing and why his approach was effective in the ways it was. Jane Addams's Hull House in Chicago, founded in 1889, had established the model: middle-class reformers residing in working-class and immigrant communities, building from their direct community contact the social programs and policy advocacy addressing the conditions of urban poverty. The innovation was not merely programmatic; it was epistemological. Addams insisted knowledge of the social conditions requiring reform had to be built from direct community experience rather than from a distance, and which reform programs designed without which direct knowledge would systematically miss what the community actually needed.

The adaptation of this model to Black urban communities in the interwar decades produced institutions combining the settlement house's epistemological commitment to knowledge-from-inside with the organizational logic of Black civic institutions: the recognition about how the Black church was the primary institutional backbone of Black community life and any effective community organization program had to work with and through the church rather than in competition with it. The Wharton Centre's collaboration with Samuel Evans and the North Philadelphia Youth Movement, organizing its Youth City program through local Black churches, was this adaptation in practice: settlement house methodology deployed through the institutional infrastructure of the Black civic world.

Barbour's social work training at the University of Pennsylvania gave him the theoretical framework for understanding what he was doing at the Wharton Centre in terms of both traditions. The settlement house tradition's epistemological commitment to knowledge-from-inside justified his survey research among gang members: understanding what the gangs were and why they existed required asking the gang members, treating them as informants capable of providing accurate knowledge about their own circumstances rather than as objects of institutional processing. The Black church tradition's organizational logic justified the Youth City program's design: reaching North Philadelphia's gang-involved teenagers required working through the institutions they recognized and trusted, not establishing new institutions whose relationship to the existing community was uncertain.

The combination of these two traditions in the Wharton Centre's approach to juvenile delinquency was, in retrospect, more sophisticated than the standard accounts of Depression-era and wartime social work acknowledge. The Neighbourhood Plan Barbour contributed to, a plan for hiring social workers to make sustained direct contact with gang members in their own neighborhoods, gaining their confidence through repeated and reliable interaction, and helping them develop constructive alternatives, anticipated several decades of subsequent social work theory about the conditions under which community-based intervention could be effective. The Plan worked not because it was theoretically elegant but because it was practically wise: it addressed the actual conditions producing gang involvement rather than the symptoms those conditions produced, and it did so through the institutional channels the community recognized rather than through the institutional channels the reformers preferred.

Barbour's graduate training at the University of Pennsylvania placed him in direct institutional relationship with the scholarly tradition W.E.B. Du Bois had established at the same institution in 1896 and 1897, and the significance of this relationship for understanding his civil rights method deserves extended treatment. Du Bois's *Philadelphia Negro* was not simply the first systematic empirical study of Black urban life in America; it was a methodological manifesto, a demonstration which the social scientific study of Black communities could be conducted with the rigor and the precision which the most demanding academic standards required, and which the knowledge produced by this study could be deployed in the service of civil rights advocacy without losing its intellectual integrity.

David Levering Lewis, in his authoritative biography of Du Bois, traces the specific circumstances of the Philadelphia Negro's creation: Du Bois's appointment by the University of Pennsylvania as an 'assistant in sociology,' a position giving him institutional affiliation without academic standing, his residence in the worst block of the seventh ward, from which he conducted his fieldwork among the community he was studying, and his production, from this position of simultaneous institutional marginality and community immersion, of the most comprehensive empirical study of Black urban life yet attempted. Lewis's account makes clear how Du Bois's methodological choice, to study Black Philadelphia from inside the community rather than from the comfortable distance of the academy, was both epistemologically necessary and personally costly, a form of scholarly discipleship anticipating, in its character, the costly discipleship Barbour's theological formation demanded of human rights work.

The methodological tradition Du Bois established at the University of Pennsylvania in 1899 was still present, at least in the form of institutional memory and scholarly reputation, when Barbour arrived to study social work at the Pennsylvania School of Social Work four decades later. The methods he learned in graduate school, the systematic empirical documentation of social conditions, the analysis of structural causes rather than individual pathologies, the deployment of research findings in advocacy arguments addressed to policymakers and the public: all of these drew on the Du Bois tradition, whether or not this tradition was explicitly named in the curriculum. Barbour's own subsequent research, from the Wharton Centre's gang surveys through the Richmond and Tucson studies to the World Affairs Institute paper on human rights, stood in direct methodological continuity with Du Bois's approach. The Philadelphia Negro was Barbour's scholarly grandfather text, even if the genealogy was not always made explicit.

The organizational environment of New York's civil rights world in the early 1940s was being transformed by the dynamics of the wartime moment. Randolph's March on Washington campaign was building the organizational infrastructure for the 1941 confrontation with Roosevelt producing Executive Order 8802. CORE was being organized from the Fellowship of Reconciliation's New York networks. The NAACP's Legal Defense Fund was developing the legal strategy producing Brown v. Board of Education of Topeka. The Brotherhood of Sleeping Car Porters was deploying the organizational capacity Randolph had built over a decade and a half in the service of the March on Washington campaign and, subsequently, of the broader wartime civil rights agenda. Barbour was living and working in the city where all of this was happening, and however thin the documentary record of his activities during these years, the organizational environment was shaping the context of his professional formation in ways which would become visible in his Denver work.

The Decision to Return: Philadelphia and Graduate School

The decision to leave New York for Philadelphia, to enroll in the Pennsylvania School of Social Work at the University of Pennsylvania, and to take up the social work position at the Wharton Centre proving to be the most intensive professional formation of his career: this decision is not documented in the surviving record with the specificity allowing a fully confident account of its making. What can be said with confidence is how the decision reflected a consistent pattern in Barbour's professional development: the willingness to move toward the work rather than toward the recognition, to take the position offering the most intensive learning opportunity rather than the position offering the most comfortable circumstances.

Philadelphia in 1944, the specific Philadelphia of North Philadelphia's Black neighborhoods in the fourth year of World War II, was not a comfortable posting. The neighborhoods were overcrowded and underserved, the juvenile gang dynamics were escalating toward the violence reaching their crisis in October 1945, and the institutional resources available to the Wharton Centre were limited by the wartime diversion of public resources toward the military effort and the chronic underfunding characterizing social services to Black communities in every period of American history. The graduate program at the University of Pennsylvania was rigorous and demanding. The combination of full-time social work practice and graduate study was, by any measure, a demanding professional schedule.

He chose it anyway. The pattern was consistent with the motto organizing his professional life. "Make Jesus King" meant doing the work the Kingdom required rather than the work the career path preferred, showing up in the institutional spaces where the need was greatest rather than the spaces where the recognition was most available. North Philadelphia's gang-involved teenagers needed someone willing to do the patient, daily work of relationship-building, which the Neighbourhood Plan required. The Wharton Centre needed a practitioner combining the community organization skills he had developed over his previous fifteen years with the social work credentials the professional world was beginning to require. The University of Pennsylvania needed students willing to bring to their academic formation the direct professional experience that deepened theoretical understanding rather than substituting for it. Barbour was all of these things, and he moved toward the place where all of these needs could be met rather than toward the place where his own needs would be most comfortably accommodated.

This is what it meant, in the career choices of William Wilbur Miller Barbour, to "Make Jesus King." Not the dramatic public act, not the celebrated confrontation, not the recognized leadership of a national organization: the daily decision to move toward the work rather than away from it, to place institutional need above personal comfort, to treat the most demanding professional option as the most faithful professional option. The motto was not a Sunday morning aspiration. It was a Monday morning choice, and a Tuesday morning choice, and a Wednesday morning choice, repeated across twenty-five years of professional life until the choices had accumulated into the career this biography documents.

Philadelphia, 1955. Three generations gathered in the living room of Mr. and Mrs. Swinton Scott. Seated on the couch, left to right: Deborah Neil (Barbour's granddaughter), Minnie Gertrude Mumford Barbour Archer (Barbour's mother), Renee Whitby (Barbour's granddaughter). Kneeling behind the couch, left to right: Cecil Scott Jr. (Barbour's grandson), Ellen Jane Barbour Simpson (Barbour's daughter), Cecil Asbury Scott (Barbour's son-in-law), Ruth Johnson Barbour (Barbour's wife), Lillian Scott, Swinton Scott. Standing at center: William Wilbur Miller Barbour. The work of a man who spent his career arguing for human dignity in legislative chambers and civic forums was rooted, finally, in this the faithfulness of a wife who bore the burden alongside him, a daughter who carried the values forward, grandchildren who had inherited the stakes. Before he built the harmonious whole from the separate parts, he tended the smaller community from which everything else drew its meaning.

Photo courtesy of Deborah Neil.

Ralph W. Schlosser in the classroom, Elizabethtown College. He had graduated with the Class of 1907, the same year he joined the faculty of a college barely eight years old. He would not leave for sixty-three years. He pressed the same conviction into every student: "Put your life on the side of those striving to consummate a constructive program for humanity. Dare to do right at any cost. Never flinch when duty calls." Here he is eighty-five, his hearing difficult, his method adapted small seminars, seated among his students rather than standing above them. He understood the teacher's deepest reward was not recognition but transformation.

Schlosser leans toward his students. They lean back toward him. This is what sixty-three years of teaching looked like at its best; not a lecture, not a performance, but a conversation. A circle of minds gathered around the questions worth spending a life on. The discussion method was not a pedagogical preference. It was a theological conviction: truth is found in community, tested in conversation, embodied in the lives of people willing to follow it wherever it leads. The students in this photograph do not know yet where it will take them. Schlosser, who had watched young people leave this college for more than half a century, had learned not to predict what the formation would produce. He had only to press the mandate into them and trust the rest.

Ralph W. Schlosser. Elizabethtown College, The High Library Special Collections.

Martha Martin, Associate Professor of Bible, Elizabethtown College. She is dressed as her faith requires; the cape dress, the prayer covering; the whole body a statement of conviction before she has spoken a single word. In the Anabaptist tradition, dress is not fashion. It is a covenant made visible. The college where she spent twenty-five years teaching Bible existed, in part, because the Commonwealth of Pennsylvania's Garb Law of 1895 had barred plain-dressed teachers from the public-school classroom. The Brethren community's answer was to build an institution where this witness could not be legislated away. Martha Martin was, at her death, the only living charter member of the Elizabethtown Church of the Brethren. She had been there from the beginning. William Wilbur Miller Barbour sat in her classroom, bringing with him the African Methodist Episcopal conviction that the Gospel is incompatible with structures of domination. Martha Martin's Brethren hermeneutic offered him a complementary lens. Two traditions. The same Bible. The same horizon.

Martha Martin. Elizabethtown College, The High Library Special Collections.

Barbour on the Elizabethtown College debate team, ca. 1930. His Middletown High School classmates had already seen it clearly enough to put it in print: here was a young man who should consider the law. At Elizabethtown, Ralph W. Schlosser took those gifts and gave them direction. Between 1930 and 1938, the college's intercollegiate debating program would compile approximately 150 contests and a formidable winning record. Schlosser coached the teams himself, understanding what the Anabaptist tradition had always understood: nonresistance did not mean silence. It meant the rejection of force in favor of the persuasive power of argument, testimony, and example. Debate, in this tradition, was a form of discipleship.

Etonian (Elizabethtown College yearbook), 1930, p. 82. Elizabethtown College, The High Library.

William Wilbur Miller Barbour with the Etonian yearbook staff, Elizabethtown College, 1932. Four years of Homer, Plato, Augustine, and Shakespeare, the full weight of a great books education, had done what such an education is designed to do: it had made him a writer. Precise in observation. Disciplined in description. Exact in word choice. The yearbook was where those skills first met a deadline and a real audience, the first practice ground for a man who would go on to write for the Denver Post, contribute to Adult Leadership magazine, and lecture at the University of Denver's World Affairs Institute.

Etonian (Elizabethtown College yearbook), 1932, p. 84. Elizabethtown College, The High Library.

Ira Herr coached at Elizabethtown College for thirty-three years, from 1928 to 1961, on terms Ralph W. Schlosser had made explicit from the beginning: the athletic field was not separate from the classroom. Victory achieved at the cost of honor was to be regarded as defeat. Special treatment for athletes; subsidies, scholarships, academic concessions based on athletic skill alone was prohibited. Herr honored this across three decades. His athletes were praised throughout Lancaster County not for winning records alone but for their sportsmanship and Christian bearing. When William Wilbur Miller Barbour, the only African American player in the frame, stood on this field, Herr coached him without exception and without qualification. When character is the measure of athletic participation rather than competitive utility, including a Black player is not a calculated risk. It is the fulfillment of a founding commitment.

Ira Herr in baseball uniform. Elizabethtown College, The High Library Special Collections.

Track Team, Miller Barbour first on left, ca. 1930. Elizabethtown College. Fair play. Perseverance. The willingness to give everything and accept the outcome with dignity. These were not merely the virtues of a good athlete. They were the virtues of a disciple and Barbour was learning them in both registers simultaneously. He carried those disciplines into every arena his life would take him: the Neighborhood Plan he developed at the Wharton Centre in North Philadelphia, the young men he coached as a liaison to the New York Black Yankees, the legislative chambers of Denver, the civic forums of Los Angeles. The geography changed. The work was the same. The track at Elizabethtown was part of the curriculum.

Track Team, Miller Barbour first on left, ca. 1930. Elizabethtown College, The High Library Special Collections.

Barbour with the Brutal Thirteen, Elizabethtown College's clandestine 1928 football squad. He is the only African American player in the frame. His presence was no accident. It was the college's founding commitment made visible. He had arrived on College Hill already formed; shaped first on the fields of Middletown High School, sharpened as headman of the Harrisburg Eleven. Here those gifts found their fullest expression. Ira Herr coached on the terms Ralph Schlosser required: the field was a place of discipleship, or it was nothing. When character is the measure of athletic participation rather than competitive utility, including a Black player is not a progressive gesture. It is obedience. The teamwork, the fair play, the perseverance built across these years did not stay on the field. They became the tools of the work that followed. 1928.

The High Library Special Collections.

William Wilbur Miller Barbour, Elizabethtown College, Class of 1932. He is twenty-three years. old, and four years of formation are written in his bearing.

Etonian (Elizabethtown College yearbook), 1932, p. 50. Elizabethtown College, The High Library.

Denver, April 6, 1951. Three men gather around the National Urban League's annual activity report. On the left, Dr. Charles J. Blackwood, Jr., the first African American to graduate from the University of Colorado School of Medicine, the first Black clinical professor at the institution, the only African American Police Surgeon on the Denver Police Force, stands in his role as Chairman of the Urban League's enrollment campaign. At center, Mayor James Quigg Newton, Jr., lawyer and reformer, renews his membership in the organization whose mission aligned with his own conviction about how a modern city must serve all of its citizens. To his right stands William Wilbur Miller Barbour, Executive Director of the National Urban League of Denver; the steady hand behind the organization's daily work of opening doors, expanding opportunity, and making the promise of American life a reality for those long denied it. He had been formed at Elizabethtown College by a three-word mandate. He was still living it out.

Photo by Dean Conger/The Denver Post via Getty Images.

Members of the Cosmopolitan Club of Denver. Front row, left to right: Clarence Holmes (dentist), James Fresquez, Lawrence Lightner, Elliott Draine, Harold Brown Sr. Back row, left to right: Clayton Hawkins (physician), Earl Mann (Ret. Lt., U.S. Army), Miller Barbour (Urban League), Paul Roberts (Dean, St. John's Episcopal Church), Yosui Minori, and others unidentified. When Barbour arrived in Denver in 1947, he did not arrive in an empty landscape. The Cosmopolitan Club had been there since 1931, founded by Dr. Clarence Holmes in the teeth of institutionalized discrimination. Its motto named the conviction at its center: Humanity above Nation, Race or Creed. Its membership drew from Denver's African American, Jewish, Japanese American, and Anglo communities; educated progressives committed to the proposition that interracial justice was not a distant ideal but a present obligation. Barbour would have recognized it immediately; not only as an ally but as a kindred institution, arrived by a different route at the same bedrock. Denver had been at this work for sixteen years before he walked through the door.

Cosmopolitan Club Group Photo, photograph by Burnis McCloud. Clarence and Fairfax Holmes Papers, WH1270, Photobox 1, FF78. Denver Public Library Special Collections.

Mayor James Quigg Newton, Jr. had been in office less than six months when, on June 19, 1947, he summoned seven citizens to his office and asked them to do something no Denver mayor had asked before: find out the truth. The Interim Survey Committee on Human Relations was charged with documenting the full scope of discrimination in Denver; social, economic, and in real estate and delivering a comprehensive report by November 1. Among the seven members, handpicked by the mayor himself, was Barbour. He was not a peripheral figure. He was one of seven people entrusted with the foundational survey that would shape Denver's entire postwar civil rights infrastructure. Barbour had been trained at Elizabethtown College to do exactly this: to move into the spaces between the law's promise and American life's reality, to document what he found there with empirical rigor, and to build from the evidence the institutional conditions genuine community required. Newton had swept into office on a wave of reform. Barbour had arrived from Philadelphia carrying a mandate pressed into him two decades earlier on College Hill. They found each other in a mayor's office in Denver in the summer of 1947, and the city would not be the same.

| 5 |

Building the Kingdom

Denver in January 1947 was cold, the Rocky Mountain winter pressing down on the city from the peaks visible to the west, the streets carrying the purposeful traffic of a city with ambitions it was not yet sure how to fulfill. The new mayor, James Quigg Newton Jr., had been in office only weeks when William Wilbur Miller Barbour arrived to take up his position as executive secretary of the National Urban League. Newton was thirty-five years old, the youngest mayor in the city's history, educated at the University of Colorado and Yale Law School, elected by 58 percent of the vote on a platform of civic modernization including, explicitly and unusually for a western city of the period, the dismantling of racial segregation in housing and racial discrimination in employment. He was a reformer in the tradition of municipal progressivism, convinced Denver could be better than its past, willing to use the power of the mayor's office to push it in this direction.

Barbour was thirty-nine years old, arriving from Philadelphia with his MSW, his Wharton Centre experience, and twenty years of formation in the two theological traditions organizing his understanding of the work before him. He and Newton shared a vision for Denver's racial future, though they came to it from very different social locations: Newton from the white reform tradition of civic progressivism, Barbour from the intersection of Anabaptist-Pietist discipleship and AME prophetic witness. The convergence of their visions, and the productive tension between their different institutional positions, would make possible the most significant civil rights advances Denver had seen.

The National Urban League occupied a distinctive position in the organizational landscape of the Long Civil Rights Movement. Founded in 1910 from the merger of three earlier organizations devoted to improving the conditions of Black Americans in northern cities, the League had developed a approach to civil rights work distinguishing it from the NAACP's primarily legal and political strategy. Where the NAACP fought racial inequality through the courts and through legislative advocacy, the Urban League worked through institutional negotiation and coalition-building: persuading employers to hire Black workers, working with city governments to improve services to Black communities, placing graduates of historically Black colleges in professional positions, and building the institutional relationships through which incremental progress could be made.

This approach was both a strength and a limitation. Its strength was its institutionalism: the Urban League worked within the established structures of American civic and economic life, building the relationships and the credibility giving it access to the decision-makers capable of producing change. Its limitation was its institutionalism: working through established agencies and organizations rather than confronting them sometimes meant accepting the pace of change those agencies set, accommodating the priorities of donors and board members whose own racial assumptions could limit the League's advocacy, and maintaining the respectability required for access at the cost of the militancy the community's situation demanded.

Barbour understood both the strength and the limitation. He had been trained in the social work tradition undergirding the Urban League's institutional approach, and he believed in the value of working through established agencies and building lasting institutional relationships. But he also carried a theological formation insisting on how discipleship was costly, which making Jesus King sometimes required confronting institutions rather than only negotiating with them, and how the standard of measure was not institutional respectability but the concrete conditions of the community the institution was supposed to serve. He would spend his Denver years navigating the tension between these two imperatives with considerable skill.

In a 1948 letter to the Elizabethtown College student newspaper, *The Etownian*, Barbour described the Denver Urban League's work in his own words, with the directness of a practitioner speaking to the institution that had formed him. "The Urban League of Denver,' he wrote, 'is a social work agency operating in the field of race relations, seeking to broaden opportunities for all minorities in a growing community. Where possible it works through established agencies and organizations and does not duplicate existing services. My task is to carry out the functions of the League under the supervision of a biracial Board of Directors." The description was accurate and spare, precise about method and governance while leaving unstated the theological conviction which organized the method: the understanding coalition-building and institutional negotiation were themselves forms of making Jesus king in the social arrangements of a western city. He knew his Elizabethtown audience would hear what was not said as clearly as what was.

Among Barbour's responsibilities in Denver was teaching sociology and social work at the University of Denver in night classes. The teaching assignment was not incidental to his human rights work; it was an extension of it, connecting the professional preparation of future social workers to the conditions of Denver's racial landscape and building, in the university's professional programs, an awareness of racial inequality as a structural problem requiring professional attention.

One of his courses was entitled 'Racial Contributions to American Life,' a title reflecting the pedagogical approach the intergroup relations movement was developing in the late 1940s: the understanding about how racial and ethnic diversity was not a problem to be managed but a contribution to be recognized, the cultural, intellectual, and civic contributions of minority communities to American life were being systematically ignored or denied by a dominant culture organized around assumptions of white supremacy, and how education had a role to play in correcting this distortion. The course was, in the vocabulary of its moment, a form of multicultural education avant la lettre, an effort to expand the horizons of the social work students who would later serve the diverse communities of a rapidly growing western city.

The University of Denver connection also provided Barbour with the academic platform for the internationalist human rights advocacy he developed in the late 1940s. The Citizens Committee of Human Rights for the World Affairs Institute, sponsored by the Social Science Foundation of the University of Denver, was the organizational vehicle for his 1951 information paper on human rights, 'The Prospect for Freedom: Human Rights: What Can be Done on the Local Level.' This paper, co-authored with Michael L. Freed and Helen L. Peterson, situated Denver's civil rights struggles within the framework of the United Nations Charter and the Universal Declaration of Human Rights, connecting local advocacy to the internationalist principles the postwar order had established.

The housing crisis Barbour confronted in Denver was not a matter of individual discrimination. It was a structural problem embedded in the legal, financial, and institutional architecture of the housing market. The human cost of this structure had specific faces. Thomas Ernest McClain, the first African American registered dentist in Colorado, had paid for a house to be built in Denver in the 1920s. When the white seller discovered Dr. McClain was African American, he refused to hand over the keys. A cross was burned on the front lawn. The structure was not abstract to McClain. Even after the United States Supreme Court held racially restrictive covenants unenforceable in 1948, they continued to be recorded and observed in Denver. When the southwest Denver subdivision of Burns Brentwood was built in 1949, its racially restrictive covenant was explicit: only persons of the Caucasian race shall own, use, or occupy any dwelling erected upon said lots or tracts. Barbour understood his work in Denver was, in part, the work of dismantling exactly this kind of documented, institutional, legally recorded exclusion.

The Mayor's Committee on Human Relations, established by Newton shortly after his inauguration in 1947, provided the institutional vehicle for an initial assessment of Denver's racial conditions. The committee's November 1947 report was a significant document in the history of Denver's civil rights movement: it named the problem, Denver, a democratic city of the USA, had ghettoes in fact, if not in name, with a directness unusual for a municipal report of the period. It attributed residential inequality to informal 'gentleman's agreements,' restrictive real estate practices, and neighborhood prejudice confining minority residents to overcrowded and deteriorating districts, documenting in terms the gap between Denver's democratic self-image and its racial reality.

Mayor Newton's November 1947 committee report named Denver's racial reality with a directness unusual for a municipal document of the period: Denver, a democratic city of the USA, has ghettoes in fact, if not in name. Barbour's own *Denver Post* column, issued as the year closed, put specific flesh on this finding. He included the candid expressions of racial ideology he had encountered in the committee's interviews, the specific, daily language of exclusion which structural racism speaks when it thinks no one uncomfortable is listening: 'We wouldn't want to have Mexican kids running around the place;' 'I tell Jews not to buy out there because it would not be good for their children, you know what I mean;' 'It is best to keep these minorities isolated to their own districts;' 'Colored folks would rather live with their own people anyway.' He documented the Platte River corridor where Denver's Black and Latino residents were concentrated: in the area along the Platte River, from 60 to 90 per cent of the housing was considered sub-standard, with conditions so bad much of the area had been marked for condemnation under the city's housing code. Ninety per cent, thirteen thousand, of Denver's Negroes; seventy-five per cent, twenty-four thousand, of its Spanish-Americans; and many of its Japanese were penned into this area, where sewage, sanitation, and recreation facilities were the poorest in the city, and infant mortality and juvenile delinquency the highest. He closed with a sentence swathed, as Newsum notes, in the iconic imagery of the American West, a land of wide-open spaces and individual liberty: 'Apart from the moral wrong involved, Denver taxpayers should be anxious to wipe out these expensive breeding grounds of crime and disease. The solution can be summed up in a few words: more freedom and space for minorities. Don't fence them in.'

This argument, about how racial discrimination was not only a moral problem but an economic one, was a staple of Barbour's human rights advocacy and reflected the formation his dual theological tradition provided. The AME tradition had always understood racial justice as a matter of prophetic moral demand; the Brethren tradition added the conviction about how the community's social arrangements had practical as well as moral consequences, a community organized around the exclusion of some of its members was paying a price for this exclusion which it could not indefinitely afford. Making Jesus King meant building the argument at both levels: the moral argument, because moral truth required naming, and the practical argument, because the people making the decisions Barbour was trying to influence were often more susceptible to practical arguments than to moral ones.

Every Minister In The City

The campaign for fair employment practices legislation in Colorado extended across four legislative sessions, from 1945 to 1951, and its history provides the most detailed documentation available of Barbour's coalition-building method in action. Each successive campaign built on the previous one, expanding the coalition, refining the argument, and pressing the legislature toward the accountability the community's needs demanded. The full story of these campaigns is recovered in Dani R. Newsum's *Cold War Colorado*, the most comprehensive scholarly analysis of the interwar civil rights movement in Colorado, and the account here draws heavily on her research.

The 1945 and 1947 campaigns failed without significant political consequence for their opponents, killed in committee by a Republican-dominated legislature regarding racial discrimination in employment as a private matter beyond the reach of public regulation. The political dynamics of Colorado in those years reflected the lingering influence of the Klan era's hostility to minority rights and the institutional conservatism of a Republican Party whose base in the state included business interests with a direct financial stake in maintaining the racial segmentation of the labor market.

The 1949 campaign achieved broader mobilization. The Unity Council coordinated with the Anti-Defamation League, the Urban League, the Mayor's Commission on Human Relations, and a coalition of religious and civic organizations to build the most comprehensive civil rights coalition Denver had yet seen. The campaign organized outreach through a Spanish American committee focused on Latino neighborhoods and an East Denver committee devoted to mobilizing African American residents, reflecting Barbour's insistence about how fair employment was a shared concern across racial and ethnic lines. On March 27, 1949, in what Barbour described as a significant organizational achievement, 'every Negro minister in this area' urged their congregants to contact state legislators in support of the fair employment bill.

The ministerial mobilization was not a tactical gimmick. It was the deployment of the deepest institutional resource the Black community possessed: the Black church's capacity to translate political demands into moral obligations and to activate the civic participation of community members who might not otherwise engage with a legislative campaign. Barbour understood this resource because he had been formed within it: the AME tradition had always used the pulpit for political as well as spiritual purposes, understanding the two as inseparable dimensions of the prophetic tradition the church inherited.

His ability to activate Black ministers in support of fair employment legislation reflected his credibility within the AME organizational network and his understanding of how the church's institutional resources could be translated into political pressure.

The 1949 campaign fell short of full FEPC legislation but produced a significant shift in public opinion. As Newsum documents, five years of intensive public education efforts had 'changed some influential minds,' and the Republican majority in the legislature acknowledged, for the first time, the political and public sentiment had shifted toward some form of fair employment regulation. The acknowledgment was itself a civil rights victory, small but real: the question in Colorado was no longer whether fair employment legislation was legitimate but what form it would take.

The arguments Barbour deployed in Denver's legislative chambers and civic forums drew their intellectual authority from a framework he had developed across two decades of reading and professional practice, and the World Affairs Institute paper of 1951 preserves it in his own words with a clarity the summary cannot fully substitute for. He told his Denver audience exactly where he located the moral foundation of the civil rights claim. 'I always emphasized,' he said, 'this was about human dignity based on the natural rights of men in Plato's *Republic*; in The Magna Carta; in The Declaration of Independence; in The Emancipation Proclamation; and in the Human Rights Charter of the United Nations.' The list was not rhetorical decoration. It was a scholarly argument, tracing the genealogy of the democratic principle from its ancient philosophical roots through its institutional expressions to the international human rights framework the postwar world had assembled. He was insisting, before a Denver audience which might have preferred a narrower frame, the racial justice he was demanding was not a special interest but the universal inheritance of Western civilization.

He understood history as the record of forces working both for and against human dignity, and he named those forces with the precision of a trained social scientist: 'the Renaissance, the Reformation and Counter-Reformation, and the French and American Revolutions brought social changes in the struggle of man for the good and for the free society but this struggle had been interrupted or side-tracked by war and slavery, the most destructive negative forces, the extreme evidences of man's failures to resolve his problems in human ways.' The habit of mind was Elizabethtown's: his education rooted in the classics had trained him to place every injustice within the broadest available historical and philosophical context, and he deployed this training consistently in his human rights advocacy. When he argued against racial discrimination in Denver, he was not making a local argument. He was making a civilizational one.

Barbour's World Affairs Institute paper included a sweeping historical survey of Colorado's own human rights record making clear he was not speaking abstractly. He reminded his Denver audience: 'In 1895, Colorado passed a Civil Rights law, an attempt to preserve the dignity of the individual by setting up the machinery to guarantee his right to equal service in places of public accommodation. As successive waves of immigration hit our state, the Russo-Germans, the Irish, the Chinese, the Italians, the Negroes, the Jews, the Japanese, and lastly the Spanish and Mexican Americans, the same sad story of ugly denials of human rights and encroachment upon the dignity of individuals recurred.' He continued with a reckoning naming the state's own most recent failure: 'In the 1920s, the fiery cross of the Ku Klux Klan burned above Clear Creek. At the height of its strength, the Klan elected the governor, the majority of legislators, judges at all levels, and filled important positions in Denver city government. The trail of violations of human rights left in its wake an ugly scar, still vivid to many older citizens.' He was telling Denver's story back to Denver, with documentation. He was making the abstract argument specific by grounding it in the city's own living memory. Several people in his audience would have been old enough to remember the Klan's dominance of Colorado government. He was not warning them about a distant possibility. He was pointing at a recent fact.

The 1951 FEPC campaign confronted the form of racial liberalism Barbour found most politically sophisticated and most intellectually dishonest. Republican state senator Frank Gill had proposed a fair employment bill widely seen as weak, an attempt to provide the appearance of reform without its substance. Gill made his position plain in words Dani Newsum preserves in her 2012 dissertation: 'They'd better accept this one or they won't get anything,' barked the senate leader. 'This will get FEP on the books and it will serve as a darn good cornerstone for good racial harmony.' The threat was unmistakable: accept the inadequate bill or receive nothing. For Barbour, this was exactly the gradualism he had identified as the civil rights movement's most persistent obstacle, not outright opposition but the permanent deferral dressed in the language of prudent progress.

Barbour's public response to Gill situated the senator's position within the framework Gunnar Myrdal had provided in *An American Dilemma*, his 1944 landmark study of American race relations. Myrdal's concept of the 'American dilemma,' the tension between the nation's democratic ideals and its racial practices, had given civil rights advocates a powerful analytical tool: it named the contradiction at the heart of American democratic identity and framed racial discrimination not merely as a social problem but as a civic failure, a betrayal of the nation's foundational commitments. Barbour used this framework to read Gill's position as an instance of precisely the racial liberalism Myrdal had analyzed: a politics committed in principle to equality but in practice to a gradualism ensuring equality's indefinite deferral.

'Gradualism might not be such a bad approach,' Barbour wrote in his 1951 information paper, 'if it were not for the fact the so-called gradualist is almost always a status-quo-er, the gradualism to take place after his departure from life. The usual period of time is my life time to five hundred years.' The wit was characteristic, but the point was serious: gradualism in the service of racial equality was rarely genuine gradualism, a steady movement toward a goal within a defined timeframe, and almost always a permanent deferral dressed in the language of prudent progress. Making Jesus king did not permit permanent deferral. The Kingdom was urgent because the people it was to serve were in need now, not in five hundred years.

The World Affairs Institute paper Barbour presented in Denver in 1951 contains some of the most eloquent writing of his career, and his voice in it deserves to be heard at length rather than summarized. He opened with a statement framing the stakes as simultaneously a theological claim, a foreign policy argument, and a civil rights demand: "From its inception, the United Nations recognized: unless the worth and dignity and rights of every inhabitant on this planet are observed and practiced, the prospects for a peaceful world are, indeed, dim. The subject matter of our discussion, Human Rights, thus assumes awesome importance: either we take concrete steps to achieve their communication in our every-day living, or humankind itself may very well perish in the vortex of international strife." He was not being hyperbolic. He was describing, with characteristic analytical precision, the connection between domestic racial justice and international peace which the Cold War had made newly urgent.

His Cold War argument was equally direct: 'The prospects for freedom in our time are inextricably linked with the willing effectiveness with which the world standard-bearer of democracy, our own country, demonstrates to the hundreds of millions of peoples on both sides of the Iron Curtain how she not only professes ideals about Human Rights but practices them as well. To win the struggle for men's minds, the United States must close, and quickly, the gap between democratic profession and performance.' The phrase 'gap between democratic profession and performance' was his own coinage, and it named with memorable precision the central failure his human rights career was devoted to addressing. He deployed it across two decades of advocacy because it was both accurate and rhetorically powerful: it framed racial discrimination not as a deviation from American values but as a betrayal of them, a failure internal to the democratic project rather than external to it.

He closed this section of the paper with a statement of the necessary relationship between policy and the organized civic effort required to translate policy into practice: 'The problem of Human Rights, with its important component part, Race Relations, has become man's most important problem. Social change is not automatic; it is effected by planned activity of citizens who actively engage in building a better society in which they want to live. To this Denver is no exception.' The final sentence was characteristic Barbour: the move from the global to the local, the insistence the abstract principle had a address, and the implicit demand his Denver audience recognize themselves as the citizens whose planned activity the abstract principle required. He was making Jesus king by closing the gap between the universal declaration and the city.

The Cold War's anticommunist pressures bore on Barbour's human rights advocacy in concrete ways. But he turned the Cold War's rhetorical framework back against those who wielded it. Newsum records the single most dramatic statement of his Colorado career, delivered at a meeting of the East Denver Improvement League: 'Your failure in making Democracy work here in Colorado has a bearing on the international situation. The killing and burial of this bill will be beamed by the Soviet radio to the lands where 1 billion seven hundred million colored people live.' He paused, then drove the point home: 'They will say how can you people trust the American offer of Democracy when one of the traditionally liberal states denies it to a portion of its own citizens?' The room understood exactly what he was saying. He was not making a human rights argument. He was making a national security argument. He was telling Colorado's legislators their local vote would register in Moscow and in every capital where the United States was asking the world's colored majority to choose the American side.

Barbour navigated these pressures with the theological framework his dual formation provided. He consistently framed his civil rights advocacy in the language of democratic principle and human rights rather than socialist or communist politics. When opponents attempted to red-bait the civil rights coalition in Colorado, he responded not with defensive denial but with a systematic analysis of the anti-civil-rights tactic itself. In his World Affairs Institute paper he enumerated five specific attitudes 'presently affecting human rights in a very negative way:' first, apathy and resignation; second, the 'There's-no-problem' position; third, the insidious association of intergroup or interracial programs with communist or socialist labels; fourth, the status-quo-ers and the gradualists, 'gradualism might not be such a bad approach if it were not for the fact the so-called gradualist is almost always a status-quo-er, the gradualism to take place after his departure from life, the usual period of time is my life time to five hundred years'; and fifth, what he called, coining a word for a condition the existing vocabulary could not adequately name, 'race-opaths', people whose attitudes in this area were, in his clinical assessment, psychopathological in nature. The taxonomy was both analytical and rhetorical: it gave the coalition's allies a precise vocabulary for identifying the forces they were up against, and it named the most dangerous of those forces, not the overt racist but the gradualist, not the Klansman but the status-quo-er, with the specificity required to counter them.

His 1951 paper on human rights deployed the Cold War's own logic against the red-baiters: if the United States was engaged in a global struggle against Soviet totalitarianism for the allegiance of the world's nonwhite populations, then racial discrimination at home was not merely a domestic injustice but a strategic liability. The Soviet propaganda apparatus was documenting American racial practices with considerable effectiveness, and the State Department was under pressure to respond. Barbour made this argument explicitly in the 1949 FEPC campaign, warning the Colorado legislature about how defeating the fair employment bill would provide Soviet propagandists with evidence of American hypocrisy precisely when American foreign policy depended on projecting racial liberalism abroad.

Mary Dudziak's *Cold War Civil Rights* demonstrates how this argument was deployed by civil rights advocates across the country in the late 1940s and 1950s, creating a form of leverage over the federal government which the domestic political dynamics alone could not have provided. Barbour's use of the international frame in his Denver advocacy placed him within this broader strategic pattern, demonstrating his awareness of the Cold War's implications for civil rights politics and his capacity to deploy this awareness in the specific legislative context of Colorado.

Standing At The Gate

The 1951 direct-action test at the Denver swimming pools was Barbour's most visible departure from the institutional negotiation and legislative advocacy characterizing most of his Denver work, and its significance lies partly in what it reveals about the range of his methodological repertoire. He was not primarily a direct-action organizer; the swimming pool test was one episode in a career defined primarily by coalition-building, legislative advocacy, and empirical research. But the episode reveals the full range of the movement's methods was available to him when circumstances warranted.

The specific choice of swimming pools as the site of direct-action testing was not arbitrary. Swimming pools were among the most viscerally contested sites of racial integration in mid-century America, because they were understood by many white Americans as spaces of particular intimacy, spaces where the logic of racial separation was most intensely felt even when its legal basis was weakest. The desegregation of swimming pools had provoked riots in multiple cities in the postwar years, and the reluctance of municipal governments to press the issue even where they had legal authority to do so reflected their awareness of its political volatility.

Sportland's affiliation with the YMCA and financial support from Denver's Community Chest underscored the argument Barbour was making: facilities funded in part by community contributions were practicing racial exclusion at their admission gates, this public money was subsidizing private discrimination, and how this contradiction was both a legal problem and a moral one. Palmer Brown's subsequent press coverage of the episode made the contradiction visible to a Denver public who might otherwise have remained unaware of it or indifferent to it. Micky Freed's criticism of national media for ignoring the story raised the broader question of how the press's indifference to nonviolent racial exclusion sustained the racial order by making it invisible to those not directly experiencing it.

The swimming pool test was, in the language of Barbour's theological formation, an act of prophetic witness: the embodied insistence, at personal cost and with personal risk, which the racial exclusion being practiced was incompatible with the democratic and Christian values the community claimed to hold. The AME tradition had always understood prophetic witness as costly discipleship: the prophet named the sin and accepted the social consequences of naming it. The Brethren tradition had understood the gathered community's witness as embodied rather than only verbal: the community demonstrated by its practices, not only by its arguments, what the Kingdom of God looked like. At the swimming pool gate in 1951, Barbour embodied both traditions simultaneously, standing in the spaces where racial exclusion operated and insisting, through his presence, how the space should be otherwise.

The National Urban League's selection of Denver to host its 1949 national convention at the University of Denver was recognition of the achievements of Barbour's first two years as executive secretary. As the first national Urban League conference convened in a western city, the choice signaled institutional confidence in the Denver League's work and in the broader reform climate cultivated through the collaboration between Barbour's organization and Mayor Newton's administration. The convention brought national civil rights leadership to Denver, provided Barbour with an opportunity to showcase the coalition-building model he had developed, and positioned Denver as a potential model for other western cities beginning to confront the civil rights challenges the postwar period was bringing to a national scale.

Recognition from the national organization was important not only institutionally but personally. Barbour had spent twenty years preparing for leadership of this kind, building the skills, the credentials, and the institutional relationships which a position like his required. The convention's presence in Denver was validation about how he had used those preparations well, the work he and Newton and the broader coalition had done in Denver was being seen and valued by the national organization whose mission he was serving.

The appointment to the Western Field Office directorship in Los Angeles in 1952 was the next step in this recognition. The creation of the Western Field Office was itself significant: it represented the National Urban League's acknowledgment about how the American West, with its rapidly growing urban populations, its complex racial and ethnic demography, and its unique combination of civil rights challenges, required dedicated institutional attention at the regional level. Naming Barbour as the first regional director was a vote of confidence in his capacity to apply the method he had developed in Denver to a larger and more complex canvas.

What He Built

The economic logic underlying Barbour's human rights work in Denver was not implicit; he stated it plainly, in words whose chain of reasoning is as clear and as demanding as any policy argument in the civil rights literature: 'When a person earns money they can afford an education, with an education their earning power increases exponentially, with increased earning power they can afford to live wherever they desire.' Three sentences. Three links in a chain connecting employment, education, and housing, the three domains his Denver Urban League work targeted simultaneously and the three domains the civil rights legislation of the 1960s would eventually address. He saw it whole in 1947, and he spent five years in Denver building the institutional and political conditions for addressing all three together.

When Barbour resigned from Denver in January 1952 and moved with Ruth to Pasadena, California, he left behind a human rights infrastructure he had spent five years building. The Denver Urban League had become, under his leadership, a nationally recognized model of municipal human rights work. The Mayor's Commission on Human Relations, on which he served, had established the institutional presence of human rights advocacy within the municipal government. The FEPC campaigns, while they had not yet produced legislation, had shifted public opinion and established the organizational relationships which would eventually produce the Colorado Anti-Discrimination Act. The interracial coalition he had built, drawing on Black church networks, labor organizations, Jewish civic organizations, and the reform community connected to Mayor Newton's administration, was a durable institutional achievement sustaining human rights advocacy in Denver beyond his departure.

He left also a personal legacy: the relationships he had built in five years of intensive civic engagement, the reputation he had established as a human rights leader of unusual combination of theological seriousness, intellectual rigor, and practical effectiveness, and the model he had demonstrated of what the integrator could accomplish in a city in a period. Denver in 1952 was not a racially equal city; Barbour would have been the first to acknowledge how the work was far from finished. But it was a city where the racial question had been publicly named, where the gap between democratic profession and democratic performance had been documented and argued over and pressed in legislative chambers and civic forums and newspaper columns, and where the institutional infrastructure for continuing this pressure was in place.

Making Jesus king, in Denver from 1947 to 1952, had looked like this: five years of coalition-building, legislative advocacy, empirical research, direct-action witness, and institutional development, sustained by the conviction about how the work was not optional but demanded, not merely professionally useful but theologically necessary. He had made the king's claim visible in the housing markets and the employment practices and the legislative chambers and the swimming pools of a western city. He carried what he had learned westward, to Los Angeles, to the larger canvas where the same work awaited.

The work Barbour did in Denver was not accomplished by Barbour alone. The Urban League's staff, board, and volunteer community were essential partners in the coalition-building and advocacy work he led, and the historical record, while incomplete on the specifics of these relationships, suggests a community of committed people whose collective effort produced the achievements gaining national recognition. Understanding Barbour as a leader requires understanding him in relation to the community of people he was leading.

The bi-racial board of directors which the Urban League's governance structure required was itself a significant organizational achievement in the Denver of the late 1940s. Assembling a board including both Black and white members, both community representatives and institutional leaders from business, religion, and civic life, in a city with the Klan's recent history and the racial geography of restricted covenants, required the combination of relationship-building capacity and moral persuasion Barbour's formation had equipped him to exercise. The board was not merely a legal requirement; it was a demonstration of the integrative possibility Barbour's human rights work was working to realize in the broader community. If the Urban League's governance could be genuinely bi-racial in Denver in 1947, then the argument about how genuine interracial collaboration was impossible in a city with Denver's racial history was demonstrably false.

Ruth

Ruth Johnson Barbour is, in the historical record, a figure who exists primarily in relation to her husband's career: she is the wife who accompanied him to Denver and Los Angeles, who suffered the stroke stealing her speech, who arranged for his body to be returned to Philadelphia after his death. This is the record's failure, not her significance. No person who married William Wilbur Miller Barbour, traveled with him across three time zones and two decades of human rights work, managed the household which made his institutional engagement possible, and survived the personal devastation of a severe stroke with enough presence of mind and enough love to make the arrangements which honored him in death was a marginal figure in the story. She was its essential support.

The family interview the author conducted with Barbour's granddaughters Renee Whitby and Deborah Neil and his great-grandson Paul Neil in September 2025 offers what the documentary record cannot: the living memory of people who knew both Ruth and William Barbour through the eyes of the next generation. The picture which emerges, however partially, is of a partnership between two people of complementary gifts and shared conviction, a marriage in which the human rights work was not his career which she accommodated but their shared commitment which they navigated together across the specific circumstances of their life.

Her migration from Arkansas to Philadelphia, her own navigation of the Great Migration's terms, gave her a formation analogous to his in important ways: the knowledge of the South's racial terms and the refusal of them, the determination to build something better in the North, the practical resourcefulness of a person who had made her way in conditions not designed for her success. Her marriage to a man devoted to the human rights work addressing the conditions she had grown up navigating suggests a shared understanding of what the work was for and why it mattered. The loss of her ability to speak following her stroke, coming in the years when her husband was doing his most visible and consequential work in Los Angeles, was a personal tragedy whose specific emotional weight on both of them can only be imagined from outside. Barbour's continuation of his work at the same level of engagement through this personal difficulty is evidence of the combination of commitment and compartmentalization which the integrator's role required.

The coalition Barbour assembled in Denver across his five years of Urban League leadership was not a single organization but an ongoing negotiation among organizations with different constituencies, different institutional cultures, and different but overlapping interests in the human rights outcomes Barbour was pursuing. Understanding the organizations in the coalition and the ways Barbour managed the relationships among them illuminates the organizational sophistication which the integrator's method required.

The Anti-Defamation League of B'nai B'rith was one of the most consistent and most practically useful coalition partners. The ADL's commitment to combating discrimination against minority groups generally, not only against Jews specifically, gave it a genuine organizational interest in the FEPC campaigns which aligned well with Barbour's goals. The specific test at the Denver swimming pools, in which ADL representative Micky Freed participated alongside Barbour and journalist Palmer Brown, exemplified the kind of interracial direct action which the coalition's organizational culture supported. Freed's subsequent criticism of national media for ignoring the episode reflected the ADL's sophistication about the role of media attention in civil rights campaigns, a sophistication complementing Barbour's own developing awareness of mass media's civil rights significance.

The Jewish community's participation in the civil rights coalition was not without its complications. Jewish Denverites were themselves a minority community facing forms of discrimination, including exclusion from certain residential neighborhoods and social clubs, and the relationship between the Jewish civil rights organizations and the Black civil rights organizations in the coalition was shaped by the dynamics of two minority communities with overlapping but not identical interests in the outcomes of civil rights campaigns. Stuart Svonkin's Jews against Prejudice provides the scholarly context for understanding how Jewish civil rights organizations, including the ADL and the American Jewish Congress, participated in the broader civil rights coalition of the postwar decades, demonstrating how the relationship was more complex and more nuanced than either the narrative of Jewish-Black solidarity or the narrative of Jewish-Black competition fully captures.

The labor unions affiliated with the CIO provided another dimension of the coalition, bringing organizational resources and political connections which the civil rights organizations alone could not supply. The CIO's commitment to organizing Black and white workers together, however imperfectly realized in locals and industries, gave it a genuine organizational stake in the success of the FEPC campaigns, because fair employment legislation would reduce the ability of employers to use racial discrimination as a tool for weakening union solidarity. Barbour's ability to work within this coalition, to understand the specific interests of each organizational partner and to frame the FEPC campaigns in terms advancing those interests as well as the broader civil rights goal, was one of the most important dimensions of his human rights effectiveness.

The Black church networks, activated through Barbour's AME connections and through the relationships he had built with Denver's Black ministers across his first years in the city, provided the community base without which the legislative coalition would have lacked the grassroots political pressure which legislative advocacy required. The March 27, 1949, mobilization in which 'every Negro minister in this area' urged congregants to contact state legislators was not an improvised event; it was the fruit of patient relationship-building across Denver's Black church community, the activation of organizational networks Barbour had been cultivating since his arrival. The ministers' willingness to mobilize their congregations reflected both their trust in Barbour's leadership and their own theological conviction, nourished by the AME and Black Baptist traditions of prophetic witness, which fair employment legislation was not merely a political demand but a moral one.

Gunnar Myrdal's *An American Dilemma: The Negro Problem and Modern Democracy*, published in 1944, was the most influential scholarly analysis of American race relations in the twentieth century, and its impact on civil rights advocacy in the postwar decade was substantial. Myrdal's central argument, about how American racial inequality represented a fundamental contradiction between the nation's democratic ideals and its actual practices, a contradiction he called the 'American dilemma,' gave civil rights advocates a framework for understanding and arguing about racial discrimination which was both analytically rigorous and morally urgent.

Barbour deployed Myrdal's framework with precision and effect in his Denver advocacy. His public letter responding to Senator Gill's defense of his weak FEPC bill situated Gill's position within Myrdal's analysis with the intellectual confidence of a person who had read the book carefully and understood its analytical power. Barbour argued Gill's position exemplified precisely the form of racial liberalism Myrdal had analyzed: a politics committed in principle to equality while in practice ensuring its indefinite deferral, a combination of authoritarian insistence on the terms of compromise and liberal reformist language about progress which revealed, in Myrdal's framework, the American dilemma in its specifically political form.

The deployment of Myrdal was itself a form of intellectual civil rights advocacy, an assertion which the analysis of racial discrimination belonged to the highest levels of social scientific inquiry and which civil rights advocates could and would engage this inquiry on its own terms. When Barbour cited Myrdal before a legislative committee or in a newspaper column, he was insisting on the intellectual seriousness of the civil rights demand: this was not merely a political preference or an emotional response to personal experience, but an argument grounded in the most sophisticated contemporary scholarship on the subject. The Elizabethtown liberal arts interdisciplinary formation taught Barbour to read primary texts carefully and to deploy theoretical frameworks in argument was paying dividends in the institutional contexts of human rights advocacy.

The Denver Commission on Human Relations, established as a permanent municipal body in 1950 following the earlier work of the Mayor's Interim Committee Newton had created upon taking office, represented the institutionalization of the civil rights advocacy Barbour had been conducting through the Urban League and the broader coalition. The Commission gave the human rights agenda a formal place within the structure of municipal governance, a presence on the organizational chart of city government translating the moral and civic arguments of the human rights coalition into an official institutional voice.

Barbour's service on the Commission placed him simultaneously inside the formal structure of municipal governance and outside it, in his parallel role as Urban League executive and coalition leader. This dual positioning was characteristic of the integrator's method: the ability to work from within formal institutions while maintaining the independence of the community organization, giving the formal institution pressure and accountability. When the Commission produced reports documenting racial discrimination in Denver's housing market, Barbour was both a contributor to those reports in his capacity with the Commission and an organizer of community pressure that gave the Commission's recommendations political weight in his capacity with the Urban League. The two roles reinforced rather than conflicted with each other.

The Commission's existence also provided a model for what Barbour would later argue was essential to integration: the development of formal institutional mechanisms for monitoring racial conditions and demanding accountability from the institutions responsible for addressing them. The integration process could not proceed on the basis of good intentions alone; it required the sustained, organized, institutionally grounded pressure of bodies capable of producing evidence of discriminatory practice and demanding a response from the institutions producing it. The Denver Commission on Human Relations was one such body, imperfect in its authority and limited in its resources but genuine in its commitment and significant in its symbolic statement about how racial equality was a matter of municipal responsibility rather than private preference.

| 6 |

War, Conscience, and Kingdom Deferred

The radio in the Barbour household would have carried, like every radio in America on the afternoon of December 7, 1941, the interrupted programming and the urgent bulletins and then, in the evening, the voices of correspondents and officials assembling from fragments a picture of what had happened in Hawaii. The attack on Pearl Harbor killed 2,403 Americans, wounded 1,178, and destroyed or damaged much of the Pacific Fleet. By the morning of December 8, when President Roosevelt addressed Congress and the American people, the United States was committed to a war on two fronts, in the Pacific and in Europe, reshaping every dimension of American life over the following four years. William Wilbur Miller Barbour was thirty-three years old. The world he had spent his adult life working to transform was about to transform itself, in ways both promising and treacherous for the civil rights cause he served.

The specific complexity of Black America's response to Pearl Harbor was compressed into the formulation the *Pittsburgh Courier* published in February 1942 and promoted aggressively through the remainder of the war: the Double V, victory over fascism abroad and victory over racial fascism at home. The Courier's campaign was both a patriotic commitment and a political demand, a statement: Black Americans would serve the nation's war effort on the condition, explicit rather than merely implied, the nation would honor its democratic promises at home. The formulation had the clarity and the urgency of a long-suppressed demand finally finding its moment, and its resonance across Black America, where the Courier's circulation expanded dramatically during the war years, reflected how thoroughly this moment had been prepared by everything preceding it.

For Barbour, the Double V expressed in popular political language the theological argument he had been carrying since Elizabethtown College: the gap between democratic profession and democratic performance was not a political inconvenience but a moral failure, which the nation claiming to fight for democracy abroad was conducting a moral argument it was simultaneously refuting at home, and this refutation demanded correction as a matter of fundamental justice rather than strategic convenience. The Double V was, in the vocabulary of his theological formation, an assertion about how making Jesus King was non-negotiable, and how His kingship could not be limited to the private lives of believers or the Sunday worship of the church while the public life of the nation organized itself around racial hierarchy. The war had made the assertion urgent at the national level in ways peacetime politics had not.

Philip Randolph, The March on Washington Movement, and The FEPC

The most consequential civil rights initiative of the immediate prewar and wartime period, and the one whose methodological significance for understanding Barbour's subsequent career is greatest, was A. Philip Randolph's threatened March on Washington of 1941 and the Fair Employment Practices Committee it produced. Randolph's campaign was a masterclass in the form of political leverage the Long Civil Rights Movement had been developing since the 1930s: the use of organized political pressure, backed by the credible threat of mass action, to force a reluctant federal government to take action against racial discrimination in a specific, limited domain where the political cost of inaction exceeded the political cost of action.

Randolph had been working since 1940 to force the Roosevelt administration to issue an executive order prohibiting racial discrimination in defense industry employment. The defense industries were expanding rapidly in response to the war in Europe and the growing recognition of inevitable American involvement, and the expansion was producing millions of new jobs being systematically closed to Black workers despite the federal government's partial financial stake in the enterprises doing the hiring. Randolph's demand was concrete: an executive order prohibiting discrimination by defense contractors and establishing a mechanism to investigate and remedy complaints. His leverage was real: he threatened to organize a mass march of 100,000 Black Americans on Washington, D.C., on July 1, 1941, if Roosevelt failed to issue the order.

The threat was credible because Randolph had, through a decade of building the Brotherhood of Sleeping Car Porters into a major labor organization, demonstrated the organizational capacity to execute it. The Brotherhood's 18,000 members and the broader Black organizational networks Randolph could activate through the National Negro Congress and his extensive personal connections gave the march threat a logistical foundation Roosevelt's advisors took seriously. Eleanor Roosevelt and New York City Mayor Fiorello La Guardia, both committed civil rights allies, urged Randolph to call off the march. He refused unless Roosevelt acted. On June 25, 1941, six days before the march was scheduled, Roosevelt issued Executive Order 8802, prohibiting discrimination in defense industry employment and creating the Fair Employment Practices Committee to investigate complaints.

Merl Reed's Seedtime for the Modern Civil Rights Movement provides the definitive scholarly account of the FEPC's creation and operation. Reed documents both the significance of the precedent the FEPC established and the limitations of its actual enforcement capacity: the committee was understaffed, underfunded, lacking sub-poena power, and dependent on the voluntary compliance of employers whose cooperation was inconsistent at best. But the precedent was real and politically important: the federal government had, for the first time since Reconstruction, formally prohibited racial discrimination in a significant domain of economic life, and the organizational leverage producing the prohibition was a model civil rights advocates at every level of the movement could draw on in their own campaigns.

Beth Tompkins Bates, in Pullman Porters and the Rise of Protest Politics in Black America, situates the March on Washington Movement within the longer arc of Black political mobilization Randolph's career represented. Bates demonstrates how the Brotherhood of Sleeping Car Porters was not merely a labor union but a political organization, and how Randolph's use of its organizational base to press for federal civil rights action represented a new model of Black political leverage combining the resources of the labor movement, the moral authority of the civil rights tradition, and the political context of a wartime emergency requiring Black cooperation for its success. This model was directly applicable to the civil rights campaigns Barbour would lead in Colorado in the late 1940s and early 1950s, and his own legislative advocacy shows clear evidence of having absorbed its lessons.

The theological tension between Barbour's two formative traditions was most acutely posed by the war, and examining it in some depth illuminates dimensions of his human rights formation the institutional and professional narrative alone cannot fully capture. The AME tradition had always connected Black military service to the assertion of citizenship: if Black men fought and died for the republic, the republic was morally and constitutionally obligated to honor its democratic promises to them. This argument had sustained Black military participation through the Revolutionary War, the Civil War, the Spanish-American War, and World War I, even when each of those wars produced its own version of the Double V's frustrated domestic promise.

The Brethren tradition offered a fundamentally different response: the nonresistant refusal of military service as a theological commitment derived from the teaching of Jesus in the Sermon on the Mount and the practice of the early church before its accommodation with the Roman Empire under Constantine. Albert N. Keim and Grant M. Stoltzfus, in *The Politics of Conscience*, trace the Historic Peace Churches' navigation of this commitment through the challenges of World War II, documenting how Civilian Public Service provided an alternative service pathway for conscientious objectors from Brethren, Mennonite, and Quaker communities, and how the Brethren Service Committee organized alternative service programs allowing peace church members to serve the nation without bearing arms.

Rachel Waltner Goossen's *Women against the Good War* complicates this story by showing how the peace church communities' conscientious objection was not only a male practice but a gendered negotiation in which women bore specific burdens and developed forms of witness the standard accounts of conscientious objection have not fully acknowledged. Goossen's analysis is relevant to understanding the Brethren institutional context within which Barbour's Elizabethtown formation had been conducted, because it reveals the full complexity of the peace church response to World War II in ways illuminating what the Brethren tradition offered as an alternative to the militarism the war demanded.

The historical record does not preserve any direct statement by Barbour about his personal position on conscientious objection or his response to the military draft. He does not appear in the Selective Service records as a conscientious objector, and the family oral history does not address this question directly. Barbour held a Class 2-A occupational deferment — social workers and community organizers had been classified as essential to civilian welfare, and the government considered his work too important to send him to the front. What can be said with confidence is how his response to the war was to intensify his human rights work in the institutional forms available to him rather than to address the war's demands primarily through the question of military service. The Wharton Centre work he undertook in 1944, the graduate study at the University of Pennsylvania he pursued simultaneously, and the development of the Neighborhood Plan he contributed to were all expressions of the same conviction shaping his entire career: the integrator's work of building genuine community across racial lines was the form of discipleship the specific circumstances demanded.

The creative tension between the AME tradition's military-service-as-citizenship argument and the Brethren tradition's nonresistance was not, for Barbour, a contradiction requiring resolution in favor of one tradition or the other. It was a productive tension, each tradition qualifying and enriching the other in ways producing a human rights practitioner more effective than either tradition alone could have formed. From the AME tradition he drew the prophetic urgency: the war's democratic claims had to be matched by democratic practice at home, and the insistence on this matching was non-negotiable. From the Brethren tradition he drew the methodological commitment: the matching had to be built, through patient institutional work, rather than merely demanded through dramatic confrontation. The integrator synthesized both.

Howard Thurman's *Jesus and the Disinherited*, published in 1949 but developed through years of lectures and sermons preceding its publication, was the most significant theological text produced for the civil rights movement in the wartime and immediate postwar period, and its significance for understanding the theological synthesis Barbour embodied deserves extended treatment. Thurman, the dean of Rankin Chapel at Howard University and later the founding co-pastor of the Church for the Fellowship of All Peoples in San Francisco, the first intentionally interracial, interdenominational congregation in American history, was developing in the 1940s exactly the theological framework serving as the intellectual bridge between Barbour's two formative traditions.

Thurman's central argument in *Jesus and the Disinherited* was: Jesus, as a poor Jew living under the Roman occupation, belonged to the company of the disinherited, the people who had their backs against the wall, and how his Gospel was therefore most directly addressed to those in analogous circumstances. For Black Americans living under American racial apartheid, Jesus's teaching was not the comfortable religion of the powerful seeking to domesticate their conscience; it was the specific, urgent, costly demand of a person who had himself lived within the conditions of domination and had found, in the response of love to fear and hatred and deception, the only path leading through those conditions without being destroyed by them. The theology was not a theology of accommodation; it was a theology of resistance, a theology insisting how authentic response to racial domination required neither the violence of retaliation nor the capitulation of accommodation but the costly, creative, dignity-preserving response of love Jesus had himself embodied.

Thurman had visited Gandhi in India in 1936, as part of a delegation from the Negro Student Christian Movement, and his conversation with Gandhi about the relevance of nonviolent resistance to the conditions of African Americans was one of the formative intellectual encounters of the civil rights movement's development. Gandhi's challenge to Thurman, which the American Negro may be the group chosen to transform the world's understanding of democracy, became one of the organizing convictions of Thurman's subsequent theological work and, through the people his theology shaped, of the civil rights movement itself. James Farmer, who had read Thurman carefully, brought this theological framework to CORE. Martin Luther King Jr., who carried a copy of Jesus and the Disinherited in his coat pocket during the Montgomery Bus Boycott, drew on it explicitly in his understanding of nonviolent resistance. The theological tradition Thurman articulated was, in important ways, the theological synthesis of the AME's prophetic tradition and the peace church's nonresistant tradition, the same synthesis Barbour had embodied through his dual formation. That dual formation, Barbour's own, had arrived at the same convergence by a different route: not through Thurman's text but through lived experience in Ebenezer AME's pews and Elizabethtown College's classrooms. He did not need the book to know what it said.

Barbour did not leave behind a direct statement of his relationship to Thurman's theology, and any claim about this relationship must be appropriately cautious. What can be said is how the theological synthesis Thurman articulated, the insistence on the specific relevance of Jesus's teaching to the conditions of the disinherited, the commitment to a form of resistance which was neither violent retaliation nor passive accommodation, and the conviction about how the Kingdom of God's values could and should be made visible in the social arrangements of everyday life, described precisely the theological framework Barbour's human rights career embodied. Whether he encountered Thurman's work directly, whether the framework was independently produced through the intersection of his two formative traditions, or whether both drew on deeper wells in the Black Christian tradition sustaining them both: any of these possibilities is consistent with the evidence, and the resemblance is too precise to be accidental.

Bayard Rustin's career provides the most precise illustration of how the peace church networks and the Black civil rights tradition intersected in the wartime years in ways directly relevant to understanding Barbour's organizational context. Rustin was born in 1912, three years before Barbour, in West Chester, Pennsylvania, into a Quaker family, and was raised in the peace church tradition in a mid-Atlantic region similar to the one shaping Barbour's formation. He joined the Fellowship of Reconciliation's staff in 1941 and became one of the central figures in the development of CORE's nonviolent direct action methodology in the early 1940s.

The parallels between Rustin's formation and Barbour's are striking and historically significant. Both were formed in the peace church world of the mid-Atlantic region. Both were deeply engaged with the Black church tradition. Both were committed to the development of the nonviolent direct action methods the civil rights movement would deploy on a national scale in the 1950s and 1960s. Both worked in the organizational networks connecting the Fellowship of Reconciliation, the Historic Peace Churches, and the Black civil rights organizations. And both were, in the 1940s, developing the methodological repertoire proving essential to the movement's subsequent success.

The difference was one of visibility and subsequent recognition: Rustin's role in organizing the March on Washington for Jobs and Freedom in 1963, his theoretical contributions to the movement's tactical development, and his eventual public recognition as one of the movement's most important strategists gave him a place in the historical record Barbour did not achieve. But the organizational work Rustin was doing in the early 1940s, building the networks and developing the methods of the peace church civil rights tradition, was happening in the same organizational world Barbour was embedded in through his Elizabethtown connections. The specific people and organizations connecting these two figures's organizational worlds would reward further archival investigation, and the similarity of their formations suggests the investigation would be productive.

John D'Emilio's *Lost Prophet*, the definitive biography of Rustin, traces the development of Rustin's civil rights career with the scholarly rigor Barbour's career has not yet received. D'Emilio's account of the wartime FOR networks, the development of CORE's methodology, and the organizational connections between the peace church tradition and the Black civil rights tradition provides the most detailed scholarly reconstruction of the organizational world Barbour was embedded in during the 1940s. Reading D'Emilio's account alongside this biography's account of Barbour's parallel formation suggests how much of the Long Civil Rights Movement's organizational infrastructure was built in the peace church networks of the mid-Atlantic and northeast, and how many of the movement's most important practitioners were formed in the intersection of those networks and the Black church tradition.

The social crisis Barbour confronted when he joined the Wharton Centre's staff in 1944 was not the product of the war alone, though the war had intensified every dimension of it. North Philadelphia's Black neighborhoods had been under pressure since the 1920s, when the Great Migration's first wave had brought more people than the available housing stock could accommodate without the overcrowding, the deterioration of services, and the social stress that rapid population growth in conditions of inadequate investment inevitably produced. The war had accelerated population growth, as defense industries drew additional workers from the South, and had directed the city's attention and resources toward the war effort in ways that left even less than usual for the social services the growing population required.

The housing situation in North Philadelphia in 1944 was, by any standard of adequacy, a crisis. The neighborhoods where Black Philadelphians were confined by racial covenants and discriminatory landlord practices were severely overcrowded, with families sharing apartments designed for far fewer people, with buildings maintained at levels far below what the city's housing codes nominally required, and with a rental market where the combination of high demand, limited supply, and the racial restriction preventing Black tenants from moving to better-maintained neighborhoods gave landlords no incentive to maintain their properties. The physical conditions of the housing stock translated directly into the health and social outcomes its residents experienced: elevated rates of tuberculosis, infant mortality, and the stress-related conditions chronic overcrowding and inadequate maintenance produced.

The schools serving North Philadelphia's Black students were overcrowded and underfunded in the way schools in poor urban neighborhoods have always been overcrowded and underfunded in the American educational system: they received fewer resources, employed less experienced teachers, and maintained facilities in worse condition than the schools serving the city's more affluent and less racially restricted neighborhoods. The employment available to North Philadelphia's Black residents was concentrated in the domestic service, unskilled labor, and service industry positions designated as appropriate for Black workers in the racial labor market, positions paying too little to allow the accumulation of the savings which would have made housing improvement or educational investment possible.

Into this environment, the wartime migration of additional Black workers from the South was adding population to neighborhoods already at or beyond their capacity to absorb it without social deterioration. The young men who were forming and joining the gangs of North Philadelphia in 1944 and 1945 were growing up in these conditions: overcrowded housing, underfunded schools, a job market confining them to the lowest-paying and least secure positions, and a civic order regarding their presence as a social problem rather than a civic responsibility. The gangs they formed were rational responses to irrational conditions: organizations providing the community, the protection, and the economic opportunity the formal institutions of the city were declining to provide on equitable terms.

The wartime transformation of Black economic and social expectations Barbour would later document in his Denver work, his 1947 observation: 'what the average Negro wants right now is a job, and not the menial type of job considered proper for him before the war,' was visible from inside the wartime city in ways the subsequent historical scholarship has not always adequately captured. The texture of Black life in wartime Philadelphia and New York, the combination of defense industry employment opening positions previously closed to Black workers with the continued operation of racial hierarchy in housing, education, and social services, produced in the communities Barbour was working with a form of rising expectation combined with continuing frustration.

Harvard Sitkoff's *A New Deal for Blacks* documents the dimensions of this transformation: the defense industry's demand for Black labor, driven by wartime necessity rather than racial liberalism, opened manufacturing positions which had previously been closed; the Double V campaign gave these economic gains a political framing; and the wartime migration of additional Black workers to northern cities gave the transformation a demographic scale making its reversal politically difficult even for those who would have preferred it. But Sitkoff also documents the limits: the defense industry's racial integration was partial and contested, typically confining Black workers to the least skilled and lowest paid positions within the industry rather than achieving genuine occupational integration, and the residential racial geography of the cities to which Black workers were migrating remained as rigidly segregated as before.

Barbour was living inside this combination of expanded opportunity and continued constraint in North Philadelphia in 1944 and 1945, and the specific form it took in the juvenile gang dynamics he was addressing at the Wharton Centre reflected the combination's consequences. The young men joining the gangs of North Philadelphia were growing up in a moment when their older brothers and fathers were earning more than their families had earned in the Depression, were working in defense plants alongside white workers, were coming home from military service with the combination of dignity and anger the Double V campaign expressed. They had higher expectations than their parents had allowed themselves to hold, and they were encountering the same structural barriers to fulfilling those expectations their parents had always encountered. The gap between expectation and attainment, in social psychological terms the conditions most reliably producing frustration and its consequent behaviors, was wider in wartime North Philadelphia than it had been in the Depression years, and the gangs were one expression of how this gap was being managed.

Understanding this dynamic, understanding the wartime transformation of Black expectations as the social context for the juvenile gang problem he was addressing, was part of what made Barbour's approach to gang work effective. He did not treat the gang members he was working with as simply delinquent, as people who had failed to develop the individual moral character required for constructive civic participation. He treated them as people responding rationally to conditions designed to frustrate them, and he directed his intervention not primarily at changing their individual behavior but at changing the conditions producing the frustration and providing the constructive alternatives rational people would choose when they were available. This was the integrator's method in embryo: not the management of individual pathology but the transformation of the social conditions producing it.

The Method

The Wharton Centre in 1944 occupied a position in the organizational landscape of North Philadelphia's Black community: it was simultaneously a settlement house in the traditional sense, a middle-class institution bringing resources and professional expertise into direct contact with a working-class community, and a specifically Black institution whose programs were organized around the specific circumstances of an African American community in a racially organized city. Samuel Evans's Youth City program represented the synthesis of these two institutional identities: a settlement house program organized through the Black church networks which were the primary institutional resource of the community the Centre served.

Evans himself was a figure whose character and organizational method shaped the context of Barbour's work at the Centre in ways deserving attention. Evans's approach to juvenile delinquency reflected the community organization tradition being developed in social work during the 1930s: the conviction about how the most effective response to community problems was the organization of the community's own resources and leadership capacity rather than the imposition of professional solutions from outside. His collaboration with local Black ministers and churches to develop the Youth City Sunday Activities program was an expression of this conviction, and its success in reducing gang activity in the neighborhoods it served provided the evidence for the Neighbourhood Plan Barbour and his colleagues subsequently developed.

The survey research Barbour conducted among gang members applied the empirical respect Du Bois had brought to his study of Black Philadelphia in 1899: treating the people whose circumstances were being studied as the best sources of information about those circumstances. V. P. Franklin, drawing on Barbour's findings in his 1998 analysis of North Philadelphia's gang dynamics, preserves the texture of what Barbour documented: all along Norris Street were a number of different gangs occasionally fighting among themselves but always united against outsiders. Among the gangs Barbour surveyed were the North Coasters at Twentieth and Montgomery Avenue; the Vogueteers, who hung out at the Vogue Theater; the Swans at Twenty-third and Montgomery Avenue; the Mohawks at Ringgold and Taylor Streets; the Tophatters at Twenty-first and Columbia Avenue; and the Master Street Gang at Twenty-third and Master. Each had up to thirty members, and Barbour noted these by no means included all the teenage gangs in the neighborhood served by the Settlement House. He was mapping a social world of considerable organizational complexity, and the map was a precondition for any intervention capable of navigating it.

North Philadelphia, October 1945

Friday evening, October 18, 1945. The Wharton Centre's regular dance was underway, one of the Wednesday and Friday events drawing young people from throughout the surrounding neighborhoods and serving simultaneously as a social gathering and as contested territory, because the Centre's position at the boundary between several gang territories made its dances a place where the geography of gang affiliation was most immediately at stake. The Villagers gang, whose territory lay to the south and west of the Centre's location, had members present with specific intentions for the night: they were look-ing for members of the Ward gang, with whom an escalating series of conflicts had been building toward confrontation.

The confrontation came. Approximately nine or ten shots were fired inside and around the Centre, in the confused and rapid se-quence of violence which gang confrontations in confined spaces pro-duce. When the shooting stopped, a thirteen-year-old girl who had been at the dance, a bystander in the most literal and most terrible sense, lay critically wounded. The medical assessment at the hospital gave her a fifty-fifty chance of survival. The surrounding streets were in what V. P. Franklin describes as 'an uproar,' the immediate after-math of sudden violence in a dense urban neighborhood: people run-ning, people seeking shelter, people trying to reach their children, people calling for help from institutions, as they always did in such neighborhoods, after the fact.

The retaliatory violence began the following day. On October 19, Mohawk members damaged a poolroom associated with the Vil-lagers. On October 20, armed Villagers entered Ward territory and fired again, wounding two additional people. The pattern was the classic cycle of gang retaliation: each act of violence producing the ra-tionale for the next, with the original grievance becoming progres-sively less relevant and the maintenance of the gang's capacity for retaliation becoming the primary organizing principle. The commu-nities surrounding these conflicts were not participants in them, but they bore their consequences: the fear, the disrupted routines, the parents keeping children inside, the elderly residents moving through their neighborhoods with the careful wariness of people who under-stood they were in a contested space.

After October 20, several Ward gang members came to Barbour. Franklin preserves the specific words spoken. 'Mr. Barbour, some-thing would have to be done and done immediately,' shouted one boy. The approach was itself significant: they came to him rather than to the police or to any other formal institution. He had not yet earned the gang members' full confidence, but he had earned enough. His response was conditional: cooperation with law enforcement through identifying the people responsible and supporting prosecution. The condition was not negotiable.

His response was conditional: cooperation with law enforcement through the identification of the people responsible for the shootings and support for prosecution. The condition was not negotiable; he did not offer to intervene without it. The reasoning behind the condition was both practical and theological. Practically: without accountability, the cycle of retaliation would continue, because the gang logic organizing violence as a response to disrespect could only be interrupted by a counter-logic holding the violence accountable to consequences the gang logic could not itself impose. Theologically: the Anabaptist tradition's insistence on accountability, on the responsibility of every person within the gathered community to the community's standards and to the moral order the community was trying to embody, applied to the gang situation with uncomfortable precision. Making Jesus King in the Ward neighborhood in October 1945 required insisting the violence had consequences.

The trip to the police station at Nineteenth and Oxford Streets was not a simple act. For young Black men from North Philadelphia to walk into a police station in 1945 and deliver formal statements about gang violence was to place themselves in the hands of an institution whose record with their community was, at best, inconsistent. The police department which these young men knew was not primarily an institution of community protection; it was an institution of community surveillance and control, whose officers exercised their discretionary power in ways reflecting and reinforcing the racial hierarchy of the surrounding social order. Walking into the station required a kind of trust: not in the police department as such, but in Barbour's judgment this cooperation with prosecution in this cases was worth the risks cooperation with the police always carried.

Barbour accompanied them to the police station at Nineteenth and Oxford Streets, where they offered their versions of the shootings. When the police captain asked why they had not come to the police before, Franklin records the reply precisely: the leader of the boys quickly pointed out they had come to the police and had also gone to various agencies in an effort to solve this problem. They were there to get protection from the police or else they would have to proceed to protect themselves. The statement was not insolence. It was civic instruction delivered by a teenager who had learned, from the experience of growing up in North Philadelphia, what official institutions did and did not reliably provide. When the Warders went to the second floor they recognized three members of the rival Villagers gang being questioned about the Sunday evening shootings. Those boys were immediately arrested, and three others involved were caught and held for hearing. Barbour's presence was not ceremonial. He was there as an institutional witness whose professional standing gave authority to the proceedings and whose sustained relationship with the Ward boys had made the proceedings possible.

Barbour's simultaneous graduate study at the Pennsylvania School of Social Work while working at the Wharton Centre was not an accident of scheduling; it reflected a deliberate strategy of integrating theory and practice in the way the best professional education requires. The social work curriculum he encountered at the University of Pennsylvania in the mid-1940s was shaped by two decades of rapid theoretical development, as the profession sought to establish both its scientific foundations and its practical methods on firmer intellectual ground than the settlement house tradition's combination of moral commitment and improvised practice had provided.

The casework tradition, associated most prominently with Mary Richmond's Social Diagnosis and its elaborations in the subsequent decades, had established the systematic, evidence-based assessment of individual and family circumstances as the foundation of professional social work practice. The group work tradition, associated with Grace Coyle at Western Reserve University and her collaborators, had developed frameworks for understanding how the group setting could be used therapeutically and organizationally in ways complementing and extending the casework focus on individuals. The community organization tradition, still in its early theoretical development in the 1940s, was beginning to articulate the principles underlying the kind of work Barbour was doing at the Wharton Centre: the mobilization of community resources and the development of community leadership capacity as the appropriate response to the structural conditions producing the problems individual casework and group intervention could address only symptomatically.

The theoretical frameworks Barbour encountered in graduate school did not teach him what he was doing at the Wharton Centre; he had been doing it before he could fully articulate it in theoretical terms. What they gave him was the vocabulary to describe and analyze his practice, the conceptual tools to place his specific interventions within a broader understanding of how communities worked and how they could be helped to work better, and the professional credentials giving his subsequent advocacy institutional credibility in the professional world of civil rights and social reform. The MSW degree was not merely a credential; it was evidence of a professional formation occurring simultaneously through academic study and direct practice, each dimension informing and deepening the other.

The University of Pennsylvania connection also placed Barbour in the institutional settings where Du Bois had conducted his Philadelphia Negro research in 1896 and 1897. The methodological tradition Du Bois had established, the systematic empirical documentation of the social conditions of Black communities paired with rigorous analysis of the causes and consequences of racial inequality, was the intellectual inheritance of the institution where Barbour was training. His own subsequent research contributions, the Richmond study, the Tucson study, and the World Affairs Institute paper on human rights, stood in direct methodological continuity with Du Bois's approach, applying the same combination of empirical rigor and moral argument to the specific civil rights challenges of the postwar West. The institutional connection was not merely historical; it was the transmission of a specific methodological tradition from one generation of Black civil rights scholarship to the next.

A New Method of Witness

The founding of the Congress of Racial Equality in 1942 was the most significant organizational innovation of the wartime civil rights movement, and its significance for understanding Barbour's subsequent career requires extended treatment because the connection between CORE's founding and Barbour's Elizabethtown formation is more direct than the standard accounts of either acknowledge. CORE emerged from the Fellowship of Reconciliation's interracial networks, and the FOR drew on the same peace church theological tradition forming Barbour during his years at Elizabethtown College.

James Farmer, who founded CORE with George Houser, Bernice Fisher, and others in 1942, had grown up in the African Methodist Episcopal Church, the same tradition which had formed Barbour at Ebenezer AME in Middletown. Farmer's father, a Methodist minister and theologian, had instilled in his son the same conviction animating Barbour's human rights formation: the incompatibility of authentic Christian faith with structures of racial domination. When Farmer encountered the Fellowship of Reconciliation and its commitment to nonviolent direct action as a tool of social change, he recognized in it the complement to the AME tradition's prophetic witness that the Brethren tradition had provided for Barbour: a method for confronting racial hierarchy in the specific, embodied, public manner the Gospel demanded without recourse to the violence both traditions rejected.

August Meier and Elliott Rudwick's *CORE: A Study in the Civil Rights Movement* provides the definitive organizational history of CORE's development from its 1942 founding through its transformation in the 1960s. Meier and Rudwick document how CORE's early actions in Chicago, the sit-ins at segregated restaurants and lunch counters in 1942 and 1943, were conducted according to principles of nonviolent discipline developed in explicit dialogue with Gandhi's campaigns in India, as transmitted through Howard Thurman's *Jesus and the Disinherited* and the Fellowship of Reconciliation's educational programs. The sit-ins required participants to maintain their dignity and their nonviolent discipline in the face of deliberate verbal and physical abuse, to insist through the embodied act of their presence that the racial exclusion being practiced was both unjust and unsustainable, and to accept the social consequences of insistence without retaliation.

Scott H. Bennett's *Radical Pacifism* traces how these tactical innovations were transmitted through the peace church and pacifist networks to become the methodology of the civil rights movement's mass phase. The chain of transmission runs from Gandhi through the FOR through CORE's founding members through the workshops and training programs preparing the participants of the 1960 sit-ins for the form of nonviolent discipline they would need to maintain. The Elizabethtown College connection, through the Brethren's peace church networks, placed Barbour within the organizational ecosystem from which this tactical tradition was emerging in the 1940s, giving him access to its development even when his specific professional activities were not directly organized around the direct-action method.

His 1951 direct-action test at the Denver swimming pools was, in this context, not an improvised gesture but the deployment of a tactical method he had been observing and understanding for nearly a decade. The specific interracial character of the action, Barbour and Brown and Freed together, reflected CORE's foundational principle of direct action against racial exclusion, which was most effective when conducted by an interracial group whose different treatment at the same admission gate made the racial character of the exclusion unmistakable. The documentation strategy, Brown's subsequent press coverage, making the discrimination visible to a public who might otherwise have remained unaware of it, reflected CORE's understanding of the media as an essential component of the direct action's effectiveness. Barbour was applying a sophisticated tactical method to a specific local target, and the sophistication of the application reflected the depth of his engagement with the tactical tradition the peace church networks had developed.

Denver Beckons

The appointment to the Denver Urban League executive secretary position came in 1947, after Barbour had earned his MSW and while his Wharton Centre work was demonstrating, at small scale, the effectiveness of the integrator's method in the conditions of a North Philadelphia neighborhood. The appointment was not a coincidence of timing. It reflected the National Urban League's awareness of a practitioner who had developed, through fifteen years of direct engagement with some of the most difficult civil rights challenges of urban America, exactly the combination of professional competence, theoretical sophistication, and practical effectiveness the Denver position required.

He was thirty-nine years old. The formation was, for practical purposes, sufficient for the work ahead. Not complete, because no human formation is complete while the person is still living and learning and being shaped by the world they move through. But sufficient: sufficient for the demands of building a municipal civil rights coalition in a postwar western city, sufficient for the legislative advocacy and the direct action and the empirical research and the community organization Denver would require, sufficient for the theological conviction sustaining the work through the inevitable frustrations and setbacks of civil rights advocacy in a city whose recent history included Klan dominance of municipal government and whose present included racially restrictive covenants in its newest residential developments.

He carried to Denver the method the Wharton Centre had refined, the intellectual resources Elizabethtown had provided, the professional credentials the University of Pennsylvania had certified, and the theological mandate organizing everything since June 1932. Make

Jesus King. In Denver in 1947, making Jesus king meant doing exactly what the motto had always demanded: showing up in the institutional spaces where the racial order operated, insisting on its contradiction with the democratic and theological principles the community claimed to honor, and building, through patient coalitional work, the conditions under which insistence could produce concrete, measurable change. The work of twenty years had been preparation. Denver was where the preparation would be tested.

"Make Jesus King." In Denver in 1947, this was what the motto demanded: the full deployment of everything fifteen years of formation had built, in the service of a city whose racial future was being contested in the legislative chambers and the housing markets and the employment offices and the swimming pools and the newspapers and the university classrooms and the mayor's conference rooms where civic life was organized and civic futures were determined. He was ready. The city was about to discover what his readiness meant.

| 7 |

The Harvest He Would Not See

Barbour began his work as Western Regional Director of the National Urban League on January 15, 1952, operating from an office in Los Angeles while living with Ruth in Pasadena, the quiet residential city just east of Los Angeles, where middle-class Black professionals had found a degree of residential stability unusual in the racially restricted housing markets of the postwar West. The Western Field Office gave him a platform and a responsibility both larger than anything he had previously held: not a single city's Urban League affiliate but the entire western United States, a region whose racial complexity exceeded the urban North in important ways, whose civil rights challenges were shaped by distinctive histories of anti-Mexican, anti-Asian, and anti-Black discrimination, and whose rapidly growing cities were repeating, as Barbour would publicly argue, the blunders committed a century earlier by eastern cities in their approach to minority communities.

He arrived at this position carrying the accumulated formation of twenty years: the Wharton Centre method, the Denver coalition model, the human rights framework developed at the World Affairs Institute, and the theological conviction organizing everything since his years at Elizabethtown College. He arrived also carrying something new, or rather something which the Los Angeles context would develop in him: a sophisticated awareness of the role mass culture could play in the integration process, an awareness shaped by daily proximity to Hollywood and the entertainment industry whose reach into American public consciousness exceeded any political organization or civic institution.

The Larger Canvas

Los Angeles in 1952 was a city in the midst of transformation making Denver's postwar growth look modest. The metropolitan area's population had grown from 1.5 million in 1940 to nearly 4 million in 1950 and was still expanding rapidly, driven by the aerospace and defense industries, the postwar suburban boom, and the migration of workers from across the United States and Latin America. The racial complexity of the metropolitan area exceeded any city Barbour had previously worked in: large communities of Black Americans concentrated in South Central Los Angeles and parts of the San Fernando Valley; large Mexican American communities in East Los Angeles and throughout the metropolitan area; significant Japanese American communities, many of them still recovering from the trauma of wartime internment; smaller Chinese American, Filipino American, and other Asian American communities; and a white majority which was itself internally diverse, including large numbers of recent migrants from the South and Midwest who brought their own racial attitudes with them.

The racial geography of Los Angeles was organized by the same mechanisms Barbour had encountered in Philadelphia and Denver, but at a scale and with a sophistication exceeding both. The Federal Housing Administration's racially discriminatory lending guidelines had structured the postwar suburban boom to exclude Black Americans from homeownership, transforming white working-class families into the American middle class. Racially restrictive covenants, though declared unenforceable by the Supreme Court in 1948's Shelley v. Kraemer, continued to be observed through informal mechanisms of social pressure and real estate steering in most of the region's residential neighborhoods. The result was a metropolitan area whose racial geography was as rigidly separated as the most explicitly segregated southern city, maintained not by statute but by the informal architecture of a racial order which had learned to operate without the embarrassment of explicit legal sanction.

Josh Sides, in *L.A. City Limits*, traces the development of Black Los Angeles from the Great Depression through the postwar period, documenting how the wartime migration of Black workers to the defense plants and shipyards had created the large Black communities which the postwar racial order was working to contain and compress. Sides shows how the combination of residential segregation and employment discrimination Black Los Angeles experienced was produced not by individual prejudice alone but by the systematic operation of institutional mechanisms: the real estate industry's racial steering practices, the mortgage lending industry's discriminatory policies, the city planning decisions locating industrial facilities and transportation infrastructure in ways reinforcing racial residential boundaries, and the zoning policies allowing industrial and commercial uses degrading the residential environments of Black neighborhoods while protecting white neighborhoods from equivalent development pressure.

This was the landscape Barbour was charged with addressing at the regional level. His mandate extended well beyond Los Angeles itself: the Western Field Office served communities throughout California, Nevada, Utah, Colorado, New Mexico, Arizona, Oregon, and Washington, a vast geography of racial inequality whose forms varied by region and community but whose underlying dynamics were recognizably similar across the entire terrain.

Barbour's exploratory study of socioeconomic problems in Richmond, California, published jointly by the United Community Defense Services and the National Urban League in 1952, was his first major research undertaking as Western Regional Director and illustrated his methodological approach at its most developed. Richmond had been, during World War II, one of the most dramatic examples of the wartime economic transformation reshaping the racial landscape of the American West. The Kaiser Shipyards, building more ships than any other shipyard in the world, had recruited African American labor from the southern United States on a massive scale, transforming a small Bay Area city into a major industrial center and a major receiving point for the Great Migration's wartime acceleration.

Shirley Ann Wilson Moore's careful reconstruction of Richmond's Black community in To Place Our Deeds documents the character of this transformation. The Black workers who came to Richmond from Louisiana, Texas, and the Gulf Coast states encountered a labor market where the wartime emergency had opened some industrial positions previously closed to them while maintaining the racial hierarchy of the union hall and the shop floor. The Boilermakers Union's treatment of its Black auxiliary members, denying them full voting rights, access to better positions, and equal representation in grievance procedures, was the labor movement's racial architecture in concentrated and unusually visible form.

By 1952, when Barbour conducted his study, the wartime emergency which had opened industrial employment to Black workers in Richmond had passed, and the racial hierarchy of the labor market was reasserting itself with the same systematic efficiency it had displayed before the war. His observation, quoted in Moore's study, about how the 'hostility toward the white southerner' in Richmond had 'modified considerably' but the 'big problem which remains is the Negro,' captured this dynamic with precision: the war had changed some racial attitudes without changing the structural mechanisms through which racial inequality was maintained. The study recommended institutional interventions: job development programs, open occupancy housing initiatives, and the formation of an Urban League affiliate to coordinate civil rights advocacy in the Richmond area.

The Richmond study also reflected Barbour's understanding of the relationship between labor and human rights which his formation in both the AME tradition and the Long Movement's broader organizational context had given him. The AME tradition had always understood economic justice as inseparable from racial justice; the freedom struggle was also an economic struggle, and no vision of racial liberation which ignored the material conditions of Black workers was adequate to the full scope of what liberation required. A. Philip Randolph had made this connection the organizing principle of his human rights career, and Barbour's work in Richmond was in direct continuity with Randolph's understanding: the racial integration of the industrial workforce was not merely a civil rights demand but an economic necessity, for both the workers excluded and the society bearing the costs of their exclusion.

Barbour's trajectory from Denver to Los Angeles was direct and swift. He started his new position on January 15, 1952, with an office in Los Angeles and he and Ruth settled in Pasadena. That same year he authored a study on socioeconomic problems affecting the Negro-White relationship in Richmond, California, and helped establish the first desegregated housing development in Victorville. The breadth of his first two years in Los Angeles illustrated the method: empirical research, institutional development, and direct civic engagement conducted simultaneously across multiple fronts.

In 1954, *House and Home* magazine published a report noting: in a Los Angeles talk, Barbour had asserted many western cities were repeating 'the blunders committed 100 years ago by eastern cities' in an 'apathetic approach to minority-group problems tending to encourage slum development.' He was naming the pattern precisely: the West was not exempt from the racial history of industrialization; it was recapitulating it, and doing so with the evidence of a century's consequences readily available.

In the spring of 1955, he moderated a panel discussion at the National Conference on Social Work, held at the University of Pennsylvania, entitled 'Integrated Housing: Social Work's Challenge and Opportunity.' The panel brought him back, institutionally if not physically, to the place where he had trained, and asked him to speak to the field which had formed him about the central problem he had spent eight years addressing. The following year, in October 1956, he delivered an address entitled 'Where Do We Stand on Racial Desegregation?' at the San Diego Open Forum. The editors who published the piece captioned it as 'the finest objective summary we have ever seen' on the topic. He was forty-seven years old, nine months from his death, and his writing was, by the editors' own assessment, the best analytical statement the field had produced.

His assessments of the West Coast hotel situation documented genuine geographic variation. San Francisco stood apart, its world-famous establishments practicing non-discrimination. But even there the pattern was inconsistent, and the smaller cities were worse. Of the cities between Los Angeles and the Oregon border, he named specific places where the welcome was genuine: Fresno, California, where apparently all establishments admitted non-white travelers; the Court John motor court in Albuquerque, unusually cordial; and Deer Lodge, near the California-Oregon border, as another notable exception. He named them because the civil rights argument required evidence, and evidence required names.

The Tucson assignment of 1954 extended Barbour's analytical and organizational framework in a direction his previous work had pointed toward but not fully developed. Tucson's demographic complexity, with its substantial Native American, Mexican American, Japanese American, Chinese American, and African American communities alongside its white majority, required a multidirectional analysis of racial conditions the Black-white binary organizing most civil rights discourse of the period could not adequately provide. Barbour's willingness to undertake this more complex analysis and his capacity to frame it within the broader principles of human dignity and democratic equality reflected the intellectual formation his Elizabethtown education rooted in the classics had provided.

His seven days in Tucson produced a study whose analytical sophistication exceeded what most civil rights reports of the period achieved. His identification of the 'Spanish-white' category as sociologically complex, noting the United States Census Bureau had designated Spanish-speaking people as Caucasian but their actual social position in many southwestern communities corresponded to minority group status, anticipated the scholarly debates about Latino racial classification which would later become central to the sociology of race and ethnicity in the United States. His observation: Tucson's border location made it 'southern in its approach to and the handling of minority problems,' because of the migration patterns bringing southern racial attitudes into a southwestern setting, demonstrated his awareness of the regional variability of racial ideology and the mechanisms through which racial attitudes traveled and adapted.

The study's most practically significant contribution was its insistence on seeing the multiethnic community as a whole rather than as a collection of separate minority group problems requiring separate interventions. Barbour posed the evaluative question: whether 'the sum total of these inter-relationships is reacting to the benefit or detriment of the community.' The question required a form of community analysis going beyond the documentation of discrimination against any single minority group to assess how the relationships among all the groups, including the relationships among minority groups themselves, were shaping the overall health and functioning of the civic community. This holistic framework anticipated the intersectional analysis later scholars would develop, and it was grounded in the same theological conviction that had organized all of Barbour's work: the conviction about how the Kingdom of God was not built group by group but community by community, which genuine integration required building a harmonious whole from all the separate parts.

Two years before the Tucson study, Barbour had stated a truth at another Urban League function which the Tucson findings confirmed: 'The Negro does not think of temporary housing units as temporary. He knows very little housing is available to him and the reasons it will not be provided.' Andrea Juliette Lightbourne, in her 2004 dissertation on Tucson's segregated Dunbar School, provides the documentary confirmation: Tucson's historic A Mountain was a segregated African American residential area; Mexican Americans lived in segregated neighborhoods as well. The majority of African

Americans in Tucson were living in the oldest sections of the city under sub-standard conditions. Barbour's study was not discovering conditions hidden from view. He was documenting conditions already known, naming them in the language of scholarship and human rights, and creating the evidentiary record on which institutional action could be built.

The Tucson Urban League Service Council's president, Laura Owen, and her assistant used Barbour's study as the basis for a programmatic agenda: a job development program with emphasis on career guidance, an open occupancy housing program for under-represented groups, and the formation of an Urban League affiliate serving the multiethnic communities of the Tucson area. These recommendations translated Barbour's analytical framework into the institutional action the integrator's method required. Analysis without institutional follow-through was, in his understanding, incomplete; the integrator's task was to move from the documentation of conditions to the building of the institutional capacity for addressing them.

Tears On The Mojave

The Supreme Court handed down its unanimous decision in Brown v. Board of Education of Topeka on May 17, 1954, the decision the reader met on the first page of the Introduction: Barbour on the highway, the radio bulletin breaking through the desert static, the tears he did not try to contain. That opening scene established both the moment and the emotional register. What the narrative now requires is the analytical sequel. The emotion subsided. The desert continued. The analysis began.

The question was not whether the decision was right. He knew it was right. The question was what came after: how you moved from the legal demolition of separate but equal to the actual building of integrated communities. Barbour had been developing his answer to this question for twenty years, in the gang work of North Philadelphia, in the coalition campaigns of Denver, in the community studies of Richmond and Tucson. The Mojave Desert moment crystallized the answer into its clearest formulation: the integrator, the person who moved into the space between legal change and human transformation and built, by patient, costly, theologically grounded work, the conditions for genuine community.

His April 1957 article in *Adult Leadership* magazine, 'Where We Stand on Racial Desegregation,' was the fullest statement of this conceptual framework. It began with the desert scene, moved through the history of the distinction between desegregation and integration, traced the institutional roles of the NAACP and the National Urban League as the twin tracks of a two-phase process, and arrived at the challenge the Brown decision posed: not whether desegregation would proceed, for the court had settled this question, but whether the country had the institutional capacity and the civic will to pursue integration, to build the harmonious whole from the separate parts, to close the gap between democratic profession and democratic performance.

Barbour's diagnosis of the forces resisting integration was precise and unsparing. He identified the five negative attitudes in specific, recognizable terms: the apathy of people who acknowledged the problem but declined to act; the denial of people who claimed there was no problem; the red-baiting of people who associated civil rights advocacy with communist subversion; the gradualism of people who in principle accepted the need for change but in practice deferred it indefinitely; and the race-opathy of people whose attitudes on racial matters were, in his clinical judgment, psychopathological. These were not abstractions. They were the specific human attitudes he had encountered in every city where he had worked, in every legislative chamber where he had testified, in every civic forum where he had argued. Naming them precisely was itself an act of making Jesus King: insisting the emperor's nakedness be called by its name.

Hollywood and The Kingdom

Among the most distinctive features of Barbour's Los Angeles years was his systematic cultivation of the entertainment industry as a partner in the integration process. His recognition of mass media's role in shaping public attitudes toward racial equality was ahead of its time in its analytical precision and its institutional implications. He understood, with a clarity the civil rights movement's national leadership was only beginning to develop, about how the mass culture produced in Hollywood was reaching audiences no political organization or civic institution could match, and its portrayal of racial relationships had direct consequences for the public attitudes on which the integration process depended.

His 1957 *Adult Leadership* article identified 'the mass media, with particular emphasis on television, along with the field of sports and entertainment,' as among the positive forces 'helping shape the integration process.' The observation was grounded in direct experience: Barbour had spent five years in Los Angeles cultivating relationships with Hollywood figures who could use their fame and platforms to advance the cause of racial equality, presenting them with the National Urban League's American Teamwork Award as recognition and incentive, and building the personal connections through which the entertainment world and the civil rights world could become partners rather than merely observers of each other.

The Third Annual Winter League Ball at the Beverly Hilton on March 1, 1957, was the most visible expression of this strategy. Dorothy Dandridge, who had become the first Black woman to be nominated for the Academy Award for Best Actress for her performance in Carmen Jones in 1954, and Glenn Ford, one of Hollywood's major box office stars of the 1950s, received the American Teamwork Award before an audience assembled in the Grand Ballroom of one of Beverly Hills's most prestigious venues. The event brought together in one room the worlds of entertainment, business, and civil rights advocacy, and it did so on terms suggesting these worlds shared a common stake in the integration process Barbour was working to advance.

Emilie Raymond's *Stars for Freedom* documents how this cultivation of celebrity civil rights support became a significant force in the movement of the late 1950s and early 1960s. The celebrities who attended the Urban League's Beverly Hills events, who received and presented its awards, and who were introduced through Barbour's efforts to the civil rights organizations doing the integration work on the ground, became the celebrity contingent of the March on Washington for Jobs and Freedom in August 1963. Josephine Baker, Harry Belafonte, Sidney Poitier, Sammy Davis Jr., Lena Horne, Marlon Brando, and others who knew Barbour's work through their Beverly Hills connections joined the march A. Philip Randolph and Bayard Rustin organized around the same economic justice themes Barbour had been articulating since his Denver years.

"Make Jesus King," in the Beverly Hilton ballroom in 1957, looked like the specific, patient cultivation of the cultural infrastructure of integration: the building of relationships between the civil rights world and the entertainment world through which the mass culture's reach could be enlisted in the service of the Kingdom's values. It was an unlikely place for discipleship. It was precisely the right place for the integrator.

The Road and The Door

Barbour's 1954 article in *Frontier* magazine, 'Breaking the Barriers: Anti-Negro Prejudice Lessens in Western Hotels,' combined personal testimony, empirical observation, and measured analytical judgment in ways characteristic of his best writing. The article documented the improving yet still deeply imperfect conditions faced by Black travelers in the American West, a topic that connects the abstract principles of racial equality to the specific, concrete, daily experience of a person navigating a racially organized landscape.

The Klamath Falls incident deserves to be heard in Barbour's own words, because the precision of his telling is itself evidence of the discipline his human rights writing brought to personal testimony. He arrived in Klamath Falls at about ten in the evening, after driving nonstop from Los Angeles. He went directly to the Winnema Hotel. 'All full,' he was told. He asked the room clerk to telephone other hotels. All of them said they too were full. He went to the police department for help. The sergeant in charge began telephoning all the hotels and motels, and so did his relief. None would accept him. Since he had been driving all day and the road ahead was not easy for a tired driver, the police did not want him to continue to the next city. In the end, after several hours on the phone, they arranged a room at a definitely inferior hotel. 'The bitterness I felt toward Klamath Falls on that night,' he wrote, 'was alleviated only by the courtesy of the police who were incensed at the refusals. Incidentally, they did not know I was a representative of the Urban League. To them, it was enough that I was an American citizen.' A curious final detail: Klamath Falls was the hometown of State Senator Phillip S. Hitchcock, who had sponsored Oregon's recently enacted Public Accommodations Law, making it unlawful to discriminate on the basis of race, color, creed, or national origin. The law was on the books. The hotels were full.

He described the practical calculus of Black travel in the American West with a specificity born of long experience: 'The standard rule for a Negro traveling is he must make reservations in advance, even for those hotels which have no open restrictive policies...one can encounter individual room clerks or assistant managers who have been known to attempt to dissuade the inexperienced non-white traveler.' And he named, with characteristic precision, the form of confusion the pattern produced: 'A confusing aspect of travel for the non-white is the fact if he attempts to stay over in small towns, he can expect consistent refusal.' He understood what this experience cost, not only in inconvenience but in the specific psychological toll of navigating a landscape organized against your presence. 'It is difficult,' he wrote, 'for a white person to understand the trepidation and confusion that beset a Negro upon beginning a long trip.' He was not asking for sympathy. He was providing evidence.

The *Frontier* article gave San Francisco specific praise, Barbour's measured empiricism leading him to acknowledge genuine improvement where he found it. 'Such world-famous hotels as the Fairmount and Mark Hopkins have a traditional policy of non-discrimination befitting a sophisticated and cosmopolitan city,' he wrote, before immediately qualifying the point with characteristic honesty: 'Yet, to point up the fact about how discrimination is not dead even in the best areas, I was turned down flatly by a third-rate hotel on Sutter street.' The contrast, the Fairmount and the Mark Hopkins practicing non-discrimination while a third-rate Sutter Street hotel refused him, was not merely ironic. It was the pattern he was documenting throughout the article: the inconsistency of racial exclusion, its persistence in unexpected places, and the impossibility of navigating it without the knowledge of which establishments in which cities had which policies on which days.

The incident captured, in miniature, the central argument of Barbour's entire human rights career: the gap between democratic profession and democratic performance, the law and the reality, the statute and the daily experience of the person the statute was supposed to protect. Making Jesus king meant closing this gap, not merely establishing the legal principle but building the human reality the principle was supposed to produce. The hotels of the American West in 1954 were legally prohibited from discriminating. They were discriminating anyway. The integrator's work was still unfinished.

His assessment of the progress being made was measured and honest. 'In general, there is no question that the Negro traveling in the West is considerably better off than he was ten, or even five years ago,' he wrote, citing examples of genuine improvement in San Francisco and Fresno and elsewhere. 'The constant education in the press and on the air, the Supreme Court decisions, the Public Accommodation Laws, the strong position taken by such organizations as the National Association for the Advancement of Colored People and the

Urban League, have all begun to have their effect.' He acknowledged progress without overstating it, named the remaining discrimination without despairing of improvement, and maintained the analytical composure distinguishing his human rights writing from the advocacy documents of less careful writers. It was the composure of a person who had been trained at Elizabethtown College to think clearly and argue honestly, and who had spent twenty years in the work discovering what those virtues required.

The Montgomery Bus Boycott began in December 1955, eighteen months after Barbour crossed the Mojave Desert with tears in his eyes and a year and a half before his death. The boycott and the emergence of Martin Luther King Jr. as the movement's most visible national leader represented a new phase in the Long Civil Rights Movement, a phase whose character was shaped by the organizational and intellectual groundwork Barbour and his generation of civil rights workers had been laying for two decades. Understanding the relationship between Barbour's work and King's emergence requires understanding both what the Long Movement had built and what the mass movement added to it.

Taylor Branch's *Parting the Waters*, the first volume of his monumental history of America in the King years, traces the organizational and theological infrastructure underlying King's emergence with the same attention to detail and the same commitment to biographical specificity this biography has tried to bring to Barbour's story. Branch shows how the Montgomery Bus Boycott was possible only because the organizational infrastructure of the Black community in Montgomery, the churches, the Women's Political Council, the NAACP branch, and the network of civic organizations had been building the capacity for collective action for years before Rosa Parks sat down on December 1, 1955. The history of the Montgomery civil rights community in the years before the boycott mirrors the history of communities like Denver, where Barbour and his colleagues had been building exactly this kind of organizational capacity throughout the late 1940s and early 1950s.

King's theology of nonviolent resistance, developed at Boston University under the influence of Howard Thurman and Benjamin Mays and expressed in the specific idiom of the Black Baptist preaching tradition, drew on some of the same intellectual and theological sources as Barbour's formation without being identical to it. King's encounter with Gandhi through Howard Thurman's *Jesus and the Disinherited*, his engagement with the Social Gospel tradition through Walter Rauschenbusch, and his philosophical training in the personalist theology of Boston's school gave him a framework for nonviolent resistance resonating with the peace church tradition's commitment to nonresistance while drawing on the Black church's tradition of prophetic confrontation. The convergences between King's formation and Barbour's are not coincidental; they reflect the shared theological sources on which the civil rights movement's most theologically serious practitioners consistently drew.

The connection was not only theological but institutional and personal. Charles Coates Walker, a Quaker descended from the founders of Coatesville, Pennsylvania and born on the family farm near Gap, enrolled at Elizabethtown College with the Class of 1941, formed in the Historic Peace Church tradition that had shaped Barbour nine years earlier at the same institution. During World War II Walker was imprisoned as a conscientious objector, refusing cooperation with the military draft in the costly and public way the peace church tradition had always demanded of its members. In the 1940s he worked for the American Friends Service Committee traveling to college campuses promoting peace and racial justice. In the 1950s he served as Middle Atlantic Regional Secretary for the Fellowship of Reconciliation in Philadelphia, placing him at the organizational center of the movement through which Bayard Rustin and the founders of CORE were developing the nonviolent direct action methodology the mass movement would deploy. In 1949 he arranged for A.J. Muste, the internationally renowned minister and father of nonviolent social activism, to speak at Crozer Theological Seminary in Chester, Pennsylvania. The young Martin Luther King Jr., in his first year of study at Crozer, attended that lecture and later cited it as his first serious exposure to pacifist thought. Throughout the 1960s Walker trained activists preparing for Freedom Rides, the 1963 March on Washington for Jobs and Freedom, and the 1964 Mississippi Freedom Summer Project. The chain runs directly: Elizabethtown's peace church formation, through Walker, to Muste, to King, to Montgomery. The standard narratives of the civil rights movement have not named this chain. It is time they did.

Barbour did not live to see the full flowering of the movement King would lead. He died in March 1957, three months after the Montgomery Bus Boycott's successful conclusion, in the moment when the mass movement was just beginning to take the form which would produce the legislative victories of the following decade. He had spent his career building the foundations; King's generation would build the edifice. The relationship between the two phases of the movement was not one of succession, the first phase completing its work and handing off to the second, but of continuation: the organizational capacity, the theological framework, the coalition relationships, and the intellectual resources the Long Movement had built remained essential to the mass movement which came after it, and the mass movement's achievements rested on those foundations even when the movement's participants were unaware of the specific people who had built them.

The Last Campaign

The weeks before Barbour's death were full in the way his entire career had been full: the Beverly Hilton gala on March 1, the ongoing work in San Bernardino and throughout the western region, the planning for future campaigns, the cultivation of the relationships that the integration process required. The *California Eagle*'s report on the gala captured the energy of the final weeks: 'Miller Barbour must be VERY busy uncorking champagne for his office staff and all his assistants who helped make the Urban League Ball of 1957 the Most. Barbour is also active in urban redevelopment in San Bernardino and has been especially concerned with race relations throughout the West Coast, especially in those areas where no local Urban League exists.'

The description, casually affectionate and unconsciously precise, captured something essential about Barbour's human rights work: the combination of the celebratory and the serious, the festive and the urgent, the Beverly Hilton gala and the urban redevelopment work in San Bernardino. Making Jesus king had never, for him, been a grim or joyless business. The warmth and the affableness his college classmates had recognized in him in 1932 were still present and still essential to the work in 1957: human rights advocacy depended on the capacity to be in a room with people of very different perspectives and interests and to find, through the warmth of genuine personal engagement, the common ground on which a coalition could be built.

On March 20, 1957, nineteen days after the Beverly Hilton gala, William Wilbur Miller Barbour died of a myocardial infarction at Good Samaritan Hospital in Los Angeles. He was forty-nine years old. The heart which had sustained twenty-five years of the integrator's work had given out. He had, by every measure available, earned the rest. The work had not.

His widow Ruth, who had lost her ability to speak following her stroke several years earlier, arranged for his body to be returned to Philadelphia. Funeral services were held on March 19, conducted by the Reverend Charles Beckett of Washington, D.C., an AME minister connecting Barbour in death to the theological tradition that had formed him from childhood at Ebenezer AME in Middletown. His father-in-law, the Reverend Dr. W. L. Johnson of Philadelphia, also an AME clergyman, was part of the community of faith from which Barbour had come and to which, in death, he was returned. Interment took place at Mount Lawn Cemetery, Lincoln Memorial Park in Delaware County, Pennsylvania, established in 1925 during an era of legally enforced segregation to provide burial space for African

Americans excluded from many white-owned cemeteries. The choice of Mount Lawn was not only civic but also family.

O'Dessa J. Shipley, Ruth's sister, who had built her own career as a pioneering African American civic activist in Philadelphia, would herself be interred at Mount Lawn when she died in May 1994 at the age of seventy-seven. The cemetery in Sharon Hill, Delaware County, held the Johnson family as it held the man Ruth had married: the Arkansas migrants who had come north in the Great Migration, had built their lives in Philadelphia's civic institutions, and were buried in the segregated ground the city's racial geography had made available to them.

Even in death, the racial geography of mid-century America asserted its claims. The cemetery at Sharon Hill and the cemetery on Iron Mine Road in Middletown are separated by sixty miles and generations of American history. They are connected by the same logic. The East Middletown Cemetery, long established as the Old Negro Burying Ground, is where the community that formed Barbour buried its dead, including his mother, Minnie, and his stepfather, Charles Henry Archer. Mount Lawn, established in 1925, is where that same racial geography, adapted to a new century and a new county, received him. He was born into a world consigning its Black dead to separate ground. He was buried in a world which still did. The racial order he had spent twenty-five years documenting and opposing in the employment offices and housing markets and legislative chambers of Philadelphia and Denver and Los Angeles outlasted him in the most literal sense available to it: it organized the ground in which he lay.

The New Pittsburgh Courier ran a brief obituary under the headline "UL Official Dies in LA." The *Baltimore Afro-American* reported on the funeral services. The civil rights community which had known his work noted his passing and moved on, because the movement which had been his life's work did not stop when one of its builders stopped. Six months after his death, Congress passed the Civil Rights Act of 1957. In 1963, the March on Washington for Jobs and Freedom drew together the celebrity world he had cultivated and the human rights world he had served. In 1964 and 1965, the Civil Rights Act and the Voting Rights Act accomplished the desegregation he had spent his career pressing for. The integrator's work, he had always understood, outlasted any individual integrator. He had planted seeds in ground he would not live to harvest. The harvest came.

The relationship between William Wilbur Miller Barbour and Elizabethtown College did not end at his graduation in June 1932. The College tracked his career through its alumni communications and student newspaper, and his connection to the institution he had attended remained a source of both pride and responsibility for both parties. *The Etownian*'s 1948 report on his Denver Urban League work, based on a letter he wrote for the student paper, documented the alumni community's awareness of what one of its members was doing in the world. The College had formed him; he was demonstrating what the formation produced.

Steven M. Nolt's institutional history of Elizabethtown College notes the College's pride in its African American graduates during the interwar years and the ways in which their subsequent careers embodied the institutional mission the College articulated through its motto. Barbour's career was the most prominent and most consequential of these careers, and its recovery through this biography represents, among other things, an opportunity for the College community to understand more fully what its formation, its motto, and its commitment to *radical inclusion* produced in the specific life of one of its graduates.

The College's motto, "Make Jesus King," was not Barbour's alone. It was the motto of an institution that, in its best moments, took it seriously as a mandate for the communities it served and the graduates it sent into the world. Barbour's life is evidence of what the motto, taken seriously, could produce: a human rights leader of unusual theological depth and unusual practical range, sustained across twenty-five years of hard, unglamorous, often frustrating work by the conviction that making Jesus King was not a metaphor but a mandate. The College which gave him this conviction gave him, in the fullest sense of the phrase, the most important thing it had to give.

The recovery of Barbour's story is, in part, a gift the present offers to the institution that formed him: the knowledge that the motto worked, which the formation it described produced, in at least one graduate, exactly the kind of life it was designed to produce. "Make Jesus King." He did. It cost him everything. It was worth every cost.

| 8 |

The Unfinished Kingdom

Six months later, Congress passed the Civil Rights Act of 1957. The legislation was limited in scope, focused primarily on voting rights and establishing a civil rights division within the Justice Department, and it was weaker than what the civil rights community had sought. But it was the first significant federal civil rights legislation since Reconstruction, and its passage came in the year of Barbour's death, at the end of a decade during which the Long Civil Rights Movement's patient organizational and legal work had created the political conditions for exactly this kind of federal action. Barbour had spent his career building those conditions. He did not live to see the legislation signed.

This is the specific poignancy of the Long Movement's builders: they built the foundations on which others erected the visible structure, and they often did not live to see the structure rise. Barbour was not alone in this. The NAACP Legal Defense Fund's lawyers who spent the 1930s developing the legal strategy for what became Brown v. Board of Education of Topeka did not all live to see the 1954 decision. The labor organizers who spent the 1930s building the CIO's industrial unions did not all live to see the Wagner Act enforced with the vigor their organizing had made possible. The peace church activists who spent the 1940s developing the methods of nonviolent direct action did not all live to see those methods deployed on a national stage in the sit-ins and the Freedom Rides of the early 1960s.

This is what it means to be a builder of foundations: the foundation outlasts the builder, and the structure rises on the builder's work without always acknowledging the work on which it stands.

The Planter

The task of assessing William Wilbur Miller Barbour's historical significance with the precision his life deserves requires resisting two temptations: the temptation to overstate, to claim for him more than the evidence supports; and the temptation to understate, to allow the obscurity the historical record has imposed on him to set the terms of the assessment. Both temptations are present in biographical writing, and both distort the historical record rather than clarifying it. The assessment offered here attempts to be precise about what Barbour actually achieved, what he contributed to the movement he served, and what he left behind.

His most concrete and most documentable achievement was the development, through fifteen years of direct practice and institutional leadership of the integrator's method: an approach to human rights work combining empirical research, coalition-building, legislative advocacy, institutional negotiation, and direct-action witness in a sequence calibrated to the specific circumstances of the city and the institutional context being addressed. This method was not his invention alone; it drew on the traditions of the Urban League, the settlement house movement, the peace church networks, the AME Church's tradition of institutional leadership, and the social work profession's developing community organization theory. But his application of these traditions to the challenges of mid-century western civil rights advocacy produced a model which the National Urban League recognized as nationally significant when it created the Western Field Office and appointed him to lead it.

His conceptual contribution, the distinction between desegregation and integration, was his most important intellectual legacy to the movement. The clarity with which he articulated this distinction in the months before his death, in his final *Adult Leadership* article, established a framework that remained analytically useful well beyond his moment. The distinction named a problem the Brown decision had made newly urgent: the problem of what came after the legal victory, of who would do the work the law could not do, and what this work required of those who did it. Every subsequent generation of civil rights workers has had to confront the same problem, and Barbour's articulation of the integrator's role as the answer provides one of the most precise and most practically useful frameworks for understanding what the work requires.

His coalition-building achievements in Denver, while less visibly dramatic than the legislative victories they helped secure, were organizational accomplishments of genuine significance. The Denver Urban League under his leadership became a nationally recognized model of municipal civil rights work, demonstrating how the combination of institutional advocacy, community organizing, direct action, and empirical research could produce measurable progress on racial equality in a city with the specific racial history and political culture of Denver. The National Urban League's selection of Denver for its 1949 national convention was recognition about how the Denver model was worth showcasing, and the appointment to the Western Field Office directorship was recognition about how the model's architect was capable of applying it at a larger scale.

His cultivation of the entertainment industry as a human rights partner in Los Angeles was a tactical innovation with consequences reaching well beyond his own career. The celebrities whose civil rights commitments he helped to activate through the Urban League's Hollywood events became significant forces in the mass movement of the late 1950s and early 1960s. When Harry Belafonte organized the celebrity contingent for the March on Washington for Jobs and Freedom in August 1963, he was drawing on relationships with civil rights organizations which had been built, in part, through the Beverly Hilton galas Barbour had chaired and the Urban League events at which Barbour had been the institutional host. The seeds he planted produced a harvest he did not live to see, in the tradition of the Long Movement's builders.

The Harvest

The legislative achievements transforming Barbour's programmatic goals into federal law deserve to be named and celebrated with the specificity they have earned. Between 1964 and 1968, Lyndon Baines Johnson signed into law the most consequential domestic legislative program in American history since the New Deal: the Civil Rights Act of 1964, which prohibited racial discrimination in employment and public accommodations; the Voting Rights Act of 1965, which enforced the Fifteenth Amendment's guarantee of the right to vote; the Fair Housing Act of 1968, which prohibited racial discrimination in the sale and rental of housing; and Executive Order 11246, which mandated affirmative action in federal contracting. Together these statutes accomplished, in the space of four years, the legislative objectives Barbour had spent twenty-five years working to build the political and institutional conditions for achieving. The Great Society was, in significant measure, the legislative harvest of the Long Civil Rights Movement's patient foundational work, and Barbour was among the most important of the Long Movement's architects.

The historiography of Johnson's Great Society has undergone significant rehabilitation in the decades since his presidency. The Vietnam War shadowed his domestic legacy for a generation, making it difficult for even admiring scholars to assess his civil rights achievements without qualification. The rehabilitation began with the work of scholars who insisted on separating the domestic record from the foreign policy catastrophe, and it has produced a body of scholarship which now gives Johnson his due as the most consequential civil rights president in American history. Robert Dallek's two-volume biography, Lone Star Rising and Flawed Giant, situates Johnson's civil rights commitment within his Texas political formation, demonstrating how his ambition and his genuine conviction about racial justice converged in the Great Society legislation. Randall Woods, in *LBJ: Architect of American Ambition*, argues Johnson's commitment to civil rights was not merely tactical but deeply personal, shaped by his experience teaching impoverished Mexican American children in Cotulla. Texas, in 1928, the same year Barbour was playing football for the Brutal Thirteen, running track, and competing on the basketball team at Elizabethtown College. Nick Kotz, in Judgment Days: Lyndon Baines Johnson, Martin Luther King Jr., and the Laws That Changed America, reconstructs the specific legislative battles through which the Civil Rights Act and the Voting Rights Act became law, documenting the combination of presidential will, congressional skill, and movement pressure producing the decisive victories.

The scholarly consensus emerging from this rehabilitation: Johnson's legislative achievement was both necessary and insufficient, necessary because the foundational work of the Long Civil Rights Movement required federal legislative action to become law, and insufficient because the legislation addressed desegregation as a matter of policy while the integration process Barbour had spent his career defining remained, as he had always insisted it would, a matter of ongoing work. Joseph Califano, Johnson's chief domestic policy advisor, wrote in The Triumph and Tragedy of Lyndon Johnson: the President told his staff repeatedly: "We shall overcome, and we will." The commitment was genuine, the achievement was historic, and the incompleteness was exactly what Barbour had predicted. Hugh Davis Graham, in The Civil Rights Era: Origins and Development of National Policy, 1960–1972, provides the most comprehensive scholarly account of how the Johnson administration translated civil rights advocacy into specific statutory language, documenting the dense policy history through which Barbour's conceptual framework, the distinction between desegregation as policy and integration as process, informed the choices the administration made about what the legislation would and would not do.

Barbour, writing in April 1957, seven years before the Civil Rights Act and four months before his death, had identified with clinical precision exactly what the legislation would achieve and what it would leave undone. Desegregation was a matter of policy: the tearing down of the legalized institutional structure of racial exclusion. Integration was a matter of process: the ongoing, costly, human work of creating the harmonious whole from the separate parts. Johnson's Great Society accomplished the first. The second remains, as Barbour always said it would, the work of the generations following. The Civil Rights Act bears Johnson's signature. The integration process bears Barbour's intellectual framework, and the framework is still needed. What Lyndon Johnson built in 1964, 1965, and 1968 rested on the foundations William Wilbur Miller Barbour spent twenty-five years building in Philadelphia, Denver, Tucson, and Los Angeles. Neither man could have achieved what he achieved without the other's contribution, separated though they were by the accident of mortality. Johnson signed the legislation. Barbour built the ground on which it could stand.

This biography's central interpretive argument, the claim that the convergence of Anabaptist-Pietist and AME theology in Barbour's formation was a distinctive and historically significant strand of human rights thought. The two theological traditions which formed Barbour were not, in the standard histories, in dialogue with each other. The Anabaptist-Pietist tradition had developed in the context of white European Christianity and was, in the early twentieth century, primarily the tradition of white rural and small-town communities whose engagement with the racial questions of their time was limited. The AME tradition had developed in the context of African American institutional life, as the organizational expression of a community's determination to build the institutions of civic and spiritual life which the surrounding white society was unwilling to provide on equitable terms. These were, in the most literal sense, worlds apart.

The convergence Elizabethtown College made possible was not the merger of these two worlds but the encounter of their theological core convictions in a single person of exceptional gifts who had been formed by both. The core conviction they shared, the insistence about how authentic Christian faith is incompatible with structures of domination, was the theological foundation of Barbour's human rights work, and the specific form it took in his career reflected the complementary emphases of the two traditions: the Brethren tradition's emphasis on patient institution-building and the AME tradition's emphasis on prophetic confrontation, synthesized by a person who understood the full range of the movement's demands required both.

The scholarly significance of this convergence extends beyond Barbour's individual biography. The history of Anabaptist engagement with racial justice has been underexamined in the scholarship of civil rights history, and the history of AME civil rights leadership has been underexamined in the scholarship of Anabaptist theology. Barbour's life sits at the intersection of these two underexamined histories and provides a specific, documentable case study in how they could and did converge in ways producing a human rights practitioner of unusual effectiveness. The recovery of his story is, among other things, an invitation to scholars in both fields to examine the convergences between them more carefully and to consider what further recoveries the examination might produce.

Mennonites Albert N. Keim and Grant M. Stoltzfus's Politics of Conscience documents the historic peace churches' engagement with the racial questions of the twentieth century, but the contributions of Anabaptist-formed individuals to human rights leadership remain largely unexamined in the scholarship. Harold S. Bender's Anabaptist Vision, articulated the tradition's core commitments in terms directly applicable to the civil rights struggle, was published in 1944, in the middle of Barbour's most intensive human rights formation.

The connection between Bender's Anabaptist Vision programmatic theology and the civil rights movement's organizational methods has not been adequately explored, and Barbour's life suggests it would reward exploration.

The argument for Barbour's inclusion in the canon of civil rights history requires precision about what the canon is and what it should be. The canonical narrative of the civil rights movement, the story centered on a decade of mass action between 1955 and 1965 and organized around the leadership of Martin Luther King Jr., Ralph Abernathy, Bayard Rustin, A. Philip Randolph, Fannie Lou Hammer, has the virtues of clarity and inspirational power. It identifies the movement's most dramatic moments, honors its most visible leaders, and provides a narrative arc which civic education can transmit and popular memory can sustain. These are real virtues, and this biography does not contest them.

What the canonical narrative has not adequately captured is the Long Movement's organizational infrastructure: the decades of patient work by people like Barbour who built the coalitions, developed the methods, conducted the research, and cultivated the institutional relationships on which the mass movement depended. Taylor Branch's Parting the Waters, the first volume of his America in the King Years trilogy, is the most accomplished biographical account of the mass movement period, and even Branch's richly detailed narrative of the Montgomery Bus Boycott makes clear how much institutional groundwork had been laid before December 1955. The Montgomery Improvement Association did not spring into existence on the night Rosa Parks was arrested; it was the activation of organizational capacity built over years of prior work.

Charles Payne's organizing tradition is the concept best capturing what Barbour contributed to the movement. Payne distinguishes the organizing tradition, the tradition of sustained, relationship-based, community capacity-building that builds the movement from the ground up, from the mobilizing tradition, the tradition of mass action and public confrontation that produces the dramatic moments the standard narratives document. Both traditions were essential to the movement; neither could sustain the other's work. The organizers built the community capacity, which the mobilizers deployed; the mobilizers created the public pressure, which opened the political space in which the organizers could continue building. Barbour was an organizer in Payne's precise sense, and his place in the movement's canon is the organizer's place: essential but largely invisible, the foundation beneath the structure.

Barbara Ransby's biography of Ella Baker provides the most illuminating comparison. Baker, like Barbour, was a builder of the movement's organizational infrastructure, a person who devoted her career to creating the conditions for other people's leadership rather than positioning herself at the center of the stage. Baker's concept of "group-centered leadership," her insistence the movement's strength lay in the organizing capacity of communities rather than the charisma of individual leaders, resonates with Barbour's institutional emphasis. Both were invisible in the way foundations are invisible: essential to the structure, hidden beneath it, present in everything the structure could support. Ransby's recovery of Baker's significance is the scholarly precedent for this biography's recovery of Barbour's, and the parallel demonstrates the Long Movement had more builders of this kind than the standard narratives have yet recovered.

Manning Marable's analysis of the relationship between the Long Movement's earlier workers and the mass movement of the 1950s and 1960s places this recovery in its broadest historiographical context. Marable argues, in *Race, Reform, and Rebellion*, that understanding the mass movement requires understanding the organizational and intellectual infrastructure built by the previous generation, and that the dramatic moments of 1955 to 1965 were not spontaneous eruptions of popular will but the political expression of decades of organizational preparation. Barbour was part of which preparation, doing his specific portion in Philadelphia, Denver, Los Angeles, and Tucson, with limited resources and no national recognition, but with the consistency and commitment the work required. His place in the movement's canon is the place of every person who built its foundations.

The Motto's Final Meaning

There is a moment, if you follow Barbour's story all the way through to its end, when three phrases converge into a single light, and you see what this life was and what it cost and what it gave. The first phrase is the one Elizabethtown College pressed into him across four years of intellectual and spiritual formation beginning in September 1928: "Make Jesus King." Not as a slogan, not as a chapel sentiment, but as an institutional mandate, the three-word answer a Church of the Brethren college gave to the question every generation of its students had to answer for themselves: what does the Kingdom of God require of you, specifically, in the conditions of the world you are entering? The second phrase reaches back behind this mandate to the Anabaptist tradition from which it came, back through the Ephrata Cloister and the printing press of 1749 and the 1,512 pages of the *Martyrs Mirror*, back to the two words the translators rendered from the Latin of the title page: "Arbeite und Hoffe," "Work and Hope." Not work and be rewarded. Not work and be recognized. Work and hope, the combination of active labor and deferred vindication which the martyrs had embodied and the tradition had crystallized, which the Amish had preserved in song and the Brethren had carried into every institution they built, including the small college in south-central Pennsylvania where Barbour arrived in the fall of 1928. The third phrase is this biography's own title, and it is the biographical name for what those two phrases together produced in a human life: A Faith Full Witness. A person who worked faithfully because the faith demanded work. Who hoped persistently because the faith sustained hope when the work produced no visible harvest. And who bore witness publicly, at the swimming pool gate, in the legislative hearing room, on the road across the Mojave, to the human dignity the Kingdom of God demands, at whatever personal cost the witness required.

These are not three different things. "Make Jesus King" and "Work and Hope" and "A Faith Full Witness" are three names for the same conviction, spoken in three theological vocabularies, across three centuries of Anabaptist-rooted Christian discipleship, arriving finally in the life of one African American man from a sundown town in south central Pennsylvania who had been formed, simultaneously, in two traditions whose deepest convictions turned out to be the same conviction. The Brethren had crossed an ocean to escape the state's power over the community of faith. The AME had walked out of St. George's to escape the racial order's power over the same. Both had arrived, by routes so different as to seem unrelated, at an identical theological bedrock: authentic Christian faith is incompatible with structures of domination, and those who claim the faith are called, not invited, not encouraged, but called, to build in the world the conditions the Kingdom of God requires. Barbour heard this from both traditions simultaneously. He spent twenty-five years doing what it asked of him. This is what a faith full witness looks like in a life.

The college motto which organized this biography's argument, the three-word imperative pressed into Barbour during his four years at Elizabethtown College and carried by him through twenty-five years of human rights work, arrives at the biography's conclusion with a meaning both consistent with its beginning and deepened by everything the narrative has placed between them. "Make Jesus King." Not as a slogan or a sentiment. As a mandate, a program, a daily obligation, a description of what the Kingdom of God requires of those who claim to follow Jesus in the conditions of a historical moment.

For Barbour, the motto's meaning was shaped by the two theological traditions in which it had been formed. In the Brethren register, it meant building institutions, communities, and coalitions organized around the values of the Kingdom rather than the imperatives of the world: institutions of *radical inclusion*, communities of voluntary commitment to mutual accountability, coalitions capable of sustaining the long work of social transformation without the dramatic victories sustaining popular attention. In the AME register, it meant confronting the forms racial hierarchy took in the specific communities where he lived and worked: naming racial discrimination as a theological error as well as a civic failure, insisting on the full humanity of every person the racial order sought to diminish, and refusing the terms of a social order organized around racial subordination as incompatible with the Kingdom of God whose kingship the motto proclaimed.

Barbour showed up for twenty-five years. He showed up in North Philadelphia's gang-contested streets and in Colorado's legislative chambers and in Denver's swimming pools and in Tucson's multiethnic community meetings and in Los Angeles's civic forums and in the Beverly Hilton's Grand Ballroom. He showed up carrying the same conviction in every institutional context, adapting its expression to the demands of the setting without ever losing its theological core. And when his heart finally gave out on March 20, 1957, he had shown up in enough places and built enough institutions and cultivated enough relationships and developed enough methods which the work he had been doing would continue after him, in the hands of other people he had helped to form and in the institutions he had helped to build.

Barbour himself had named the incompleteness in words which this biography's own argument has tried to honor. In the conclusion of his 1951 World Affairs Institute paper, written six years before his death, at the midpoint of his human rights career, he wrote: "Progress has been made in direct relation to the efforts in its behalf. If it is to be a living, continuing factor, we must strive all the more intently, from a moral basis as all-inclusive as is our physical community. For if progress is to lead to true democracy, then the road will be interminable so long as democracy remains a fraction, present for so many persons of such and such races, creeds and religions, and non-existent for such and such races, creeds and religions. In short, democracy confined is simply not democracy, but rather fragments of the Great Dream, waiting to be pieced together, waiting to be augmented by more and more fragments." The phrase arrives with the force of a life's work compressed into a sentence. Fragments of the Great Dream, waiting to be pieced together. He spent twenty-five years adding fragments. The dream is still waiting for more.

The Anabaptist tradition of discipleship informing Elizabethtown College's motto, which organized Barbour's formation had a precise word for what he was doing, a word the tradition distinguished carefully from mere occupation. Keith Graber Miller, Mennonite scholar of religion and vocation, preserves the story of a sixteenth-century Anabaptist who drew the distinction with the clarity the tradition always brought to theological precision: "I am a follower of Jesus Christ. That is my vocation. I make my living as a cobbler." The cobbler knew what he was. His occupation was the means by which he supported his life; his vocation was the call organizing the meaning of his life. Barbour's occupation, in the institutional language of successive employer descriptions, was social worker, sociologist, Urban League executive, Western Field Director. His vocation was the twenty-five-year project of closing the gap between the America the Declaration of Independence had promised and the America its institutions had built. He worked at his vocation with the combination of active labor and deferred vindication the *Martyrs Mirror* had named two centuries before his birth: "Work and Hope."

The environmental thinker, farmer, essayist, and poet Wendell Berry defines the concept in terms any Anabaptist community would have recognized immediately: "The old and honorable idea of vocation is simply this: we each are called, by God, or by our gifts, or by our preference, to a kind of good work for which we are particularly fitted." Barbour was particularly fitted for the work he did: the combination of theological conviction, intellectual formation, rhetorical skill, and institutional patience required to move between the antagonistic communities the integration process required to be bridged. The formation fitting him was dual and specific: the AME Church's prophetic insistence on racial dignity and the Brethren institution's patient organizational commitment to building the Kingdom in the specific arrangements of community life. Dietrich Bonhoeffer, the German theologian whose Cost of Discipleship had argued: authentic Christian faith demanded engagement with the world rather than retreat from it, wrote "through the incarnation of Jesus, the whole human race recovers the dignity of the image of God." This was exactly the theological claim Barbour's human rights career embodied: the insistence, against every institutional arrangement organized to deny it, the dignity of the image of God was the birthright of every person the racial order sought to diminish.

In the words of Pericles: "What you leave behind is not what is engraved in stone monuments, but what is woven into the lives of others." Barbour left nothing engraved in stone. He left the framework distinguishing desegregation from integration, the institutional relationships making the Urban League's western expansion possible, the coalitions making Denver's civil rights campaigns of the late 1940s a model for other western cities, and the understanding of what the integrator's role required informing the civil rights movement's next generation. He left his work woven into the lives of others. The lasting impact of the work is far more important than the person who did the work. "Work and Hope."

The editors of the 1949 yearbook remembered three sentences above all others from Schlosser's teaching as the essential distillation of what he had spent a career trying to press into his students: "Put your life on the side of those striving to consummate a constructive program for humanity. Dare to do right at any cost. Never flinch when duty calls." Barbour had absorbed those sentences. He had put his life, literally, on the side of those striving to consummate a constructive program for humanity, across twenty-five years in Philadelphia and Denver and Los Angeles and Tucson. He had dared to do right at any cost and refused to flinch when duty called, from the Philadelphia police station in October 1945 to the Mojave Desert road in May 1954. And Schlosser had also found the deepest satisfactions of his teaching career in the philosophy voiced by Robert Browning: "a man's reach should exceed his grasp, and what he aspired to be and was not comforts him." Barbour had absorbed this philosophy too. He had spent twenty-five years reaching. He had fallen short of the Kingdom he was reaching for, as every person who genuinely reaches for a kingdom must fall short in a single lifetime. But Schlosser's lines apply to him with a precision the mentor could not have anticipated: what Barbour aspired to be and was not, the integrator of a fully equal American democracy, comforts us, because the aspiration was genuine, the effort was total, and the fragments he pieced together are real.

What The Kingdom Still Requires

The Kingdom of God, in the theological traditions which shaped Barbour's understanding of his human rights work, is not a static destination but a dynamic process: the ongoing transformation of human social arrangements in the direction of the values Jesus proclaimed in the Sermon on the Mount, the ongoing creation of communities in which the dignity and brotherhood of every human person is not merely affirmed but enacted in the specific, concrete, measurable conditions of everyday life. The Kingdom is never finished, in the eschatological sense Christians have always understood: its completion awaits the full consummation which lies beyond human history. But it is also never merely deferred: its demands are immediate, its claims are present, and its requirements of those who claim to follow Jesus are non-negotiable.

Barbour understood this with the precision of a person formed in two theological traditions which had each, in different ways, insisted on the immediate and the costly character of genuine discipleship. The Kingdom was not something to be waited for; it was something to be built, one institution at a time, one coalition at a time, one legislative campaign at a time, one Direct Action test at a time, one community survey at a time. The building was the discipleship, the specific form making Jesus King took in the historical moment of mid-century America.

In 2026, as the United States marks its 250th anniversary, the building continues. The legal structures of explicit racial discrimination Barbour spent his career fighting have largely been dismantled. The formal equality of citizenship which the Fifteenth Amendment had promised in 1870 and the civil rights legislation of the 1960s had finally enforced is now the law of the land. The integration process Barbour distinguished from desegregation, the building of the harmonious whole from the separate parts, remains unfinished. The racial wealth gap, the residential racial segregation, the racial disparities in education and health and criminal justice: these persist in the second decade of the twenty-first century as they persisted in the fifth decade of the twentieth, and they persist for reasons directly traceable to the structural mechanisms Barbour spent his career documenting and working to dismantle.

The integrator's work, in other words, is still needed. The practitioner who can move between antagonistic groups and institutions, who can frame human rights demands in terms accessible to the full range of audiences whose cooperation the integration process requires, who can combine the prophetic confrontation of the AME tradition with the patient institution-building of the Brethren tradition, who can sustain twenty-five years of hard, unglamorous, often frustrating work in the conviction about how the work is demanded by the God whose Kingdom requires it: this practitioner is still needed, and the supply of such practitioners has never been adequate to the demand.

There is one further evidence of Barbour's significance which this biography is honored to record. The "Educate for Service: Service to Humanity Award" from Elizabethtown College, described in the Sources section of Chapter One, was presented posthumously to his grandchildren and great-grandchildren at Return to the Nest, the college's annual celebration for alumni of fifty or more years, in 2026, nearly seventy years after his death. The event takes its name from the Blue Jay, Elizabethtown's mascot, whose name was given by Ira Herr, the coach who had walked the college's sidelines during Barbour's own years there. The author served as keynote speaker, delivering remarks on Barbour's legacy and the mentorship of Ralph W. Schlosser that had shaped the man the award was honoring.

Barbour's significance was recognized not only by his own alma mater. Whittier College, in Whittier, California, established the W. Miller Barbour Award, granted to an undergraduate student who in the judgment of the Sociology faculty demonstrates the most excellence and promise in the fields of research and design, community organizations, and intergroup relations. The award carries his name into a continuing institutional future at a California Quaker, Historic Peace Churches, liberal arts college whose social justice commitments resonated with his own, a college whose most famous alumnus, Richard Nixon, himself a product of Whittier's Quaker tradition and its Historic Peace Church commitments, would later sign the Equal Employment Opportunity Act of 1972 fulfilling one of the central legislative goals Barbour had pursued in Denver and Los Angeles. The Whittier College award and the Elizabethtown College Educate for Service: Service to Humanity Award together constitute a posthumous institutional recognition spanning both coasts of the country he spent his life trying to bring closer to its founding ideals.

This biography is offered as a contribution to their formation: a specific, documented, historically situated account of what the integrator's work required of one person in one historical moment, recovered from the obscurity which the historical record had imposed on it and offered as evidence of what was possible and what it cost.

There is one image this biography returns to, as it must return, at the end: the photograph on the wall of the Jay's Nest. The Brutal Thirteen, posed in the informal arrangement of young men who know they are doing something their institution has not officially sanctioned and who are proud of it anyway. The autumn light of Lancaster County, 1928. And among them, squinting into the light, a single African American student. Peter DePuydt passed the photograph every day for years without knowing his name. Now we know it. William Wilbur Miller Barbour, Class of 1932, twenty years old, son of Great Migration parents, raised in Ebenezer AME and in the sundown town of Middletown, Pennsylvania, about to spend four years at a Brethren college which would press into him the discipleship mandate he would spend the rest of his life fulfilling. He is squinting into the light. He does not yet know what the light will ask of him: the police stations and the legislative chambers, the swimming pools and the hotel lobbies, the Mojave Desert road in May 1954 when he pulled to the shoulder and wept, the Beverly Hilton ballroom in March 1957, nineteen days before his death. He does not yet know any of it. He is just a young man squinting into the autumn light of a Lancaster County afternoon in a county whose racial geography has not arranged a place for him on this field or anywhere near it.

He is there anyway. He was always there anyway. He will keep being there, in the spaces where his presence is not arranged for and not expected, for the next twenty-five years, until his heart gives out. This is what "Work and Hope" looks like before the working begins: a young man squinting into the light, not yet knowing what it will cost, already having decided to show up. This is what it means to "Make Jesus King."

SOURCES AND METHOD

The Scholarly Formation

The scholarly framework through which these sources were assembled and interpreted was shaped by teachers whose influence pervades every chapter. To understand Barbour's world within the National Urban League and the urban human rights tradition, I drew on the scholarship of Kenneth L. Kusmer, one of the foremost historians of African American urban life in the United States, who was my professor and advisor at Temple University. Few scholars have mapped the rise of the Black urban experience with greater precision or deeper humanity, and his influence shaped my understanding at every turn, in the seminar room, across the desk, and on the written page.

This biography is accompanied by a documentary film which emerged from the same sustained research. 'The Prospect for Freedom: W. Miller Barbour's Human Rights Journey,' released in 2025, I produced, directed, wrote, edited, and designed. The film traces Barbour's life from his childhood in Middletown, Pennsylvania, through his graduation as Elizabethtown College's second African American student and the first African American student athlete to play college football in Lancaster County, as well as a member of the track and basketball teams, to his work as an Urban League leader in Denver and Los Angeles. It documents his foundational role in defining the two central goals of the civil rights movement, ending racial discrimination in employment and housing, and his place in the longer arc of human rights advocacy preceding the mass movement of 1954 to 1968. Since its release the film has received multiple public screenings throughout 2025 and 2026, sponsored and hosted by institutions whose commitment to civil rights history gave the screenings their civic weight: the Governor's Advisory Commission on African American Affairs in the Office of Governor Josh Shapiro, the Greater Harrisburg Area NAACP, the Popel Shaw Center for Race and Ethnicity at Dickinson College, and the Pennsylvania Chautauqua. The documentary has been named an official selection at the Hollywood International Indie Film Festival, scheduled for December 2026. Readers wishing to engage Barbour's story in both scholarly and visual form are encouraged to seek out the documentary alongside this volume.

The article I authored for the Journal of the Lancaster County Historical Society, forthcoming in December 2026, 'Addressing Dignity Deferred: Post Desegregation and the Process of Integration: The Life and Legacy of Race Relations Leader W. Miller Barbour (1908–1957), Elizabethtown College Class of 1932,' served as the primary biographical source for this biography. The article synthesized all of the primary sources described above into a chronological account of Barbour's life and career, and the biography builds on which foundation, expanding and deepening the scholarly engagement with the historiographical literature, reconstructing in greater narrative detail the specific scenes and episodes which the article's scholarly format could only summarize, and developing the theological argument connecting Barbour's Elizabethtown formation and his AME formation into the interpretive framework organizing this biography's central claims.

The Institutional Partners

A biography of this kind depends on the cooperation and the generosity of institutions and individuals whose assistance no amount of scholarly diligence alone could have supplied. The Elizabethtown College community provided the institutional support and the scholarly environment without which this project could not have been completed. The acknowledgments page of this volume names the individuals whose contributions were most significant, but the collective intellectual community of Elizabethtown College deserves recognition as the institutional context within which this scholarship was possible.

The Elizabethtown College Honors Program, sponsored by the Hershey Company, provided the student research partnerships through which portions of the primary source research were conducted. The Honors students named in the acknowledgments brought to the project the combination of energy, intelligence, and commitment to historical accuracy which characterizes the best undergraduate research collaboration. Their contributions, shaped and directed by my scholarly leadership, were genuine contributions to the project rather than merely useful assistance to a scholar who would have accomplished the same work without them.

On Method

The biographical method employed in this volume reflects several decades of development in scholarly biography as a genre, and the choices I have made about how to handle the gaps in the evidence, the uncertainty about episodes and inner experiences, and the relationship between the individual life and the historical context in which it was lived deserve explicit statement. Biography is not a genre whose methodological conventions are self-evident; they require as much explicit articulation as the conventions of any other scholarly genre, and the readers who will use this biography most effectively are those who understand the choices I have made and the reasons those choices were made.

The most fundamental methodological choice in this biography is my decision to treat William Wilbur Miller Barbour as a significant historical figure whose life and work deserve the same quality of scholarly attention which the standard civil rights biographies have given to figures like Ella Baker, A. Philip Randolph, Thurgood Marshall, and Martin Luther King Jr. This choice is itself an argument:

the argument that the criteria by which the historical record decides who deserves sustained biographical attention have systematically excluded people like Barbour, and which the exclusion has produced a historical record which misrepresents the character, the scope, and the institutional depth of the civil rights movement it claims to document.

The secondary methodological choice, one with implications for nearly every chapter, is my decision to employ what I call the 'surround strategy' when the direct documentary record is thin: the reconstruction, in granular detail, of the world Barbour moved through, the events he witnessed, the texts he would have read, and the people he knew, in order to create for the reader the texture of a life lived in a historical moment even in the gaps where direct documentation fails. This strategy has precedents in the best biographical writing, and I employ it in this biography in ways always signaled explicitly rather than presented as direct documentation. The prose in which it is expressed owes a debt I am glad to name: my maternal grandmother, Mary Pierantoni, was a lifelong student of history with an extraordinary gift for storytelling, and the capacity to make the past vivid and specific and fully human, to set a listener inside a moment rather than merely above it, is an inheritance I have gratefully received from her.

The third methodological choice involves the handling of the theological argument that is this biography's most distinctive interpretive contribution. The claim: Barbour's human rights work was rooted in the convergence of two theological traditions, the Anabaptist-Pietist tradition of Elizabethtown College and the prophetic tradition of the AME Church, is an interpretive argument rather than a directly documented fact. Barbour did not leave behind a theological autobiography explaining how his two formative traditions shaped his human rights method. What he left behind is a career whose methods, arguments, and institutional choices are consistent with exactly the theological formation I attribute to him, and the interpretive argument is how the consistency is not coincidental. The argument rests on the documented evidence of his formation, the documented evidence of his career, and the documented evidence of the theological traditions from which both drew, assembled into an interpretive framework which the evidence supports even when it does not require.

For the political history undergirding every chapter of this biography, the arc from Roosevelt through Truman and Kennedy to Johnson, which gave Barbour's human rights work its terrain, no guide proved more essential than James W. Hilty, a historian of rare depth and clarity whose mastery of American political life illuminated the currents carrying Barbour forward and sometimes pushing back against him. Of all the remarkable scholars I encountered at Temple University, Hilty served as my doctoral dissertation advisor. His particular genius lay in understanding the presidency not as an abstraction but as a living, breathing force touching the lives of ordinary Americans struggling for justice. He taught me to read the political landscape of mid-century America not as a backdrop to the civil rights movement, but as its very terrain.

To place Barbour's thinking within the charged atmosphere of the Cold War, to understand why his human rights advocacy was simultaneously a domestic justice argument and an international human rights argument, I turned to the work of Richard H. Immerman, whose command of American foreign relations and intelligence in the post-World War II era is without peer. Immerman was among my professors and advisors at Temple, and he brought to his students the intimate, often troubling relationship between domestic justice and international power, a tension defining Barbour's world as surely as it defined the age itself. To sit in Immerman's seminars was to understand foreign policy as something far more than a matter of governments and treaties; it was a force reaching into the lives of every American who dared to speak for justice during the long decades of the Cold War.

The urgency which moved Santos Books to publish this biography at the Semiquincentennial was also Barbour's urgency. In the last year of his life, he gave it his own voice. Barbour wrote in the last year of his life: 'This desegregation-integration problem is a national problem and all of us, as citizens, carry the obligation and responsibility for the intelligent action which is necessary to eliminate this last barrier to our becoming the truly great democracy originally intended.' He was writing about a moment, 1957, when the Brown decision was three years old and the Civil Rights Act of 1957 had not yet been passed. The specific legislative achievements he was calling for came, within the following decade, in the Civil Rights Act of 1964, the Voting Rights Act of 1965, and the Fair Housing Act of 1968. They came, but the integration he was calling for, the building of the harmonious whole from the separate parts, the closing of the gap between democratic profession and democratic performance, the making visible in the social arrangements of everyday life of the values the Declaration proclaimed, integration has not come.

Two hundred and fifty years after the Declaration's proclamation, the racial wealth gap it identified as a structural consequence of the racial hierarchy its proclaimed ideals contradicted persists in forms which the civil rights legislation of the 1960s has been insufficient to address. The residential racial segregation produced by the Federal Housing Administration's racially discriminatory guidelines and sustained by decades of discriminatory practice persists in metropolitan areas across the country. The racial disparities in educational opportunity, criminal justice, and health care Barbour spent his career documenting and addressing persist in forms which would have been recognizable to him as the same basic problem in new institutional dress. The integration process, the ongoing work of creating a new harmonious whole from the separate parts, remains unfinished at the Semiquincentennial as it was unfinished at Barbour's death.

I bring to this biography more than three decades of scholarship on the Anabaptist and plain church communities whose institutional world it reconstructs. The scholarly authority behind the plain dress passage in Chapter Two rests on a body of published work I began building at Eastern Mennonite University in 1991, with an undergraduate senior thesis on the Old Order Mennonite Church of Virginia, continued through a master's thesis at Millersville University of Pennsylvania in 1993, and sustained across four peer-reviewed articles on Old Order Mennonite history published between 1993 and 1997 in the *Mennonite Historical Bulletin, Pennsylvania Mennonite Heritage,* and *Pennsylvania Folklife.* I do not write about plain dress, the believer's church tradition, or the plain people of Lancaster County from the outside. That scholarship is my own, and it is the foundation on which this biography's theological passages stand.

To all of this I added a fourth lens, one forged not in graduate seminars but in the undergraduate classrooms of Eastern Mennonite University, where Albert N. Keim first opened my eyes to the sweep and significance of the Anabaptist tradition. The relationship developed between us went well beyond the lecture hall. As Keim's research assistant and teaching assistant, I worked alongside him in the daily labor of scholarship, tracking down sources, helping shape the material he brought to his students, and absorbing, almost without realizing it, his entire way of seeing the past. Keim was a historian unlike any other I encountered, a man who had himself lived the history he taught, having served as a conscientious objector in postwar Europe, building villages for refugees and discovering in the process a world far richer than the one he had been born into. He brought to the study of nonconformity, conscientious objection, social justice, and peacemaking not the detachment of a scholar working at a safe remove, but the earned conviction of someone who had made hard choices of his own. It was Keim who first taught me to ask not only what happened, but at what cost, and to whom, and whether those who bore the cost did so with courage and clarity of conscience. This Anabaptist lens did not narrow the inquiry into Barbour's life, it deepened it. It pressed always toward the harder questions of conscience and courage Barbour's story so compellingly raises, and reminded me at every turn: history, at its best, is not merely the record of what powerful people decided, but of what ordinary people endured, resisted, and chose. This biography is dedicated to his memory.

When I arrived at Elizabethtown College to begin my own teaching career, I found waiting there a fifth mentor, one who would prove as formative in the classroom as any I had known in graduate school. J. Kenneth Kreider, Professor of European History and long-time chair of the history department, was everything a young historian could hope to find in a senior colleague, rigorous, principled, fearless, and deeply humane. Kreider had lived the convictions he brought to his teaching just as surely as Keim had lived his. A conscientious objector who had served in postwar Europe with the Brethren Volunteer Service, who had helped resettle refugees in the ruins of a world torn apart by war, and who had stood his ground on his own campus when speaking against Vietnam cost him the goodwill of colleagues and community alike, Kreider understood from the inside what it meant to hold a minority position in a majority world. Over more than thirty years teaching together at Elizabethtown College, he modeled for me, day after day, what it looks like to bring the full weight of one's convictions into the work of historical scholarship and teaching, without flinching, without posturing, and without ever losing sight of the students sitting in the chairs before you. He was the living proof the College's motto worked in a person.

I bring something else as well, something no academic credential can confer. My maternal grandparents and my paternal grandparents were Lancaster Conference Mennonites. My mother and my father grew up in the Lancaster Conference, and in their childhood and youth they wore plain clothes, the cape dress, the prayer covering, and the plain coat, in accordance with the tradition of the community in which they were formed. In my extended family, aunts and uncles and cousins who have been Mennonites, Amish, and Church of the Brethren have at various points in their lives and spiritual formation followed the tradition of dressing plain in accordance with their membership in these Anabaptist communities.

The conversation did not stay in Lancaster County. Both sides of my family were involved in Mennonite church planting in urban settings, in New York City and in Philadelphia, where the challenges of dressing plain in secular, urbane environments were of a different order than anything the farms of Lancaster County posed. A woman in a prayer covering riding the subway. A man in a standing collar plain coat on a Philadelphia street corner, or walking into a New York office building for a meeting.

In the public schools of those cities, my mother and my aunts paid a specific, personal price for their plain dress. Their classmates, who could not comprehend why any girl would wear a cape dress to school or why any woman would cover her hair with a prayer covering, subjected them to verbal taunts and, on more than one occasion, to physical assault: the coverings pulled from their heads, the cape dresses grabbed and mocked, the daily gauntlet of children whose cruelty was the cruelty of incomprehension rather than of ideology, but whose cruelty was no less real for its innocence of theological motive.

My mother and my aunts stood their ground. They wore what their faith required. They absorbed the cost of visibility in spaces not designed for their presence, and they carried themselves with the same dignity Elizabeth Myer had carried into Millersville State Normal School in 1885, the dignity of a person who has chosen, publicly and deliberately and at cost, to show what she believes. Those stories were shared with me by family members who had lived them, and they are woven into every page of this biography where plain dress appears. The visibility, the contempt, and the daily negotiation between theological commitment and social pressure were not abstractions in my family.

The Pennsylvania Garb Law was designed, among other things, to remove precisely this visibility from public institutional spaces. My family's urban church planting stories gave me an understanding of what such removal would mean: not merely the loss of a garment, but the forced concealment of a covenant, the state requiring a person to hide what she had most publicly, most deliberately, most theologically chosen to show. When I write in this biography about what plain dress means, about Gelassenheit and the baptismal covenant and the world's arrangements of rank refused in cloth, I am drawing on my family's formation as much as on the footnoted scholarship. Elizabeth Myer walked into Millersville State Normal School in September 1885 in plain garb and decided to stay when Principal Shaub told her she would be respected for her convictions. I know, at a level below the archival record, what the cost was and what it meant. It was at Hager's Department Store at 25 West King Street in Lancaster, where Lillian Risser managed the plain dress department after the garb law ended her teaching career, where my mother, my aunts, and my cousins purchased their prayer coverings. This knowledge belongs in this preface.

What Kusmer, Immerman, Hilty, Keim, and Kreider gave me was not simply a set of arguments to deploy or a bibliography to cite. They gave me a way of standing before students and before the past, with rigor, with empathy, and with an unflinching willingness to follow the evidence wherever it leads, however uncomfortable the destination. For more than thirty years in the classroom, I have tried to honor the inheritance they passed on. I have tried to bring to my own students something of what these five men brought to me: the conviction: history is not an academic exercise but a moral one; the figures we study were real people who made real choices under real pressure; and understanding those choices demands everything we have to give. If this work reflects even a portion of what they modeled, then the years of study, the long hours in the archives, and the slow, difficult work of putting it all into words will have been more than worthwhile. They will have been, in the deepest sense, what education is supposed to be.

On Sources

This biography rests on a foundation of primary sources I assembled over several years of research and synthesis. The core biographical source is my article "'Addressing Dignity Deferred:' Post Desegregation and the Process of Integration: The Life and Legacy of Race Relations Leader W. Miller Barbour (1908–1957), Elizabethtown College Class of 1932," forthcoming in the *Journal of the Lancaster County Historical Society* (December 2026), which synthesizes newspaper archives from across Barbour's career, city and county records, university records from the University of Pennsylvania and Elizabethtown College, National Urban League publications and correspondence, government documents, academic dissertations and theses, and the family interviews I conducted in September 2025 with Barbour's granddaughters Renee Whitby and Deborah Neil and his great-grandson Paul Neil. These family interviews, representing the living memory of those who knew Barbour personally, provide irreplaceable detail about his character, his family life, and the dimensions of his experience the documentary record cannot reach.

Barbour's own writings provide the most direct window into his mind and his theological convictions. His April 1957 article in *Adult Leadership* magazine, "Where We Stand on Racial Desegregation: What Forces Are Aiding Racial Desegregation in the United States? What Forces Are Holding It Back?" is his most sustained and mature statement of the distinction between desegregation and integration, and the biography treats it as a primary source of the first importance. His 1951 information paper on human rights, prepared for the World Affairs Institute at the University of Denver in collaboration with Michael L. Freed and Helen L. Peterson, reveals the internationalist framework within which he understood his local human rights work. His 1954 study of racial conditions in Tucson, Arizona, demonstrates his methodological rigor as a social scientist and his capacity for multiethnic analysis. His 1954 article in *Frontier* magazine on racial discrimination in western hotels combines personal testimony, empirical observation, and measured assessment of incremental progress in ways characteristic of his best writing.

The institutional context for Barbour's college years draws on three scholarly essays prepared specifically for this project: an essay on the founding and theological heritage of Elizabethtown College, an essay on the college's campus culture during the interwar decades, and an essay on the theological convergences between the Church of the Brethren and the AME Church. These essays synthesize the scholarship of Steven M. Nolt, whose revised third edition of The Brethren Heritage of Elizabethtown College is the authoritative institutional history; my earlier co-authored work with Peter J. DePuydt; and my peer-reviewed article with Steven M. Nolt, "Plain Dress in the Docket," published in *Pennsylvania History* in 2021, which reconstructs in archival detail the Lillian Risser garb law case and its significance for Elizabethtown's institutional identity. Together, these essays reconstruct the intellectual and theological environment in which Barbour was formed, providing the scholarly foundation for the biography's central claim about the college's role in his human rights development.

Where the historical record is thin, this biography employs what may be called the surround strategy: reconstructing in granular detail the world Barbour moved through, the events he witnessed, the texts he would have read, the people he knew, and the theological frameworks he carried, so the reader can feel his presence even in the gaps the documentary record leaves. The biography signals explicitly when it moves from documented fact to informed inference, using the subjunctive and conditional where appropriate. It never fabricates quotations or invents scenes presented as fact. The scholarly integrity this kind of biography requires demands absolute honesty about the limits of the evidence, and this biography observes this demand throughout.

A note on the subject's name: his birth certificate recorded him as William Henry Barber. In adulthood he used the name William Wilbur Miller Barbour, a formulation signaling both continuity and reinvention. He was widely known in his professional life as W. Miller Barbour or simply Miller Barbour. This biography uses his full name, William Wilbur Miller Barbour, on first reference in each chapter, and "Barbour" on subsequent references, treating him with the scholarly dignity every major historical figure deserves. The parenthetical rendering "William (Wilbur) Miller Barbour," which appears in some earlier scholarship, is not used here; it misrepresents a name he chose and used with intention.

The recognition Barbour so long lacked from the historical record has, in the years surrounding this biography's publication, begun to arrive through the institutions which knew him best. In the academic year 2025 to 2026, Elizabethtown College awarded William Wilbur Miller Barbour, posthumously, the Educate for Service: Service to Humanity Award, its highest honor for alumni. The award was presented to his grandchildren and great-grandchildren; the living bearers of the family whose sacrifices made his human rights career possible. The Educate for Service Award represents the highest distinction Elizabethtown College extends to its alumni, celebrating those who embody the College's founding mission of using education as a foundation for service to the world. It honors individuals whose lives reflect a deep commitment to making a positive impact through leadership, innovation, humanitarian work, and community engagement, those who lead with empathy, give generously, and inspire meaningful change across professions, communities, and borders. It is, in the three words the College's original official motto has always expressed, the recognition of a life spent making Jesus King. For Barbour, who crossed the stage of the Student Alumni Gymnasium and Auditorium at Elizabethtown College in June 1932 carrying a degree and a mandate, the award is the alma mater's long-delayed acknowledgment of what he did with both.

He deserves, finally, to be known. The movement he served has been written and rewritten, debated and theorized, celebrated and contested across sixty years of scholarship. He belongs in the conversation. The pages following are his overdue introduction to it.

Any serious account of William Wilbur Miller Barbour's human rights work requires sustained engagement with the scholarship of Black religious life, because his work was rooted in this life in ways the secular frameworks of standard civil rights historiography cannot adequately capture. The scholarship of Evelyn Brooks Higginbotham, C. Eric Lincoln, Lawrence H. Mamiya, James H. Cone, and Albert

Raboteau has established, across several decades of patient historical and theological work, the indispensable institutional and intellectual role of the Black church in African American civic life and in the civil rights struggle specifically. Higginbotham's concept of the Black Baptist church as a "public sphere," a space where Black communities organized political and social life across the boundaries of class and gender, applies with equal force to the AME tradition in which Barbour was formed. Lincoln and Mamiya's comprehensive study of the Black church demonstrates how the institution served simultaneously as spiritual fortress, community center, political organization, and economic base, providing in the absence of a responsive state the full range of social services and civic functions a community required for its flourishing.

Cone's liberation theology, developed most fully in works including *The Spirituals and the Blues* and *God of the Oppressed*, provides the theological framework within which the AME tradition's prophetic witness can be most precisely understood. Cone's central claim, which the God of the Christian Gospel is the God who takes the side of the oppressed against the oppressor, and which authentic Christian theology must therefore be developed from the vantage point of those on the underside of history, was not a novelty Cone invented in the 1960s. It was a recovery and articulation of what the AME tradition had been practicing since Richard Allen walked out of St. George's in 1792. Barbour's human rights work was, in Cone's sense, theology: it was the embodiment, in civic action, of the conviction: God's character and God's will were incompatible with racial hierarchy and demanded its dismantling.

The scholarship of Anabaptist and Church of the Brethren history, particularly the work of Donald F. Durnbaugh, Carl F. Bowman, and Albert N. Keim, illuminates the other stream of Barbour's theological formation with comparable rigor. Durnbaugh's *Fruit of the Vine*, the authoritative history of the Brethren from their 1708 origins through the late twentieth century, traces the development of the Brethren's distinctive commitments to nonresistance, community accountability, and separation from the coercive mechanisms of the state across three centuries of North American life. Bowman's *Brethren Society* analyzes the transformation of Brethren culture in the twentieth century, tracing how a tradition shaped by rural isolation and ethnic distinctiveness navigated the pressures of modernity without losing the theological core which gave it its identity. Keim's biography of Harold S. Bender demonstrates how the Anabaptist Vision, Bender's programmatic articulation of the tradition's central commitments, was not merely a work of Reformation historiography but a living theological resource for communities navigating the demands of twentieth-century life.

The convergence this biography traces, the meeting of these two theological traditions in a single human rights leader, has not been the subject of prior scholarly attention. This is in part because the historiographical traditions illuminating each tradition have operated in parallel rather than in conversation with each other. The scholarship of Black religious history and the scholarship of Anabaptist history have rarely spoken to each other, because the communities they study have rarely spoken to each other. Barbour's life offers an occasion for which conversation, and the theological essay assembled for this volume begins it in productive ways. The convergence this biography documents is not the exception which proves a rule of separation. It is evidence two traditions arriving at similar hermeneutical convictions from very different historical starting points had more to say to each other than either had previously recognized.

Barbour's concept of the integrator deserves extended attention as an intellectual contribution to the civil rights movement's theory of social change, not merely as a description of his own professional role. The distinction he drew between desegregation and integration, between the tearing down of legal structures of exclusion and the building of genuine community across the lines those structures had drawn, was analytically precise in ways the movement's standard vocabulary did not always achieve. It named a problem the Brown decision had made newly urgent: the problem of what came after the legal victory, of who would do the work the law could not do, and of what this work required of those who did it.

The concept anticipated, with some precision, the debates the mass movement of the late 1950s and early 1960s would be forced to conduct. When the lunch counter sit-ins of 1960 desegregated lunch counters in city after city across the South, the question Barbour had been asking since 1954 asserted itself in practical form: desegregating the lunch counter was one thing; building the community of genuine fellowship across racial lines which would make the desegregated lunch counter a meaningful human achievement was something else, something requiring the patient, relationship-based, institutionally grounded work of the integrator. When the Civil Rights Act of 1964 prohibited racial discrimination in employment and public accommodations, the same question arose: the law had changed the policy; the process of integration remained to be built.

The historiography of community organizing provides a framework for understanding Barbour's role and his method. Charles Payne's I've Got the Light of Freedom develops the concept of the organizing tradition in the civil rights movement, the tradition of patient, persistent, relationship-based community organizing building the movement from the ground up. Payne distinguishes this tradition from the mobilizing tradition of the movement, the tradition of mass action and public confrontation which produces the dramatic moments captured in photographs and remembered in anniversaries. Both traditions were essential to the movement; neither could sustain the other's work. Barbour operated primarily in the organizing tradition, building the coalitions and the institutional relationships and the community capacity which the mobilizing tradition would deploy when its moment arrived.

Barbara Ransby's essential biography of Ella Baker illuminates the contributions this tradition made and the specific person it required. Baker, like Barbour, was a builder of the movement's organizational infrastructure, a person who devoted her career to creating the conditions for other people's leadership rather than positioning herself at the center of the stage. Baker's concept of "group-centered leader-ship," her insistence that the movement's strength lay in the organizing capacity of communities rather than in the charisma of individual leaders, resonates with the institutional emphasis of Barbour's work. He was not building his own leadership. He was building the Urban League's capacity, the coalition's capacity, the community's capacity for the sustained work of integration. The difference is not small. It is the difference between a movement which lasts and one which ends when its leader leaves.

This biography makes an argument not only about William Wilbur Miller Barbour but about the kind of civil rights history we write and the consequences of the choices we make in writing it. The canonical narrative of the civil rights movement, the narrative of heroic leaders, dramatic confrontations, and legislative victories, has served important purposes: it has made the movement memorable, has given it a shape which civic education can transmit, and has honored the courage and sacrifice of the people at its center. But it has also obscured what Hall calls the "long, hot civil rights movement" preceding the canonical decade, and it has systematically underrepresented the contributions of the organizers, the educators, the institution-builders, and the theologically grounded practitioners who built the foundations on which the canonical victories rested.

The recovery of Barbour's story is part of the ongoing effort to write a more complete and more accurate history of the movement and of the American democratic tradition it was working to fulfill. This effort matters not only for historiographical reasons but for practical ones. A society understanding the civil rights movement primarily through the lens of its most dramatic moments is a society without adequate models for the slower, less dramatic, more institutionally demanding work the movement also required and which the unfinished project of integration still requires. If the only model of civil rights action is the dramatic confrontation, the march and the sit-in and the speech, then the daily, institutional, coalition-building work of the integrator has no model and no language. Barbour provides both.

How the Research Unfolded

The primary sources for this biography were assembled across several years of research in multiple repositories and through multiple methodologies. The Earl H. and Anita F. Hess Archives at Elizabethtown College, under the care of archivist Rachel Grove Rohrbaugh, provided the documentary foundation for the chapters covering Barbour's college years: the yearbooks, the student newspaper, the correspondence of college president Ralph W. Schlosser, the athletic director's files, and the theatrical production programs which together reconstruct the institutional environment of Elizabethtown College in the late 1920s and early 1930s.

The newspaper databases, particularly Newspapers.com and ProQuest Historical Newspapers, provided access to the contemporary press coverage of Barbour's human rights work in Philadelphia, Denver, Tucson, and Los Angeles, coverage spanning the period from the late 1920s through his death in March 1957. *The Denver Post*, the *Rocky Mountain News*, the *Colorado Statesman,* the *Denver Star*, the *California Eagle,* the *Pittsburgh Courier,* the *Baltimore Afro-American*, the *New Pittsburgh Courier,* the *Arizona Daily Star*, and the *Elizabethtown Etownian* all contributed to the documentary record of his career. The experience of reading these newspapers in sequence, following Barbour's name through two decades of human rights advocacy in several cities, was among the most vivid experiences of the research process: the gradual emergence of a career, and of the person pursuing it, from the fragments of press coverage which are the primary documentary trace most civil rights workers of the Long Movement leave behind.

The family interviews I conducted in September 2025 with Barbour's granddaughters Renee Whitby and Deborah Neil and his great-grandson Paul Neil provided the irreplaceable human dimension of the biography, the living memory of people who knew William and Ruth Barbour through the eyes of children and grandchildren and who could give flesh and specificity to the person whose public record the newspapers documented. The interviews took place in a single session over the course of a September afternoon, and their content, incorporated throughout the biography with appropriate attribution and appropriate epistemic caution about the nature of family memory as a historical source, significantly deepened the portrait which the documentary record alone could have produced.

The recovery of Barbour's story did not begin with this biography. On January 21, 2019, Martin Luther King Jr. Day, Carl J. Strikwerda, then President of Elizabethtown College, sent to the campus community a presidential communication titled 'Pioneer for Social Justice.' In it, Strikwerda named Barbour directly, quoted his writing, described his career in Denver and Los Angeles, and conveyed Barbour had written to the alumni office about 'many fond memories of my days on the campus at Elizabethtown College.' The communication closed with Barbour's own words from his final Adult Leadership article: 'All of us, as human beings and citizens, carry the obligation and responsibility for the intelligent action necessary to eliminate this last barrier to our becoming the truly great democracy originally intended. Are we up to this great task? The world awaits our answer.' That was 2019. The institutional momentum has been building since January 21, 2019, and the posthumous award to Barbour of the Educate for Service: Service to Humanity Award in 2025 to 2026 is its most recent expression. He is being recovered. The work and the hope are continuing.

This is not a cause for despair. It is a cause for the kind of patient, theologically grounded, institutionally sophisticated human rights work Barbour practiced across twenty-five years, work this biography attempts to document and honor. The fragments he pieced together are real. The institutions he built continue to serve the communities he cared about. The methods he developed continue to be available to human rights practitioners willing to learn from them. And the theological conviction he carried, the conviction about how making Jesus king was not a private spiritual aspiration but a civic mandate, about how the values of the Kingdom of God had to be made visible in the specific, concrete, measurable social arrangements of specific communities, remains as radical and as urgent in 2026 as it was in 1947 or 1957.

May this book advance broader scholarly and public conversations about the long and complex effort to build a constitutional representative democracy. Civil rights history remains central to understanding our 250-year-old democratic republic. The story of William Wilbur Miller Barbour is part of this history, and his recovery from historical obscurity is a contribution to the democratic project he served. He deserves to be known. He deserves to be remembered. He deserves, most of all, to be continued. Santos Books publishes this volume in the conviction shared by its mission: every story is sacred, the work of an author discovering and telling a story is itself a form of witness, and Barbour's story, allowed to disappear for nearly seventy years, was always sacred, always worth the recovery, always worth the telling.

A Note on Santos Books

Santos Books is a religious social justice publisher based in Elizabethtown, Pennsylvania, committed to publishing scholarly and popular works that advance the cause of human dignity and democratic equality. The publisher's mission, rooted in the same Elizabethtown community that formed William Wilbur Miller Barbour, reflects the conviction that publishing serious civil rights scholarship is itself a form of the public discipleship described in the Church of the Brethren's motto. Drawing inspiration from the life and legacy of W. Miller Barbour, Santos Books publishes works whose scholarly quality and moral seriousness match the significance of the subjects they address.

The decision to publish this biography as the United States marks its Semiquincentennial reflects Santos Books' commitment to the public engagement of civil rights history at the moments when this engagement is most needed. The 250th anniversary of the Declaration of Independence is such a moment: a moment when the gap between the Declaration's proclaimed ideals and the nation's actual practices is as visible and as contested as it has been in any previous generation, a moment when the historical record of how Americans have worked to close this gap is most urgently needed as both inspiration and instruction. William Wilbur Miller Barbour spent his life working to close the gap. This book is offered in the same spirit.

NOTES

The notes below are organized by chapter. Each entry is keyed to the text by the closing words of the passage it supports. Readers wishing to pursue any dimension of the biography's argument in greater depth are encouraged to consult the works cited here.

Chapter One

"this was truly one of our nation's finest hours." W. Miller Barbour, "Where We Stand on Racial Desegregation: What Forces Are Aiding Racial Desegregation in the United States? What Forces Are Holding It Back?" *Adult Leadership* 5 (April 1957): 4.

"integrator." Barbour, "Where We Stand on Racial Desegregation," 4.

"claims upon the social arrangements of mid-century America." Ibid., 4. For the broader context of this distinction in civil rights thought, see Thomas J. Sugrue, *Sweet Land of Liberty: The Forgotten Struggle for Civil Rights in the North* (New York: Random House, 2008), 1–30.

"and ultimate defeat." Jacquelyn Dowd Hall, "The Long Civil Rights Movement and the Political Uses of the Past," *Journal of American History* 91, no. 4 (March 2005): 1233–1263, 1235. For important responses and extensions, see Steven F. Lawson, "Long Origins of the Short Civil Rights Movement, 1954–1968," in *Freedom Rights: New Perspectives on the Civil Rights Movement*, ed. Danielle L. McGuire and John Dittmer (Lexington: University Press of Kentucky, 2011), 9–37; and Sundiata Keita Cha-Jua and Clarence Lang, "The 'Long Movement' as Vampire: Temporal and Spatial Fallacies in Recent Black Freedom Studies," *Journal of African American History* 92, no. 2 (Spring 2007): 265–288.

"quiescence." Patricia Sullivan, *Days of Hope: Race and Democracy in the New Deal Era* (Chapel Hill: University of North Carolina Press, 1996), 1–20. Glenda Gilmore, *Defying Dixie: The Radical Roots of Civil Rights, 1919–1950* (New York: W. W. Norton, 2008), 1–15.

"have unfolded as it did." Manning Marable, *Race, Reform, and Rebellion: The Second Reconstruction in Black America, 1945–1990*, 2nd ed. (Jackson: University Press of Mississippi, 1991), 20–40.

"imperatives of power." Donald F. Durnbaugh, *Fruit of the Vine: A History of the Brethren, 1708–1995* (Elgin, IL: Brethren Press, 1997), 3–25. Jean-Paul Benowitz, "The Brethren Heritage of Elizabethtown College: Founding Ideals, Institutional Identity, and the Persistence of Anabaptist-Pietist Values in Higher Education" (lecture, Elizabethtown College, developed over thirty years of teaching), 2–5.

"degradation." James T. Campbell, *Songs of Zion: The African Methodist Episcopal Church in the United States and South Africa* (New York: Oxford University Press, 1995), 14–32. Richard S. Newman, *Freedom's Prophet: Bishop Richard Allen, the AME Church, and the Black Founding Fathers* (New York: New York University Press, 2008).

"Black." Jean-Paul Benowitz, "Prophetic Dissent and the Politics of Liberation: Theological Convergences Between the Church of the Brethren and the African Methodist Episcopal Church" (lecture, Elizabethtown College, developed over thirty years of teaching), 7–15. For the broader scholarly context of convergences between Anabaptist and Black liberation theologies, see J. Denny Weaver, *Becoming Anabaptist: The Origin and Significance of Sixteenth-Century Anabaptism* (Scottdale, PA: Herald Press, 1987).

"the conditions for genuine community." "Make Jesus King" was the official motto of Elizabethtown College during Barbour's years there from 1928 to 1932 and for an undetermined period thereafter. At some point in the post–World War II era, the College's operative motto gradually shifted to its current formulation, "Educate for Service." This biography makes no claim about the institutional motivations or theological implications of the change beyond noting its existence and the limits of the current documentary record regarding it.

"not only aspiration." Jean-Paul Benowitz, "Addressing Dignity Deferred: Post Desegregation and the Process of Integration: The Life and Legacy of Race Relations Leader W. Miller Barbour (1908–1957), Elizabethtown College Class of 1932," *Journal of the Lancaster County Historical Society* (forthcoming, December 2026). Interview with Renee Whitby, granddaughter of W. Miller Barbour; Deborah Neil, granddaughter of W. Miller Barbour; and Paul Neil, great-grandson of W. Miller Barbour, conducted by Jean-Paul Benowitz, September 17, 2025.

"the dimensions of his experience the documentary record cannot reach." Barbour, "Where We Stand on Racial Desegregation," 1–9. W. Miller Barbour, Michael L. Freed, and Helen L. Peterson, "What Can Be Done on the Local Level: An Informational Paper," World Affairs Institute, University of Denver, August 1951. W. Barbour, *A Study of Race Relations: A Preliminary Evaluation of Racial Minority Conditions in Tucson, Arizona and of the Tucson Urban League Service Council* (unpublished report, Tucson, 1954). W. Miller Barbour, "Breaking the Barriers: Anti-Negro Prejudice Lessens in Western Hotels," *Frontier* 6, no. 11 (November 1954): 8–9.

"his best writing." Benowitz, "Brethren Heritage," 1–20. Jean-Paul Benowitz, "'Make Jesus King': The Golden Era of Elizabethtown College and the Formation of Anabaptist-Pietist Leaders for Peace and Justice, 1920–1945" (lecture, Elizabethtown College, developed over thirty years of teaching), 1–15. Steven M. Nolt, *The Brethren Heritage of Elizabethtown College*, rev. 3rd ed. (Elizabethtown, PA: Elizabethtown College, 2024). Jean-Paul Benowitz and Steven M. Nolt, "Plain Dress in the Docket: Lillian Risser, the Pennsylvania Garb Law, and the Free Exercise of Anabaptist Religion, 1908–1910," *Pennsylvania History: A Journal of Mid-Atlantic Studies* 88, no. 3 (2021): 1–30.

"development." Evelyn Brooks Higginbotham, *Righteous Discontent: The Women's Movement in the Black Baptist Church, 1880–1920* (Cambridge, MA: Harvard University Press, 1993), 1–18. For important extensions and critiques of Higginbotham's argument, see Fredrick Harris, *Something Within: Religion in African-American Political Activism* (New York: Oxford University Press, 1999).

"its flourishing." James H. Cone, *The Spirituals and the Blues: An Interpretation* (New York: Seabury Press, 1972), 1–25. C. Eric Lincoln and Lawrence H. Mamiya, *The Black Church in the African American Experience* (Durham, NC: Duke University Press, 1990), 1–15.

"dismantling." Charles M. Payne, *I've Got the Light of Freedom: The Organizing Tradition and the Mississippi Freedom Struggle* (Berkeley: University of California Press, 1995), 1–25.

"communities navigating the demands of twentieth-century life." Barbara Ransby, *Ella Baker and the Black Freedom Movement: A Radical Democratic Vision* (Chapel Hill: University of North Carolina Press, 2003), 1–25.

"integration remained to be built." Payne, *I've Got the Light of Freedom*, 1–25. Ransby, *Ella Baker*, 1–25.

"arrived." Hall, "Long Civil Rights Movement," 1233–1263.

"lasts and one which ends when its leader leaves." Ransby, *Ella Baker*, 1–25.

Chapter Two

"something new from its materials." "Pennsylvania, U.S. Birth Certificates, 1906–1914," s.v. "Wm Henry Barber," September 20, 1908, Ancestry.com. For the broader context of naming practices in African American families during the Great Migration era, see Isabel Wilkerson, *The Warmth of Other Suns: The Epic Story of America's Great Migration* (New York: Random House, 2010), 177–210.

Plessy v. Ferguson, 163 U.S. 537 (1896). For the social history of Jim Crow's development and consolidation, see C. Vann Woodward, *The Strange Career of Jim Crow*, 3rd rev. ed. (New York: Oxford University Press, 1974). For a more recent treatment, see Leon Litwack, *Trouble in Mind: Black Southerners in the Age of Jim Crow* (New York: Alfred A. Knopf, 1998).

Tuskegee Institute, Lynching Statistics, cited in Robert L. Zangrando, *The NAACP Crusade against Lynching, 1909–1950* (Philadelphia: Temple University Press, 1980), 6. For the social function of lynching as a mechanism of racial control, see Amy Louise Wood, *Lynching and Spectacle: Witnessing Racial Violence in America, 1890–1940* (Chapel Hill: University of North Carolina Press, 2009).

David Levering Lewis, *W.E.B. Du Bois: Biography of a Race, 1868–1919* (New York: Henry Holt, 1993), 386–402. For the founding of the NAACP, see Patricia Sullivan, *Lift Every Voice: The NAACP and the Making of the Civil Rights Movement* (New York: New Press, 2009).

"National Urban League," VCU Libraries, Social Welfare History Project, accessed June 2, 2025, https://socialwelfare.library.vcu.edu/organizations/national-urban-league/. For the National Urban League's institutional history, see Nancy J. Weiss, *The National Urban League, 1910–1940* (New York: Oxford University Press, 1974).

"Pennsylvania Death Certificates, 1906–1970," s.v. "William Barbour," September 2, 1917, Ancestry.com. "Marriage License," *The Evening News*, Harrisburg, Pennsylvania, January 28, 1920. Interview with Whitby, Neil, and Neil, September 17, 2025.

"Find a Grave Index," database, FamilySearch, entry for Minnie Mumford Archer, burial in East Middletown Cemetery, Middletown, Dauphin County, Pennsylvania, record ID 13874512. For documentation of the cemetery and its USCT veterans, see "Old Negro Cemetery, Middletown, PA," Pennsylvania Grand Review, House Divided Project, Dickinson College, March 26, 2010. For the tenant farming system's function as a mechanism of racial economic subordination in the post-Reconstruction South, see Edward Royce, *The Origins of Southern Sharecropping* (Philadelphia: Temple University Press, 1993).

1920 U.S. Census, Plymouth, Montgomery County, Pennsylvania, digital image, s.v. "William Barbour," Ancestry.com. Interview with Whitby, Neil, and Neil, September 17, 2025.

"Pennsylvania, U.S. Birth Certificates, 1906–1914," Ancestry.com. "Pennsylvania Death Certificates, 1906–1970," Ancestry.com. "Marriage License," The Evening News, January 28, 1920. Interview with Whitby, Neil, and Neil, September 17, 2025.

Wilkerson, Warmth of Other Suns, 9–15. For a synthetic treatment of the Great Migration's causes, patterns, and consequences, see also Joe William Trotter Jr., ed., *The Great Migration in Historical Perspective: New Dimensions of Race, Class, and Gender* (Bloomington: Indiana University Press, 1991).

Notes and Queries, Historical, Biographical and Genealogical, Relating Chiefly to the Interior of Pennsylvania (Harrisburg, PA: Harrisburg Publishing Company, 1895), 15. For Middletown's development as a transportation and industrial hub, see the records of the Middletown Area Historical Society.

"Black History in Middletown," in *35th Annual Middletown Fair: A Tribute to the Black Influence of Middletown* (Middletown, PA: Middletown Area Historical Society, 2010), 4–5.

James W. Loewen, *Sundown Towns: A Hidden Dimension of American Racism* (New York: The New Press, 2005), 3–30. "Central Pa. 'Sundown Towns' and the Legacy of Racism: 'It's Still Here,'" *PennLive Patriot-News, February 22, 2024.* Candacy Taylor, *Overground Railroad: The Green Book and the Roots of Black Travel in America* (New York: Abrams Press, 2020).

Act of June 8, 1881, P.L. 76; Allen v. Meadville School Directors, 9 W.N.C. 509 (Pa. 1881); Pennsylvania Equal Rights Act, Act of June 27, 1935, P.L. 744. Matthew J. Countryman, *Up South: Civil Rights and Black Power in Philadelphia* (Philadelphia: University of Pennsylvania Press, 2006), 11–34. Thomas J. Sugrue, *The Origins of the Urban Crisis: Race and Inequality in Postwar Detroit* (Princeton, NJ: Princeton University Press, 1996), 3–29.

John E. Bodnar, "Peter C. Blackwell and the Negro Community of Steelton, 1880–1920," *Pennsylvania Magazine of History and Biography* 97, no. 2 (April 1973): 199–200. "The Great Migration (1910–1970)," National Archives, African American Heritage.

For the Wagner Act's failure to prohibit racial discrimination by labor unions, see Paul D. Moreno, *Black Americans and Organized Labor: A New History* (Baton Rouge: Louisiana State University Press, 2006), 150–190.

For the FHA's racially discriminatory lending guidelines, see Ira Katznelson, *When Affirmative Action Was White: An Untold History of Racial Inequality in Twentieth-Century America* (New York: W. W. Norton, 2005), 113–141.

Minutes of the Philadelphia Annual Conference of the African Methodist Episcopal Church, 1920–1939, listings for Ebenezer AME Church, Middletown, Pennsylvania.

Higginbotham, *Righteous Discontent*, 1–18. Lincoln and Mamiya, *Black Church*, 1–15.

Cone, *Spirituals and the Blues*, 1–25. Albert J. Raboteau, *Slave Religion: The "Invisible Institution" in the Antebellum South* (New York: Oxford University Press, 1978), 1–30.

Campbell, *Songs of Zion*, 14–32. Newman, *Freedom's Prophet*, 1–30.

"Middletown Notes," *Harrisburg Telegraph*, February 21, 1927, 6.

Interview with Whitby, Neil, and Neil, September 17, 2025. For the character of Black childhood in the post-Reconstruction South, see Leon Litwack, *Trouble in Mind*, 1–60.

1932 Etonian, Earl H. and Anita F. Hess Archives and Special Collections, Elizabethtown College, Elizabethtown, Pennsylvania. Benowitz, "Addressing Dignity Deferred," 10.

"60 H.S. Grads To Enter College," The Evening News (Harrisburg, PA), September 13, 1928. For Lincoln University's role in the formation of Black intellectual and professional leadership during this period, see Raymond Wolters, *The New Negro on Campus: Black College Rebellions of the 1920s* (Princeton, NJ: Princeton University Press, 1975).

Chapter Three

"and which had long since stopped noticing the gap." Benowitz, "Brethren Heritage," 3–7. Nolt, Brethren Heritage of Elizabethtown College, 1–15. Jean-Paul Benowitz and Peter J. DePuydt, *Elizabethtown College* (Charleston, SC: Arcadia Publishing, 2014), 7–15.

1930 *Etonian Yearbook*, Elizabethtown College, 52. 1933 *Etonian Yearbook*, Elizabethtown College, 48. Benowitz, "Addressing Dignity Deferred," 11.

1932 *Etonian*, Elizabethtown College Archives.

"plain sects took courage from her example." Durnbaugh, *Fruit of the Vine*, 3–30. Benowitz, "Brethren Heritage," 5–10. For the theological development of Anabaptism in the sixteenth century, see George Hunston Williams, *The Radical Reformation*, 3rd ed. (Kirksville, MO: Sixteenth Century Journal Publishers, 1992).

"her plain dress in a Pennsylvania public school." Carl F. Bowman, *Brethren Society: The Transformation of a "Peculiar People"* (Baltimore: Johns Hopkins University Press, 1995), 1–25. For the Brethren's development in Pennsylvania from their 1719 arrival, see Donald F. Durnbaugh, ed., *The Brethren in Colonial America* (Elgin, IL: Brethren Press, 1967).

"commitment." Benowitz, "Brethren Heritage," 8–12. Benowitz and DePuydt, *Elizabethtown College*, 9. The founding charter's language is quoted in Schlosser, *History of Elizabethtown College*, 8.

Jean-Paul Benowitz and Steven M. Nolt, "Plain Dress in the Docket: Lillian Risser, the Pennsylvania Garb Law, and the Free Exercise of Anabaptist Religion, 1908–1910," *Pennsylvania History: A Journal of Mid-Atlantic Studies* 88, no. 3 (2021): 1–30. Benowitz, "Brethren Heritage," 12–18. For Elizabeth Myer's biography and her role as the College's first faculty member, see Schlosser, *History of Elizabethtown College*, 118–119.

"dress fashionably is to assert it." Donald B. Kraybill, *The Riddle of Amish Culture*, rev. ed. (Baltimore: Johns Hopkins University Press, 2001), 25–50. For Gelassenheit as the foundational theological concept underlying plain dress in Anabaptist communities, see ibid., 25–35. For plain dress as the enacted baptismal covenant across Mennonite, Amish, and Brethren communities in Lancaster County, see also Donald B. Kraybill and Carl F. Bowman, *On the Backroad to Heaven: Old Order Hutterites, Mennonites, Amish, and Brethren* (Baltimore: Johns Hopkins University Press, 2001), 1–30.

"arrangement of the world organized around human exploitation." George Fox, statement of 1656, in *The Works of George Fox* (Philadelphia: Marcus T. C. Gould, 1831), vol. 8, 10. For John Woolman's wearing of undyed cloth as a testimony against slavery, see John Woolman, *The Journal of John Woolman and A Plea for the Poor* (Secaucus, NJ: Citadel Press, 1972), 150–160. For the Quaker testimony of simplicity and its theological relationship to the Anabaptist plain dress tradition, see Thomas D. Hamm, *The Quakers in America* (New York: Columbia University Press, 2003), 1–30.

Ralph W. Schlosser, *History of Elizabethtown College: 1899–1970* (Elizabethtown, PA: Elizabethtown College, 1971), 121–126. Jean-Paul Benowitz, interview with Sue Hostetter, July 14, 2025.

R. W. Schlosser to Ira Herr, November 3, 1928, Office of the President correspondence, Elizabethtown College Archives, Director of Athletics, EC III C.4, Box 2, Folder 9. Benowitz, "Make Jesus King," 4–7.

Benowitz, "Make Jesus King," 5–6. Schlosser, *History of Elizabethtown College*, 140–141. For the Great Books tradition and its educational philosophy, see Eva Brann, *Paradoxes of Education in a Republic* (Chicago: University of Chicago Press, 1979).

"their necessary fulfillment." Benowitz, "Make Jesus King," 5–8. Schlosser, *History of Elizabethtown College*, 141–145.

"convictions rather than the imperatives of the surrounding society." Barbour, "Where We Stand on Racial Desegregation," 1.

"generation before Bender gave it its landmark scholarly expression." Schlosser, *History of Elizabethtown College*, 140–141. Benowitz, "Make Jesus King," 9–11. For the content of the intercollegiate debate curriculum during this period, see also the Forensic Arts Club records in the Elizabethtown College Archives.

1932 *Etonian*, Elizabethtown College Archives. Benowitz, "Addressing Dignity Deferred," 12–13.

Theatrical production program leaflet, Earl H. and Anita F. Hess Archives. Benowitz, interview with Hostetter, July 14, 2025.

1932 *Etonian*, Elizabethtown College Archives.

Gerald Huesken Jr., "'The Brutal Thirteen': Elizabethtown College's Lone Season of Collegiate Football and How It Made History in Lancaster County, Pennsylvania," *Journal of Plain Anabaptist Communities* 1, no. 1 (2019): 10–11, 19–20.

Schlosser to Herr, November 3, 1928, Elizabethtown College Archives. For Ira R. Herr's career as Director of Athletics, his recognition as 'Dean of Coaches' in Lancaster County, the dedication of Ira Herr Field (May 7, 1966), and his continued coaching at the Patton Masonic School for Boys after retirement, see Schlosser, *History of Elizabethtown College*, 208–211.

Benowitz, "Brethren Heritage," 8–12. Harold S. Bender, "The Anabaptist Vision," *Church History* 13, no. 1 (March 1944): 3–24.

Bender, "Anabaptist Vision," 3–24. Albert N. Keim, *Harold S. Bender, 1897–1962* (Scottdale, PA: Herald Press, 1998), 300–340.

James D. Anderson, *The Education of Blacks in the South, 1860–1935* (Chapel Hill: University of North Carolina Press, 1988), 1–32. Adam Fairclough, *A Class of Their Own: Black Teachers in the Segregated South* (Cambridge, MA: Harvard University Press, 2007), 1–30.

"Elizabethtown College Commencement June 6," *Lancaster New Era*, May 24, 1932, 14.

Jean-Paul Benowitz, "Work and Hope," in *Voices of Vocation: Stories of Purposeful Life Work in Teaching, Mentoring, and Leading* (Elizabethtown, PA: Elizabethtown College, 2017), 27–52. For the *Martyrs Mirror* and its publication history, see John S. Oyer and Robert S. Kreider, *Mirror of the Martyrs* (Intercourse, PA: Good Books, 1990). For the Ephrata Cloister printing press and the production of the Martyrs Mirror, see Jeff Bach, *Voices of the Turtledoves: The Sacred World of Ephrata* (University Park: Pennsylvania State University Press, 2003), 1–30.

Minutes of the Board of Trustees of Elizabethtown College, July 29, 1915, Hess Archives, Elizabethtown College, recording the formal adoption of the motto "Make Jesus King." Benowitz, "Make Jesus King," 3–5.

Walter Rauschenbusch, *A Theology for the Social Gospel* (New York: Macmillan, 1917), 1–30. H. Richard Niebuhr, *Christ and Culture* (New York: Harper and Row, 1951), 1–30. For the "social Kingship of Christ" in early twentieth-century Protestant thought, see also Gary Dorrien, *The Making of American Liberal Theology: Idealism, Realism, and Modernity, 1900–1950* (Louisville: Westminster John Knox Press, 2003).

Board of Trustees report, 1913, Hess Archives, Elizabethtown College, quoted in Benowitz, "Make Jesus King."

"Racial prejudice contradicts the teachings of Jesus." "The Inter-Racial Problem," resolution adopted by the Annual Conference of the Church of the Brethren, 1935. On the Church of the Brethren's racial justice commitments in this period, see Durnbaugh, *Fruit of the Vine*, 400–420.

"completed achievement." Durnbaugh, *Fruit of the Vine*, 400–420. For the gap between Brethren racial commitments and institutional practice, see also Bowman, *Brethren Society*, 200–230.

"into a broader program of racially integrated summer service." Keim and Stoltzfus, *Politics of Conscience*, 50–80. For Clarence Pickett and the American Friends Service Committee's interracial work camp program, see Lawrence S. Wittner, *Rebels against War: The American Peace Movement, 1933–1983* (Philadelphia: Temple University Press, 1984), 1–30.

"expressions of the same theological commitment." Keim and Stoltzfus, *Politics of Conscience*, 100–150. Tracy, *Direct Action*, 1–30.

"most urgent intellectual support." Benowitz, "Make Jesus King," 12–15. For Bonhoeffer's influence on the American peace church tradition, see Victoria Barnett, *For the Soul of the People: Protestant Protest against Hitler* (New York: Oxford University Press, 1992).

"College's motto." For the Barmen Declaration, see Arthur Cochrane, *The Church's Confession under Hitler* (Philadelphia: Westminster Press, 1962). For Karl Barth's broader theological project and its civil rights implications, see George Hunsinger, *How to Read Karl Barth: The Shape of His Theology* (New York: Oxford University Press, 1991).

Chapter Four

"into hunger." Sullivan, *Days of Hope*, 1–44. For Black unemployment during the Great Depression, see Harvard Sitkoff, *A New Deal for Blacks: The Emergence of Civil Rights as a National Issue* (New York: Oxford University Press, 1978), 35–57.

"absorb." Benowitz, "Addressing Dignity Deferred," 14.

"enforce the racial geography their legal instruments had established." "Echoes From the Class of 1932," *Our College Times*, May 16, 1933.

"collective life in conditions designed to prevent it." Langston Hughes, *The Big Sea* (New York: Alfred A. Knopf, 1940), 228. For the Harlem Renaissance and its political dimensions, see David Levering Lewis, *When Harlem Was in Vogue* (New York: Alfred A. Knopf, 1981).

"which capacity were deployed in more visible campaigns." Gilmore, *Defying Dixie*, 1–30.

"press functioned as a civil rights institution in its own right." 1940 U.S. Census, Philadelphia, Philadelphia County, Pennsylvania, s.v. "Miller Barbour," Ancestry.com. Interview with Whitby, Neil, and Neil, September 17, 2025.

"and its aspiration." For racial discrimination in New Deal public assistance administration, see Katznelson, *When Affirmative Action Was White*, 37–79.

"participants and its audiences even when they were not made explicit." "Barbour, Urban League Official, Speaking In City," *Arizona Daily Star*, March 21, 1954, 2. For the racial dimensions of probation and parole in the 1930s and 1940s, see David Oshinsky, *Worse Than*

Slavery: Parchman Farm and the Ordeal of Jim Crow Justice (New York: The Free Press, 1996).

"caseloads under conditions of chronic institutional stress." Sullivan, *Days of Hope*, 44–78. Ira Katznelson, *When Affirmative Action Was White*, 37–79.

"carrying the most administrative burden and the most social stigma." Sullivan, *Days of Hope*, 78–115. For the CIO's organizing drives and their racial dimensions, see Robert H. Zieger, *The CIO, 1935–1955* (Chapel Hill: University of North Carolina Press, 1995), 83–138.

"seeing its operations from the caseworker's side of the desk." Katznelson, *When Affirmative Action Was White*, 113–141. For the FHA's discriminatory guidelines, see also Kenneth T. Jackson, *Crabgrass Frontier: The Suburbanization of the United States* (New York: Oxford University Press, 1985), 190–218.

"connection with medical institutions." For Charles Hamilton Houston's legal strategy and its development at Howard University Law School, see Genna Rae McNeil, *Groundwork: Charles Hamilton Houston and the Struggle for Civil Rights* (Philadelphia: University of Pennsylvania Press, 1983).

"Psychiatry gave him professional access to such understanding." Beth Tompkins Bates, *Pullman Porters and the Rise of Protest Politics in Black America, 1925–1945* (Chapel Hill: University of North Carolina Press, 2001), 1–30.

"outline." Scott H. Bennett, *Radical Pacifism: The War Resisters League and Gandhian Nonviolence in America, 1915–1963* (Syracuse, NY: Syracuse University Press, 2003), 80–130. James Tracy, *Direct Action: Radical Pacifism from the Union Eight to the Chicago Seven* (Chicago: University of Chicago Press, 1996), 1–30.

"rather than residential stability." Interview with Whitby, Neil, and Neil, September 17, 2025.

"as moral failures." 1940 U.S. Census, Philadelphia, Philadelphia County, Pennsylvania, s.v. "Miller Barbour," Ancestry.com.

"and the integrator had to be prepared to work with both versions." Sullivan, *Days of Hope*, 44–78.

"rights tool." Sullivan, *Days of Hope*, 78–115.

"designed to stabilize the agricultural economy." Katznelson, *When Affirmative Action Was White,* 37–79. For the AAA's treatment of sharecroppers, see Pete Daniel, *Breaking the Land: The Transformation of Cotton, Tobacco, and Rice Cultures since 1880* (Urbana: University of Illinois Press, 1985).

"to perpetuate substantive inequality." For the NRA's racial wage differentials, see Katznelson, *When Affirmative Action Was White,* 37–79.

"American cities through the remainder of the twentieth century." Kenneth T. Jackson, *Crabgrass Frontier: The Suburbanization of the United States* (New York: Oxford University Press, 1985), 190–218.

"equality." Donn Rogosin, *Invisible Men: Life in Baseball's Negro Leagues* (New York: Atheneum, 1983), 1–30.

"deploy." Ibid., 50–100. For the Negro Leagues' civic significance, see also ibid., 100–130.

"knowledge would systematically miss what the community actually needed." For the settlement house tradition and Jane Addams's Hull House, see Victoria Bissell Brown, *The Education of Jane Addams* (Philadelphia: University of Pennsylvania Press, 2004), 1–30. For the adaptation of settlement house methods to Black urban communities, see Elisabeth Lasch-Quinn, *Black Neighbors: Race and the Limits of Reform in the American Settlement House Movement, 1890–1945* (Chapel Hill: University of North Carolina Press, 1993).

"Black civic world." For Samuel Evans and the North Philadelphia Youth Movement, see *W. E. B. Du Bois, Race and the City: The Philadelphia Negro and Its Legacy*, ed. Michael B. Katz and Thomas J. Sugrue (Philadelphia: University of Pennsylvania Press, 1998), 156–160.

"without losing its intellectual integrity." David Levering Lewis, *W.E.B. Du Bois: Biography of a Race, 1868–1919* (New York: Henry Holt, 1993), 179–210. For the methodological significance of Du Bois's Philadelphia Negro, see also Elijah Anderson and Douglas S. Massey, eds., *Problem of the Century: Racial Stratification in the United States* (New York: Russell Sage Foundation, 2001).

"theological formation demanded of human rights work." Lewis, *W.E.B. Du Bois*, 179–210.

Chapter Five

"rights cause he served." Patrick S. Washburn, *A Question of Sedition: The Federal Government's Investigation of the Black Press during World War II* (New York: Oxford University Press, 1986), 1–30. For the Double V campaign specifically, see John Modell, Marc Goulden, and Sigurdur Magnusson, "World War II in the Lives of Black Americans: Some Findings and an Interpretation," *Journal of American History* 76, no. 3 (December 1989): 838–848.

"everything preceding it." Bates, Pullman Porters, 150–190. For Executive Order 8802 and the Fair Employment Practices Committee, see Merl E. Reed, *Seedtime for the Modern Civil Rights Movement: The President's Committee on Fair Employment Practice, 1941–1946* (Baton Rouge: Louisiana State University Press, 1991).

"inaction exceeded the political cost of action." For the Tuskegee Airmen and their civil rights significance, see J. Todd Moye, *Freedom Flyers: The Tuskegee Airmen of World War II* (New York: Oxford University Press, 2010).

"failed to issue the order." Bennett, *Radical Pacifism*, 100–130. Tracy, *Direct Action*, 1–30. Rachel Waltner Goossen, *Women against the Good War: Conscientious Objection and Gender on the American Home Front, 1941–1947* (Chapel Hill: University of North Carolina Press, 1997), 1–30.

"Employment Practices Committee to investigate complaints." "The Wharton Centre," accessed February 16, 2024, https://futureslab.community/story/wharton-centre. Benowitz, "Addressing Dignity Deferred," 16.

"advocacy shows clear evidence of having absorbed its lessons." W. E. B. Du Bois, *Race and the City: The Philadelphia Negro and Its Legacy, ed. Michael B. Katz and Thomas J. Sugrue* (Philadelphia: University of Pennsylvania Press, 1998), 156.

"nation without bearing arms." V. P. Franklin, "The Wharton Centre and the Juvenile Gang Problem in Philadelphia, 1945–1958," in *Du Bois, Race and the City*, 206.

"demanded." Ibid., 206–207.

"intellectual bridge between Barbour's two formative traditions." Ibid., 206–207. The philosophy of social work intervention underlying the Neighborhood Plan drew on the community organization theory being developed by Murray Ross and others during the same period; see Murray G. Ross, *Community Organization: Theory and Principles* (New York: Harper, 1955).

"himself embodied." Franklin, "Wharton Centre," 206–207. Interview with Whitby, Neil, and Neil, September 17, 2025.

"synthesis Barbour had embodied through his dual formation." "UL Official Dies in LA," *New Pittsburgh Courier*, March 30, 1957, 4. For the Pennsylvania School of Social Work and its curriculum during this period, see John H. Ehrenreich, *The Altruistic Imagination: A History of Social Work and Social Policy in the United States* (Ithaca, NY: Cornell University Press, 1985).

"action methodology in the early 1940s." For the founding of CORE and its organizational development, see August Meier and Elliott Rudwick, *CORE: A Study in the Civil Rights Movement, 1942–1968* (New York: Oxford University Press, 1973).

"than usual for the social services the growing population required." Howard Thurman, *Jesus and the Disinherited* (Nashville: Abingdon-Cokesbury Press, 1949), 1–40. For Thurman's place in the development of civil rights theology, see Luther E. Smith Jr., *Howard Thurman: The Mystic as Prophet* (Washington, DC: University Press of America, 1981).

"chronic overcrowding and inadequate maintenance produced." *Thurman, Jesus and the Disinherited*, 1–40. For the relationship between Thurman's theology and Martin Luther King Jr.'s civil rights thought, see David J. Garrow, *Bearing the Cross: Martin Luther King, Jr., and the*

Southern Christian Leadership Conference (New York: William Morrow, 1986), 43–45.

"tradition." For Thurman's 1936 visit with Gandhi and its significance, see Walter Earl Fluker and Catherine Tumber, eds., *A Strange Freedom: The Best of Howard Thurman on Religious Experience and Public Life* (Boston: Beacon Press, 1998), 1–30.

"form of rising expectation combined with continuing frustration." John D'Emilio, *Lost Prophet: The Life and Times of Bayard Rustin* (New York: The Free Press, 2003), 1–50.

"as rigidly segregated as before." Ibid., 50–100. For Rustin's organizational connections to CORE and the Fellowship of Reconciliation, see also Tracy, *Direct Action*, 1–30.

"resource of the community the Centre served." "Not Alms, but Opportunity," *Rocky Mountain News*, May 25, 1947, 35. Barbour, "Where We Stand on Racial Desegregation," 4.

"developed." Sitkoff, *A New Deal for Blacks*, 35–57. For the dimensions of wartime Black employment in defense industries, see also Karen Tucker Anderson, "Last Hired, First Fired: Black Women Workers during World War II," *Journal of American History* 69, no. 1 (June 1982): 82–97.

"toward confrontation." For the Pennsylvania School of Social Work's curriculum during this period, see Ehrenreich, *Altruistic Imagination*, 1–30. For community organization theory's development during the 1940s, see Murray G. Ross, *Community Organization: Theory and Principles* (New York: Harper, 1955).

"of people who understood they were in a contested space." For Denver's postwar growth, see the Mayor James Quigg Newton Jr. Papers, WH1327, Western History Collection, Denver Public Library. For the broader context of postwar western urban growth, see Carl Abbott, *The Metropolitan Frontier: Cities in the Modern American West* (Tucson: University of Arizona Press, 1993).

"had consequences." Jackson, *Crabgrass Frontier*, 190–218. For the application of FHA guidelines to Denver's residential development, see

Kristin Jones, "The Thread That Ties Segregation to Gentrification," *The Colorado Trust*, 2018.

"practice had provided." For the Five Points neighborhood and Denver's Black community during this period, see the research files of the Denver Public Library's Western History Collection.

"casework and group intervention could address only symptomatically." Keim and Stoltzfus, *Politics of Conscience*, 100–150. For the Brethren Service Committee's interracial work camps, see also Durnbaugh, *Fruit of the Vine*, 400–430.

"scholarship to the next." A. Brayman, "W. Miller Barbour, Executive Secretary Urban League, Denver, Aids Social Work," *The Etownian*, May 14, 1948.

"his years at Elizabethtown College." For the National Urban League's western expansion and the creation of the Western Field Office, see Weiss, *National Urban League*, 1–30. For the distinctive character of civil rights challenges in the American West, see Quintard Taylor, *In Search of the Racial Frontier: African Americans in the American West, 1528–1990* (New York: W. W. Norton, 1998).

"violence both traditions rejected." Taylor, *In Search of the Racial Frontier*, 1–30.

"accept the social consequences of insistence without retaliation." Barbour, "Breaking the Barriers," 8–9. For the Green Book and its civil rights significance, see Candacy Taylor, *Overground Railroad*, 1–30.

Chapter Six

"to use the power of the mayor's office to push it in this direction." Mayor James Quigg Newton Jr. Papers, WH1327, Western History Collection, Denver Public Library. Benowitz, "Addressing Dignity Deferred," 18. For Newton's political career and civic reform agenda, see also Dani R. Newsum, "Cold War Colorado: Civil Rights Liberals and the Movement for Legislative Equality" (MA thesis, University of Colorado, 2012), 15–30.

"progress could be made." Benowitz, "Addressing Dignity Deferred," 18–19.

"cost of the militancy the community's situation demanded." For the National Urban League's organizational history and methods, see Weiss, *National Urban League*, 1–30.

"audience would hear what was not said as clearly as what was." A. Brayman, "W. Miller Barbour, Executive Secretary Urban League, Denver, Aids Social Work," *The Etownian*, May 14, 1948.

"the diverse communities of a rapidly growing western city." Linda Gordon, *The Second Coming of the KKK: The Ku Klux Klan of the 1920s and the American Political Tradition* (New York: Liveright, 2015), 3–5, 72–76, 141–150. For Colorado Klan history specifically, see Robert Goldberg, *Hooded Empire: The Ku Klux Klan in Colorado* (Urbana: University of Illinois Press, 1981).

"the internationalist principles the postwar order had established." Kristin Jones, "The Thread That Ties Segregation to Gentrification," The Colorado Trust, 2018. For the FHA's racial covenants, see Jackson, *Crabgrass Frontier*, 190–218.

Newsum, "Cold War Colorado," 85–87.

"its racial reality." "Segregation Practices Spread Poverty," *Denver Post*, December 18, 1947.

Newsum, "Cold War Colorado," 60–75. For the broader history of FEPC campaigns at the state level during this period, see Herbert Hill, *Black Labor and the American Legal System: Race, Work, and the Law* (Washington, DC: Bureau of National Affairs, 1977).

"account here draws heavily on her research." Miller Barbour, "Speech Made at Luncheon of East Denver Business Men," Colorado Statesman, April 9, 1949.

"maintaining the racial segmentation of the labor market." Newsum, "Cold War Colorado," 71. For the intergroup relations movement and its relationship to civil rights liberalism, see Stuart Svonkin, *Jews against Prejudice: American Jews and the Fight for Civil Liberties* (New York: Columbia University Press, 1997).

"legislators in support of the fair employment bill." Ibid., 28.

"what form it would take." Barbour, Freed, and Peterson, "What Can Be Done on the Local Level," 1.

Ibid., 1–5.

"in practice to a gradualism ensuring equality's indefinite deferral." James Zeigler, *Red Scare Racism and Cold War Black Radicalism* (Jackson: University Press of Mississippi, 2023), 3–18. Mary L. Dudziak, *Cold War Civil Rights: Race and the Image of American Democracy* (Princeton, NJ: Princeton University Press, 2000), 1–30.

"not in five hundred years." Newsum, "Cold War Colorado," 151–152. For CORE's direct action tactics during this period, see Meier and Rudwick, CORE, 1–60.

"1949 Confab of Nat'l Urban League in Denver Sept. 4," *Omaha Star,* April 22, 1949, 1.

"projecting racial liberalism abroad." "Heads of New NUL Departments," *The Voice* 6, no. 25 (April 17, 1952).

"of its political volatility." For the racial geography of postwar Los Angeles, see Josh Sides, *L.A. City Limits: African American Los Angeles from the Great Depression to the Present* (Berkeley: University of California Press, 2003), 1–30. For the broader context of racial exclusion in western cities during the postwar period, see Quintard Taylor, *In Search of the Racial Frontier,* 1–30.

"invisible to those not directly experiencing it." Benowitz, "Addressing Dignity Deferred," 26–27.

"rights challenges the postwar period was bringing to a national scale." Shirley Ann Wilson Moore, *To Place Our Deeds: The African American Community in Richmond, California, 1910–1963* (Berkeley: University of California Press, 2000), 53.

"rights advocacy in Denver beyond his departure." Ibid., 53. For the Kaiser Shipyards and wartime Black labor migration to Richmond, see also Katherine Archibald, *Wartime Shipyard: A Study in Social Disunity* (Berkeley: University of California Press, 1947).

"Denver's racial history was demonstrably false." "Barbour, Urban League Official, Speaking in City," *Arizona Daily Star*, March 21, 1954, 2. Barbour, *A Study of Race Relations*, iv.

"together across the specific circumstances of their life." Barbour, *A Study of Race Relations*, 13.

"developing awareness of mass media's civil rights significance." Barbour, "Where We Stand on Racial Desegregation," 3–4.

"the narrative of Jewish-Black competition fully captures." Ibid., 3.

"analytically rigorous and morally urgent." Ibid., 7–8. For the broader context of Myrdal's influence, see Walter A. Jackson, *Gunnar Myrdal and America's Conscience: Social Engineering and Racial Liberalism, 1938–1987* (Chapel Hill: University of North Carolina Press, 1990).

"the human rights coalition into an official institutional voice." Newsum, "Cold War Colorado," 94. For the Denver Commission on Human Relations and its institutional development, see the Mayor James Quigg Newton Jr. Papers, WH1327, Western History Collection, Denver Public Library.

"rather than private preference." Newsum, "Cold War Colorado," 94–100.

Chapter Seven

"communities." For the racial geography of postwar Los Angeles, see Josh Sides, *L.A. City Limits*, 1–30. For the broader context of racial exclusion in western cities during the postwar period, see Quintard Taylor, *In Search of the Racial Frontier*.

"who brought their own racial attitudes with them." Benowitz, "Addressing Dignity Deferred," 26–27.

"explicit legal sanction." Shirley Ann Wilson Moore, *To Place Our Deeds: The African American Community in Richmond, California, 1910–1963* (Berkeley: University of California Press, 2000), 53.

"protecting white neighborhoods from equivalent development pressure." Ibid., 53. For the Kaiser Shipyards and wartime Black labor migration to Richmond, see also Katherine Archibald, *Wartime Ship-*

yard: A Study in Social Disunity (Berkeley: University of California Press, 1947).

"Migration's wartime acceleration." "Barbour, Urban League Official, Speaking in City," *Arizona Daily Star*, March 21, 1954, 2. Barbour, *A Study of Race Relations*, iv.

"form." Barbour, *A Study of Race Relations*, 13.

"provided." Ibid., 10–11.

"through which racial attitudes traveled and adapted." Barbour, "Where We Stand on Racial Desegregation," 3–4.

"The analysis began." Ibid., 3.

"between democratic profession and democratic performance." Ibid., 7–8.

"the integration process depended." Benowitz, "Addressing Dignity Deferred," 28–29. For Hollywood's role in the civil rights movement, see Emilie Raymond, *Stars for Freedom: Hollywood, Black Celebrities, and the Civil Rights Movement* (Seattle: University of Washington Press, 2015).

"rather than merely observers of each other." Barbour, "Where We Stand on Racial Desegregation," 7–8.

"process Barbour was working to advance." "W. Miller Barbour Stricken," *California Eagle*, February 21, 1957, 1.

"themes Barbour had been articulating since his Denver years." Ransby, *Ella Baker*, 1–25. Marable, *Race, Reform, and Rebellion*, 20–40. Taylor Branch, *Parting the Waters: America in the King Years, 1954–63* (New York: Simon and Schuster, 1988), 1–25.

Barbour, "Breaking the Barriers," 8. For the history of the Green Book and Black travel in the mid-twentieth century, see Candacy Taylor, *Overground Railroad*.

"W. Miller Barbour Stricken," *California Eagle*, February 21, 1957, 1.

"asserted its claims." "Funeral Services Held for Miller Barbour," *The Baltimore Afro-American*, March 30, 1957, 4. Interview with Whitby, Neil, and Neil, September 17, 2025. For O'Dessa J. Shipley, Ruth Johnson Barbour's sister, and her career as a pioneering African American civic activist in Philadelphia, see 'O'Dessa Shipley, 77, Civic

Activist,' *Philadelphia Inquirer,* May 24, 1994, 34. For Mount Lawn Cemetery Lincoln Memorial Park, established in 1925 to serve African American families excluded from racially segregated cemeteries in Delaware County, see the cemetery's institutional records.

"inclusion produced in the specific life of one of its graduates." Taylor Branch, *Parting the Waters,* 1–25. King enrolled at Crozer in September 1948; Walker arranged the Muste lecture in 1949, during King's first year of study.

Chapter Eight

"appointed him to lead it." Albert N. Keim and Grant M. Stoltzfus, *The Politics of Conscience: The Historic Peace Churches and America at War, 1917–1955* (Scottdale, PA: Herald Press, 1988), 1–30. Bennett, *Radical Pacifism,* 1–30. For the broader history of Anabaptist engagement with racial justice, see Perry Bush, *Two Kingdoms, Two Loyalties: Mennonite Pacifism in Modern America* (Baltimore: Johns Hopkins University Press, 1998).

"requires." Barbour, "Where We Stand on Racial Desegregation," 4.

"the movement's demands required both." Katznelson, *When Affirmative Action Was White, 113–163. For the impact of the Civil Rights Act of 1964 and the Fair Housing Act of 1968,* see Hugh Davis Graham, *The Civil Rights Era: Origins and Development of National Policy, 1960–1972* (New York: Oxford University Press, 1990).

"exploration." Barbour, "Where We Stand on Racial Desegregation," 3–4.

"of prior work." Payne, I've Got the Light of Freedom, 1–25. Ransby, *Ella Baker,* 1–25.

"beneath the structure." Hall, "Long Civil Rights Movement," 1233–1263.

"kind than the standard narratives have yet recovered." Robert Dallek, *Flawed Giant: Lyndon Johnson and His Times, 1961–1973* (New York: Oxford University Press, 1998), 112–230. Randall B. Woods, *LBJ: Architect of American Ambition* (New York: Free Press, 2006), 1–30.

"is the place of every person who built its foundations." Nick Kotz, *Judgment Days: Lyndon Baines Johnson, Martin Luther King Jr., and the Laws That Changed America* (Boston: Houghton Mifflin, 2005), 1–50. Graham, *Civil Rights Era*, 1–50.

Joseph A. Califano Jr., *The Triumph and Tragedy of Lyndon Johnson: The White House Years* (New York: Simon and Schuster, 1991), 55. Graham, *Civil Rights Era*, 150–200.

For the Philadelphia Tribune's role in the Black civil rights movement during the 1930s, see Patrick S. Washburn, *A Question of Sedition: The Federal Government's Investigation of the Black Press during World War II* (New York: Oxford University Press, 1986), 1–30. For E. Washington Rhodes's leadership of the Tribune, see also *Countryman, Up South*, 25–40.

For the settlement house tradition and Jane Addams's Hull House, see Victoria Bissell Brown, *The Education of Jane Addams* (Philadelphia: University of Pennsylvania Press, 2004), 1–30. For the adaptation of settlement house methods to Black urban communities, see Elisabeth Lasch-Quinn, *Black Neighbors: Race and the Limits of Reform in the American Settlement House Movement, 1890–1945* (Chapel Hill: University of North Carolina Press, 1993).

For Samuel Evans and the North Philadelphia Youth Movement, see Du Bois, *Race and the City*, 156–160.

Lewis, *W.E.B. Du Bois*, 179–210. For the methodological significance of Du Bois's Philadelphia Negro, see also Elijah Anderson and Douglas S. Massey, eds., *Problem of the Century: Racial Stratification in the United States* (New York: Russell Sage Foundation, 2001).

Lewis, *W.E.B. Du Bois*, 179–210.

For the Harlem Renaissance in its civic dimensions, see Lewis, *When Harlem Was in Vogue*, 1–30. For the character of New York's Black civic world in the early 1940s, see Marable, *Race, Reform, and Rebellion*, 1–20.

Howard Thurman, *Jesus and the Disinherited* (Nashville: Abingdon-Cokesbury Press, 1949), 1–40. For Thurman's place in the development of civil rights theology, see Luther E. Smith Jr., *Howard Thurman: The Mystic as Prophet* (Washington, DC: University Press of America, 1981).

Thurman, *Jesus and the Disinherited*, 1–40. For the relationship between Thurman's theology and Martin Luther King Jr.'s civil rights thought, see David J. Garrow, *Bearing the Cross: Martin Luther King, Jr., and the Southern Christian Leadership Conference* (New York: William Morrow, 1986), 43–45.

For Thurman's 1936 visit with Gandhi and its significance, see Walter Earl Fluker and Catherine Tumber, eds., *A Strange Freedom: The Best of Howard Thurman on Religious Experience and Public Life* (Boston: Beacon Press, 1998), 1–30.

John D'Emilio, *Lost Prophet: The Life and Times of Bayard Rustin* (New York: The Free Press, 2003), 1–50.

Ibid., 50–100. For Rustin's organizational connections to CORE and the Fellowship of Reconciliation, see also Tracy, *Direct Action*, 1–30.

"Not Alms, but Opportunity," *Rocky Mountain News*, May 25, 1947, 35.

Barbour, "Where We Stand on Racial Desegregation," 4.

Sitkoff, *A New Deal for Blacks*, 35–57. For the dimensions of wartime Black employment in defense industries, see also Karen Tucker Anderson, "Last Hired, First Fired: Black Women Workers during World War II," *Journal of American History* 69, no. 1 (June 1982): 82–97.

For the Pennsylvania School of Social Work's curriculum during this period, see Ehrenreich, *Altruistic Imagination*, 1–30.

For Denver's postwar growth, see the Mayor James Quigg Newton Jr. Papers, WH1327, Western History Collection, Denver Public Library.

Jackson, Crabgrass Frontier, 190–218.

For the Five Points neighborhood and Denver's Black community during this period, see the research files of the Denver Public Library's Western History Collection.

Keim and Stoltzfus, *Politics of Conscience*, 100–150. For the Brethren Service Committee's interracial work camps, see also Durnbaugh, *Fruit of the Vine*, 400–430.

Brayman, "W. Miller Barbour, Executive Secretary Urban League, Denver, Aids Social Work," *The Etownian*, May 14, 1948.

For the National Urban League's western expansion and the creation of the Western Field Office, see Weiss, *National Urban League,* 1–30.

Taylor, *In Search of the Racial Frontier,* 1–30.

Barbour, "Breaking the Barriers," 8–9.

Taylor, *Overground Railroad,* 1–30. For the Green Book and its civil rights significance, see also Gretchen Sorin, *Driving While Black: African American Travel and the Road to Civil Rights* (New York: Liveright, 2020).

For the character of Powhatan County's post-Reconstruction racial economy, see Litwack, *Trouble in Mind,* 1–60.

Royce, *Origins of Southern Sharecropping,* 1–30.

Litwack, *Trouble in Mind,* 1–60.

Wilkerson, *Warmth of Other Suns,* 9–15. Joe William Trotter Jr., ed., *The Great Migration in Historical Perspective,* 1–30.

For the Pennsylvania Railroad's labor recruitment in the South during the Great Migration years, see Trotter, *Great Migration in Historical Perspective,* 1–30.

"Black History in Middletown," Middletown Area Historical Society, 4–5. Interview with Whitby, Neil, and Neil, September 17, 2025.

"Middletown Notes," *Harrisburg Telegraph,* February 21, 1927, 6. Ebenezer African Methodist Episcopal Church, Middletown, membership rolls, 1920s.

Loewen, *Sundown Towns,* 3–30.

Campbell, *Songs of Zion,* 14–32. For the Philadelphia Conference of the AME, see Dickerson, *Religion, Race, and Region,* 1–20.

Minutes of the Philadelphia Annual Conference of the African Methodist Episcopal Church, 1920–1939.

"Middletown Notes," *Harrisburg Telegraph,* February 21, 1927, 6.

Dickerson, *Religion, Race, and Region*, 1–20. For the AME's organizational structure as a framework for civic leadership development, see also Campbell, *Songs of Zion*, 100–130.

1920 U.S. Census, Plymouth, Montgomery County, Pennsylvania, s.v. "William Barbour," Ancestry.com. "Marriage License," *The Evening News*, January 28, 1920.

1932 *Etonian*, Elizabethtown College Archives.

Bodnar, "Peter C. Blackwell and the Negro Community of Steelton," 199–200.

1930 *Etonian Yearbook*, Elizabethtown College, 52. 1933 *Etonian Yearbook*, 48.

For the structural obstacles facing Black students in northern public schools during the 1920s, see Anderson, *Education of Blacks in the South*, 1–32.

1932 Etonian, Elizabethtown College Archives. Benowitz, "Addressing Dignity Deferred," 10.

"Middletown Notes," *Harrisburg Telegraph*, February 21, 1927, 6.

Jean-Paul Benowitz, *Elizabethtown Pennsylvania, Images of America Series* (Charleston, SC: Arcadia Publishing, 2015), 7–10. For the founding of Elizabethtown Borough and the subsequent development of the borough through the Brethren migration of 1868, see also Benowitz and DePuydt, Elizabethtown College, 7–15. For the Peace Church opposition to military industrial development in Elizabethtown in 1942 and 1951, see Keim and Stoltzfus, *Politics of Conscience*, 150–200.

For the character of Lancaster County's Brethren and Reformed communities in the late nineteenth and early twentieth centuries, see Durnbaugh, *Brethren in Colonial America*, 1–30.

Loewen, Sundown Towns, 3–30. For Lancaster County's racial geography specifically, see Huesken, "'The Brutal Thirteen,'" 1–25.

Bowman, Brethren Society, 1–25. For the Brethren's navigation of modernity's institutional demands, see also Durnbaugh, *Fruit of the Vine*, 300–350.

Benowitz and Nolt, "Plain Dress in the Docket," 1–30.

Durnbaugh, *Fruit of the Vine*, 3–30. For the Brethren's founding of colleges as an expression of theological engagement with modernity, see also Bowman, *Brethren Society*, 50–80.

Schlosser, *History of Elizabethtown College*, 140–145. Benowitz, "Make Jesus King," 5–8.

Ibid., 140–141. For the intercollegiate debate circuit in the period, see also the Forensic Arts Club records in the Elizabethtown College Archives.

Schlosser, History of Elizabethtown College, 125. The Class of 1949 identified this passage as emblematic of Schlosser's teaching philosophy. Benowitz, interview with Hostetter, July 14, 2025.

Ralph W. Schlosser, quoted in Schlosser, *History of Elizabethtown College.*

Schlosser, *History of Elizabethtown College.* The Browning lines are from "Andrea del Sarto," in Robert Browning, *Men and Women* (London: Chapman and Hall, 1855).

"Elizabethtown College Commencement June 6," *Lancaster New Era,* May 24, 1932, 14.

For Charles Coates Walker, Class of 1941, and his role in the American civil rights and peace movements, see Nat Hentoff, *Peace Agitator: The Story of A. J. Muste* (New York: Macmillan, 1963), 1–30. For Walker's arrangement of A. J. Muste's lecture at Crozer Theological Seminary and Martin Luther King Jr.'s account of its significance, see Taylor Branch, *Parting the Waters*, 82–85.

Benowitz, "Make Jesus King," 8–12. On Martha Martin's teaching career and the Bible Terms and Bible Institutes, see Schlosser, *History of Elizabethtown College*, 133–135.

Ibid. For the Brethren hermeneutical tradition and its approach to biblical interpretation, see Dale W. Brown, *Understanding Pietism* (Grand Rapids, MI: Eerdmans, 1978), 1–30.

Schlosser, *History of Elizabethtown College*, 121–126. Benowitz, interview with Hostetter, July 14, 2025.

Ibid. For the Brethren revival tradition, see Durnbaugh, *Fruit of the Vine*, 300–340.

Newsum, "Cold War Colorado," 94. For the Denver Commission on Human Relations and its institutional development, see the Mayor James Quigg Newton Jr. Papers, WH1327, Western History Collection, Denver Public Library.

Newsum, "Cold War Colorado," 94–100.

Brayman, "W. Miller Barbour, Executive Secretary Urban League, Denver, Aids Social Work," *The Etownian*, May 14, 1948. For Carter G. Woodson's contributions to African American history, see Jacqueline Goggin, *Carter G. Woodson: A Life in Black History* (Baton Rouge: Louisiana State University Press, 1993).

BIBLIOGRAPHY

1. Manuscript Collections and Archival Sources

1932 Etonian Yearbook. Earl H. and Anita F. Hess Archives and Special Collections, Elizabethtown College, Elizabethtown, Pennsylvania.

Barbour, W. Miller. *A Study of Race Relations: A Preliminary Evaluation of Racial Minority Conditions in Tucson, Arizona and of the Tucson Urban League Service Council.* Unpublished report, Tucson, 1954.

Barbour, W. Miller, Michael L. Freed, and Helen L. Peterson. "What Can Be Done on the Local Level: An Informational Paper." World Affairs Institute, University of Denver, August 1951.

Ebenezer African Methodist Episcopal Church, Middletown, Pennsylvania. Membership rolls and quarterly conference minutes, 1920s–1930s.

Elizabethtown College Archives. Office of the President Correspondence. EC III C.4, Box 2, Folder 9, "Correspondence of Ira Herr, 1928–1988." Elizabethtown, Pennsylvania.

Mayor James Quigg Newton Jr. Papers. WH1327. Western History Collection, Denver Public Library, Denver, Colorado.

Minutes of the Philadelphia Annual Conference of the African Methodist Episcopal Church, 1920–1939. Listings for Ebenezer AME Church, Middletown, Pennsylvania.

Theatrical Production Program Leaflet, Senior Class Production of Othello, 1932. Earl H. and Anita F. Hess Archives and Special Collections, Elizabethtown College, Elizabethtown, Pennsylvania.

2. Newspapers and Periodicals

Adult Leadership (New York)

Arizona Daily Star (Tucson)

Baltimore Afro-American

California Eagle (Los Angeles)

Colorado Statesman (Denver)

Denver Post
Elizabethtown Etownian
Frontier (Los Angeles)
Harrisburg Evening News
Harrisburg Telegraph
Lancaster New Era
New Pittsburgh Courier
Omaha Star
Our College Times (Elizabethtown)
Philadelphia Inquirer
PennLive Patriot-News (Harrisburg)
Rocky Mountain News (Denver)
The Voice (Philadelphia)
Tucson Citizen

3. Published Primary Sources
Barbour, W. Miller. "Breaking the Barriers: Anti-Negro Prejudice Lessens in Western Hotels." *Frontier* 6, no. 11 (November 1954): 8–9.
Barbour, W. Miller. "Where We Stand on Racial Desegregation: What Forces Are Aiding Racial Desegregation in the United States? What Forces Are Holding It Back?" *Adult Leadership* 5 (April 1957): 1–9.
Bender, Harold S. "The Anabaptist Vision." *Church History* 13, no. 1 (March 1944): 3–24. Reprinted in *Mennonite Quarterly Review* 18, no. 2 (April 1944): 67–88.
Schlosser, Ralph W. *History of Elizabethtown College: 1899–1970.* Elizabethtown, PA: Elizabethtown College, 1971.
Strikwerda, Carl J. 'Pioneer for Social Justice.' E-Moment presidential communication, Elizabethtown College, January 21, 2019. https://www.etown.edu/offices/president/e-moments/ 2019-01-21-pioneer-for-social-justice.
Truman, Harry S. Executive Order No. 9980: Establishing the Fair Employment Board. Federal Register 13, no. 147 (July 30, 1948): 4311–4313.

4. Secondary Sources: Books

Anderson, James D. *The Education of Blacks in the South, 1860–1935.* Chapel Hill: University of North Carolina Press, 1988.

Archibald, Katherine. *Wartime Shipyard: A Study in Social Disunity.* Berkeley: University of California Press, 1947.

Bates, Beth Tompkins. *Pullman Porters and the Rise of Protest Politics in Black America, 1925–1945.* Chapel Hill: University of North Carolina Press, 2001.

Bennett, Scott H. *Radical Pacifism: The War Resisters League and Gandhian Nonviolence in America, 1915–1963.* Syracuse, NY: Syracuse University Press, 2003.

Benowitz, Jean-Paul. "The Brethren Heritage of Elizabethtown College: Founding Ideals, Institutional Identity, and the Persistence of Anabaptist-Pietist Values in Higher Education." Lecture, Elizabethtown College, developed over thirty years of teaching.

Benowitz, Jean-Paul. "'Make Jesus King': The Golden Era of Elizabethtown College and the Formation of Anabaptist-Pietist Leaders for Peace and Justice, 1920–1945." Lecture, Elizabethtown College, developed over thirty years of teaching.

Benowitz, Jean-Paul. "Prophetic Dissent and the Politics of Liberation: Theological Convergences Between the Church of the Brethren and the African Methodist Episcopal Church." Lecture, Elizabethtown College, developed over thirty years of teaching.

Benowitz, Jean-Paul, and Peter J. DePuydt. *Elizabethtown College.* Charleston, SC: Arcadia Publishing, 2014.

Bowman, Carl F. *Brethren Society: The Transformation of a "Peculiar People."* Baltimore: Johns Hopkins University Press, 1995.

Branch, Taylor. *Parting the Waters: America in the King Years, 1954–63.* New York: Simon and Schuster, 1988.

Brann, Eva. *Paradoxes of Education in a Republic.* Chicago: University of Chicago Press, 1979.

Bush, Perry. *Two Kingdoms, Two Loyalties: Mennonite Pacifism in Modern America.* Baltimore: Johns Hopkins University Press, 1998.

Campbell, James T. *Songs of Zion: The African Methodist Episcopal Church in the United States and South Africa.* New York: Oxford University Press, 1995.

Cha-Jua, Sundiata Keita, and Clarence Lang. "The 'Long Movement' as Vampire: Temporal and Spatial Fallacies in Recent Black Freedom Studies." *Journal of African American History* 92, no. 2 (Spring 2007): 265–288.

Cone, James H. *God of the Oppressed.* New York: Seabury Press, 1975.

Cone, James H. *The Spirituals and the Blues: An Interpretation.* New York: Seabury Press, 1972.

Countryman, Matthew J. *Up South: Civil Rights and Black Power in Philadelphia.* Philadelphia: University of Pennsylvania Press, 2006.

Dickerson, Dennis C. *Religion, Race, and Region: Research Notes on AME Church History.* Nashville: AME Sunday School Union, 1995.

Du Bois, W. E. B. *Race and the City: The Philadelphia Negro and Its Legacy.* Edited by Michael B. Katz and Thomas J. Sugrue. Philadelphia: University of Pennsylvania Press, 1998.

Du Bois, W. E. B. *The Souls of Black Folk.* Chicago: A. C. McClurg, 1903.

Dudziak, Mary L. *Cold War Civil Rights: Race and the Image of American Democracy.* Princeton, NJ: Princeton University Press, 2000.

Durnbaugh, Donald F. *Fruit of the Vine: A History of the Brethren, 1708–1995.* Elgin, IL: Brethren Press, 1997.

Ehrenreich, John H. *The Altruistic Imagination: A History of Social Work and Social Policy in the United States.* Ithaca, NY: Cornell University Press, 1985.

Fairclough, Adam. A Class of Their Own: Black Teachers in the Segregated South. Cambridge, MA: Harvard University Press, 2007.

Fairclough, Adam. *Race and Democracy: The Civil Rights Struggle in Louisiana, 1915–1972.* Athens: University of Georgia Press, 1995.

Garrow, David J. *Bearing the Cross: Martin Luther King, Jr., and the Southern Christian Leadership Conference.* New York: William Morrow, 1986.

Gilmore, Glenda. *Defying Dixie: The Radical Roots of Civil Rights, 1919–1950*. New York: W. W. Norton, 2008.

Goldberg, Robert. *Hooded Empire: The Ku Klux Klan in Colorado*. Urbana: University of Illinois Press, 1981.

Goossen, Rachel Waltner. *Women against the Good War: Conscientious Objection and Gender on the American Home Front, 1941–1947*. Chapel Hill: University of North Carolina Press, 1997.

Gordon, Linda. *Pitied but Not Entitled: Single Mothers and the History of Welfare*. New York: The Free Press, 1994.

Gordon, Linda. *The Second Coming of the KKK: The Ku Klux Klan of the 1920s and the American Political Tradition*. New York: Liveright, 2015.

Graham, Hugh Davis. *The Civil Rights Era: Origins and Development of National Policy, 1960–1972*. New York: Oxford University Press, 1990.

Califano, Joseph A., Jr. *The Triumph and Tragedy of Lyndon Johnson: The White House Years*. New York: Simon and Schuster, 1991.

Dallek, Robert. *Flawed Giant: Lyndon Johnson and His Times, 1961–1973*. New York: Oxford University Press, 1998.

Dallek, Robert. *Lone Star Rising: Lyndon Johnson and His Times, 1908–1960*. New York: Oxford University Press, 1991.

Kotz, Nick. *Judgment Days: Lyndon Baines Johnson, Martin Luther King Jr., and the Laws That Changed America*. Boston: Houghton Mifflin, 2005.

Woods, Randall B. *LBJ: Architect of American Ambition*. New York: Free Press, 2006.

Harris, Fredrick. *Something Within: Religion in African-American Political Activism*. New York: Oxford University Press, 1999.

Higginbotham, Evelyn Brooks. *Righteous Discontent: The Women's Movement in the Black Baptist Church, 1880–1920*. Cambridge, MA: Harvard University Press, 1993.

Hill, Herbert. *Black Labor and the American Legal System: Race, Work, and the Law*. Washington, DC: Bureau of National Affairs, 1977.

Hughes, Langston. *The Big Sea*. New York: Alfred A. Knopf, 1940.

Jackson, Kenneth T. *Crabgrass Frontier: The Suburbanization of the United States*. New York: Oxford University Press, 1985.

Katznelson, Ira. *When Affirmative Action Was White: An Untold History of Racial Inequality in Twentieth-Century America.* New York: W. W. Norton, 2005.

Keim, Albert N. *Harold S. Bender, 1897–1962.* Scottdale, PA: Herald Press, 1998.

Keim, Albert N., and Grant M. Stoltzfus. *The Politics of Conscience: The Historic Peace Churches and America at War, 1917–1955.* Scottdale, PA: Herald Press, 1988.

Bowman, Carl F. *Brethren Society: The Cultural Transformation of a Peculiar People.* Baltimore: Johns Hopkins University Press, 1995.

Hamm, Thomas D. *The Quakers in America.* New York: Columbia University Press, 2003.

Kraybill, Donald B. *The Riddle of Amish Culture.* Rev. ed. Baltimore: Johns Hopkins University Press, 2001.

Kraybill, Donald B., and Carl F. Bowman. *On the Backroad to Heaven: Old Order Hutterites, Mennonites, Amish, and Brethren.* Baltimore: Johns Hopkins University Press, 2001.

Woolman, John. *The Journal of John Woolman and A Plea for the Poor.* Secaucus, NJ: Citadel Press, 1972.

Yoder, John Howard, ed. and trans. *The Schleitheim Confession.* Scottdale, PA: Herald Press, 1977.

Lewis, David Levering. *W.E.B. Du Bois: Biography of a Race, 1868–1919.* New York: Henry Holt, 1993.

Lewis, David Levering. *When Harlem Was in Vogue.* New York: Alfred A. Knopf, 1981.

Lincoln, C. Eric, and Lawrence H. Mamiya. *The Black Church in the African American Experience.* Durham, NC: Duke University Press, 1990.

Litwack, Leon. *Trouble in Mind: Black Southerners in the Age of Jim Crow.* New York: Alfred A. Knopf, 1998.

Loewen, James W. *Sundown Towns: A Hidden Dimension of American Racism.* New York: The New Press, 2005.

Marable, Manning. *Race, Reform, and Rebellion: The Second Reconstruction in Black America, 1945–1990*. 2nd ed. Jackson: University Press of Mississippi, 1991.

McNeil, Genna Rae. *Groundwork: Charles Hamilton Houston and the Struggle for Civil Rights*. Philadelphia: University of Pennsylvania Press, 1983.

Meier, August, and Elliott Rudwick. *CORE: A Study in the Civil Rights Movement, 1942–1968*. New York: Oxford University Press, 1973.

Moore, Shirley Ann Wilson. *To Place Our Deeds: The African American Community in Richmond, California, 1910–1963*. Berkeley: University of California Press, 2000.

Moreno, Paul D. *Black Americans and Organized Labor: A New History*. Baton Rouge: Louisiana State University Press, 2006.

Moye, J. Todd. *Freedom Flyers: The Tuskegee Airmen of World War II*. New York: Oxford University Press, 2010.

Myrdal, Gunnar. *An American Dilemma: The Negro Problem and Modern Democracy*. New York: Harper and Brothers, 1944.

Newman, Richard S. *Freedom's Prophet: Bishop Richard Allen, the AME Church, and the Black Founding Fathers*. New York: New York University Press, 2008.

Nolt, Steven M. The Brethren Heritage of Elizabethtown College. Rev. 3rd ed. Elizabethtown, PA: Elizabethtown College, 2024.

Oshinsky, David. *Worse Than Slavery: Parchman Farm and the Ordeal of Jim Crow Justice*. New York: The Free Press, 1996.

Payne, Charles M. *I've Got the Light of Freedom: The Organizing Tradition and the Mississippi Freedom Struggle*. Berkeley: University of California Press, 1995.

Raboteau, Albert J. Canaan Land: A Religious History of African Americans. New York: Oxford University Press, 1999.

Raboteau, Albert J. *Slave Religion: The "Invisible Institution" in the Antebellum South*. New York: Oxford University Press, 1978.

Ransby, Barbara. *Ella Baker and the Black Freedom Movement: A Radical Democratic Vision*. Chapel Hill: University of North Carolina Press, 2003.

Raymond, Emilie. *Stars for Freedom: Hollywood, Black Celebrities, and the Civil Rights Movement.* Seattle: University of Washington Press, 2015.

Reed, Merl E. *Seedtime for the Modern Civil Rights Movement: The President's Committee on Fair Employment Practice, 1941–1946.* Baton Rouge: Louisiana State University Press, 1991.

Rogosin, Donn. *Invisible Men: Life in Baseball's Negro Leagues.* New York: Atheneum, 1983.

Royce, Edward. *The Origins of Southern Sharecropping.* Philadelphia: Temple University Press, 1993.

Sides, Josh. *L.A. City Limits: African American Los Angeles from the Great Depression to the Present.* Berkeley: University of California Press, 2003.

Sitkoff, Harvard. *A New Deal for Blacks: The Emergence of Civil Rights as a National Issue.* New York: Oxford University Press, 1978.

Sugrue, Thomas J. *The Origins of the Urban Crisis: Race and Inequality in Postwar Detroit.* Princeton, NJ: Princeton University Press, 1996.

Sugrue, Thomas J. *Sweet Land of Liberty: The Forgotten Struggle for Civil Rights in the North.* New York: Random House, 2008.

Branch, Taylor. *Parting the Waters: America in the King Years, 1954–1963.* New York: Simon and Schuster, 1988.

Hentoff, Nat. *Peace Agitator: The Story of A. J. Muste.* New York: Macmillan, 1963.

Tracy, James. *Direct Action: Radical Pacifism from the Union Eight to the Chicago Seven.* Chicago: University of Chicago Press, 1996.

Walker, Charles C. *A World Peace Guard: An Unarmed Corps for Constructive Action.* Hyderabad, India: Navajivan Karyalaya, 1981.

Sullivan, Patricia. *Days of Hope: Race and Democracy in the New Deal Era.* Chapel Hill: University of North Carolina Press, 1996.

Sullivan, Patricia. *Lift Every Voice: The NAACP and the Making of the Civil Rights Movement.* New York: New Press, 2009.

Svonkin, Stuart. *Jews against Prejudice: American Jews and the Fight for Civil Liberties.* New York: Columbia University Press, 1997.

Taylor, Candacy. *Overground Railroad: The Green Book and the Roots of Black Travel in America*. New York: Abrams Press, 2020.

Taylor, Quintard. *In Search of the Racial Frontier: African Americans in the American West, 1528–1990*. New York: W. W. Norton, 1998.

Trotter, Joe William, Jr., ed. *The Great Migration in Historical Perspective: New Dimensions of Race, Class, and Gender*. Bloomington: Indiana University Press, 1991.

Tyson, Timothy B. *Radio Free Dixie: Robert F. Williams and the Roots of Black Power*. Chapel Hill: University of North Carolina Press, 1999.

Washburn, Patrick S. *A Question of Sedition: The Federal Government's Investigation of the Black Press during World War II*. New York: Oxford University Press, 1986.

Weaver, J. Denny. *Becoming Anabaptist: The Origin and Significance of Sixteenth-Century Anabaptism*. Scottdale, PA: Herald Press, 1987.

Weiss, Nancy J. *The National Urban League, 1910–1940*. New York: Oxford University Press, 1974.

Wilkerson, Isabel. *The Warmth of Other Suns: The Epic Story of America's Great Migration*. New York: Random House, 2010.

Williams, George Hunston. *The Radical Reformation*. 3rd ed. Kirksville, MO: Sixteenth Century Journal Publishers, 1992.

Wolters, Raymond. *The New Negro on Campus: Black College Rebellions of the 1920s*. Princeton, NJ: Princeton University Press, 1975.

Wood, Amy Louise. *Lynching and Spectacle: Witnessing Racial Violence in America, 1890–1940*. Chapel Hill: University of North Carolina Press, 2009.

Woodward, C. Vann. *The Strange Career of Jim Crow*. 3rd rev. ed. New York: Oxford University Press, 1974.

Zangrando, Robert L. *The NAACP Crusade against Lynching, 1909–1950*. Philadelphia: Temple University Press, 1980.

Zeigler, James. *Red Scare Racism and Cold War Black Radicalism*. Jackson: University Press of Mississippi, 2023.

Zieger, Robert H. *The CIO, 1935–1955*. Chapel Hill: University of North Carolina Press, 1995.

5. Secondary Sources: Articles and Book Chapters

Benowitz, Jean-Paul. "Addressing Dignity Deferred: Post Desegregation and the Process of Integration: The Life and Legacy of Race Relations Leader W. Miller Barbour (1908–1957), Elizabethtown College Class of 1932." *Journal of the Lancaster County Historical Society* (forthcoming, December 2026).

Benowitz, Jean-Paul. "Work and Hope." *In Voices of Vocation: Stories of Purposeful Life Work in Teaching, Mentoring, and Leading,* edited by Tracy Wenger Sadd, 27–52. Elizabethtown, PA: Elizabethtown College, 2017.

Benowitz, Jean-Paul, and Steven M. Nolt. "Plain Dress in the Docket: Lillian Risser, the Pennsylvania Garb Law, and the Free Exercise of Anabaptist Religion, 1908–1910." *Pennsylvania History: A Journal of Mid-Atlantic Studies* 88, no. 3 (2021): 1–30.

Benowitz, Jean-Paul. 'The Dissatisfied Ones: Change and Adaptation Within the Old Order Mennonite Church of Virginia, 1901–1991.' Senior thesis, Eastern Mennonite University, 1991.

Benowitz, Jean-Paul. 'Community and Conflict: The Structuring of the Old Order Mennonite Church in Virginia.' Master's thesis, Millersville University of Pennsylvania, 1993.

Benowitz, Jean-Paul. "Elizabethtown Store Was Longtime Regional Leader in Clothing for Plain-Dress Religions." *Elizabethtown Advocate* 8, no. 2 (January 12, 2017).

Benowitz, Jean-Paul. "Maintaining Mennonite Identity: The Old Order Mennonite Church in Pennsylvania and Virginia." *Pennsylvania Folklife* 46 (Winter 1997): 71–82.

Benowitz, Jean-Paul. "Mennonites of Pennsylvania: A House Divided." *Pennsylvania Folklife* 46 (Autumn 1996): 2–19.

Benowitz, Jean-Paul. "One Hundred Years of Old Order Mennonite Church Community." *Mennonite Historical Bulletin* 64 (October 1993): 8–11.

Benowitz, Jean-Paul. "The Old Order Mennonite Division of 1893: An Interpretation." *Pennsylvania Mennonite Heritage* 16 (October 1993): 14–17.

Benowitz, Jean-Paul. *Review of The Original Joe Wenger: The Life Story of Bishop Joseph O. Wenger, 1868–1956,* by Elvin S. Eberly. *Journal of Plain Anabaptist Communities* 5, no. 1 (2024): 96–98.

Bodnar, John E. "Peter C. Blackwell and the Negro Community of Steelton, 1880–1920." *Pennsylvania Magazine of History and Biography* 97, no. 2 (April 1973): 199–209.

Franklin, V. P. "The Wharton Centre and the Juvenile Gang Problem in Philadelphia, 1945–1958." In W. E. B. Du Bois, *Race and the City: The Philadelphia Negro and Its Legacy,* edited by Michael B. Katz and Thomas J. Sugrue, 200–215. Philadelphia: University of Pennsylvania Press, 1998.

Hall, Jacquelyn Dowd. "The Long Civil Rights Movement and the Political Uses of the Past." *Journal of American History* 91, no. 4 (March 2005): 1233–1263.

Huesken, Gerald, Jr. "'The Brutal Thirteen': Elizabethtown College's Lone Season of Collegiate Football and How It Made History in Lancaster County, Pennsylvania." *Journal of Plain Anabaptist Communities* 1, no. 1 (2019): 1–25.

Lawson, Steven F. "Long Origins of the Short Civil Rights Movement, 1954–1968." *In Freedom Rights: New Perspectives on the Civil Rights Movement,* edited by Danielle L. McGuire and John Dittmer, 9–37. Lexington: University Press of Kentucky, 2011.

Modell, John, Marc Goulden, and Sigurdur Magnusson. "World War II in the Lives of Black Americans: Some Findings and an Interpretation." *Journal of American History* 76, no. 3 (December 1989): 838–848.

6. Theses and Dissertations

Lightbourne, Andrea Juliette. "Shining Through the Clouds: An Historical Case Study of Dunbar, a Segregated School in Tucson, Arizona." PhD diss., University of Arizona, 2004.

Newsum, Dani R. "Cold War Colorado: Civil Rights Liberals and the Movement for Legislative Equality." MA thesis, University of Colorado, 2012.

ABOUT THE AUTHOR

Jean-Paul Benowitz is the Director of Public Heritage Studies in the School of Arts and Humanities at Elizabethtown College in Elizabethtown, Pennsylvania, where he has served on the faculty since 1993 teaching in the Departments of History and Religious Studies. He holds a Bachelor of Science in History from Eastern Mennonite University and a Master of Arts in History from Millersville University of Pennsylvania. He completed doctoral studies at Temple University, where his dissertation, *James Wadsworth Symington: The Best Man*, examined the political career of United States Congressman James Wadsworth Symington in the Eisenhower, Kennedy, and Johnson administrations.

His scholarly work spans three interconnected fields: the history of the Church of the Brethren and the Anabaptist-Pietist tradition; the political history of the United States in the twentieth century, with particular emphasis on the civil rights movement and presidential politics; and the theory and practice of place-based and community-engaged learning in higher education. He served as Scholar in Residence at the Young Center for Anabaptist and Pietist Studies at Elizabethtown College, during which time he produced several scholarly works on Pennsylvania Dutch culture and the Historic Peace Churches of the mid-Atlantic region.

The scholarly authority which this biography brings to its account of plain dress, the Anabaptist believer's church tradition, and the plain people of Lancaster County rests on a body of published work Benowitz has developed across more than thirty years. His engagement with Old Order Mennonite history began at Eastern Mennonite University, where his 1991 undergraduate senior thesis, "The 'Dissatisfied Ones:' Change and Adaptation Within the Old Order Mennonite Church of Virginia, 1901–1991," examined the Old Order

Mennonite Church of Virginia. His 1993 master's thesis at Millersville University of Pennsylvania, "Community and Conflict: The Structuring of the Old Order Mennonite Church in Virginia," reconstructed the structuring of the Old Order Mennonite Church in Pennsylvania and Virginia. In the same year, 1993, he published two peer-reviewed articles: "One Hundred Years of Old Order Mennonite Church Community" in the *Mennonite Historical Bulletin* and "The Old Order Mennonite Division of 1893: An Interpretation" in *Pennsylvania Mennonite Heritage,* establishing the scholarly record of Old Order Mennonite institutional history on which the biography's theological passages draw. In 1996 and 1997 he published two articles in *Pennsylvania Folklife*: "Mennonites of Pennsylvania: A House Divided" and "Maintaining Mennonite Identity: The Old Order Mennonite Church in Pennsylvania and Virginia," both of which documented the specific Lancaster County and Virginia plain church communities whose theological commitments the biography's plain dress section explains. In 2024, he published a book review essay on Elvin S. Eberly's *The Original Joe Wenger: The Life Story of Bishop Joseph O. Wenger, 1868–1956* in the *Journal of Plain Anabaptist Communities.* These works, taken together with the definitive account of the Pennsylvania Garb Law co-authored with Steven M. Nolt, "Plain Dress in the Docket: Lillian Risser, the Pennsylvania Garb Law, and the Free Exercise of Anabaptist Religion, 1908–1910," published in *Pennsylvania History: A Journal of Mid-Atlantic Studies* in 2022, establish Benowitz as a recognized scholarly authority on Old Order Mennonite history of the mid-Atlantic region, the tradition at the institutional and theological heart of Elizabethtown College and of this biography.

His authority on this subject is not only academic. His maternal and paternal grandparents were Lancaster Conference Mennonites. His parents grew up in the Lancaster Conference wearing plain clothes in their childhood and youth. His extended family has included Mennonites, Amish, and Church of the Brethren members who have at various points in their spiritual formation dressed plain in accordance with their membership in Anabaptist communities.

The plain church world this biography describes is not, for its author, a subject encountered only in archives. It is a world he grew up adjacent to and observed in his own family across decades of ordinary life. Both sides of his family were involved in Mennonite church planting in urban settings, in New York City and in Philadelphia, where the challenge of dressing plain in secular, urbane environments was lived rather than theorized. The family stories shared with the author about this urban visibility gave him an understanding of what the Pennsylvania Garb Law was actually removing when it prohibited religious dress in public institutional spaces. It was not removing a garment. It was requiring the concealment of a covenant. This understanding is woven into the biography's plain dress section, and it could not have come from the archives alone.

His other publications include *Elizabethtown College*, co-authored with Peter J. DePuydt and published in the Arcadia Publishing Campus History Series in 2014, a pictorial history of the institution from its 1899 founding through its twentieth-century development; and Elizabethtown, published in the *Arcadia Publishing Images of America Series in 2015*, a pictorial history of the borough. His most recent book, *Sarah Tyson Rorer: The Pure Food Movement and Mount Gretna's Rorer Hall of Cookery*, published in 2026 by the Mount Gretna Area Historical Society and the Lebanon County Historical Society, extends his commitment to regional public history into the history of food reform and the distinctive cultural landscape of the Mount Gretna Pennsylvania Chautauqua community. He has also authored two Mennonite institutional histories for Tabor Community Services in Lancaster: *Make Yourself at Home: Tabor Community Services: Housing and Financial Counseling; Forty Years of Rebuilding Lives and Community, 1968–2008* (2009) and its tenth-anniversary addendum, *Welcome Home: Fifty Years of Tabor Community Services* (2018).

Benowitz has authored and edited monographs published by the National Collegiate Honors Council on teaching honors students through the Place as Text® and City as Text® pedagogies of community engagement, including his chapter "Transforming Community

Based Learning Through City As Text" in *Place, Text, Community: City As Text in the Twentieth Century*, published by the University of Nebraska–Lincoln and the National Collegiate Honors Council in 2021. His most recent contribution to this body of work is his role as editor of the NCHC Celebratory Monograph – *Festschrift: The 50th Anniversary of Place as Text*, published in 2026, in which he also authored the chapter "Les Trois Flaneuses: The Progenitrices of Place as Text® and City as Text®," a scholarly account of the intellectual origins and founding figures of the pedagogical tradition he has practiced and advanced across three decades. A 2024 article in Honors in Practice, "Teaching Honors Leadership Courses with Relevance," further extends this body of work on pedagogical innovation in honors education. These publications, grounded in his three decades of teaching community-based learning courses in the Elizabethtown College Honors Program, document an approach to undergraduate education connecting classroom learning to the historical and civic dimensions of the communities surrounding educational institutions. He serves on national committees of the National Collegiate Honors Council concerned with teaching, advising, and the development of honors education. His reflections on vocation and calling appear in the essay "Work and Hope," published in *Voices of Vocation: Stories of Purposeful Life Work in Teaching, Mentoring, and Leading* (Elizabethtown College, 2017).

His work in the Office of Prestigious Scholarships and Fellowships, which he directs, has supported Elizabethtown College students in pursuing nationally competitive scholarships including the Rhodes, Goldwater, Fulbright, and Gilman programs. He serves on national committees of the National Association of Fellowship Advisors and has presented scholarship on fellowship advising at the association's national conferences.

His teaching reflects the full breadth of his scholarly interests and ranges across twentieth-century American political history, with particular emphasis on presidential history and the Roosevelt, Kennedy, and Johnson administrations; American domestic and foreign policy since 1928; and American historical biography. His courses also engage American culture, Americana, and American studies; local and regional history, public history, and historic preservation; and the impact of religion on American history, culture, and politics. He teaches as well on the intersections of French and American history and on the enduring influence of French culture on the founding and development of the United States. This range of teaching is complemented by community-engaged honors seminars in which students conduct original historical research in the communities surrounding the college.

Benowitz received the Peace Prize from the Rockland Fellowship of Reconciliation in the spring of 1987, a recognition from within the same organizational tradition the biography identifies as central to the peace church civil rights network shaping Elizabethtown College's institutional character. The Rockland FOR award placed him, at the outset of his academic career, in the living fellowship of the tradition whose history this biography reconstructs. The Historic Preservation Trust of Lancaster County later presented him with the Smedley Award, given to an educator who has shown extraordinary support for historic preservation in Lancaster County. He has been active in the Historic Harrisburg Association, the Historic Preservation Trust of Lancaster County, the Marietta Restoration Associates, the Lancaster Historical Society, the Lebanon County Historical Society, the Mount Gretna Area Historical Society, and the Pennsylvania Chautauqua. He authored a regular column on regional history in the *Elizabethtown Advocate* and has contributed to numerous local history publications, documentary films, and public history programs throughout the south-central Pennsylvania region.

In addition to this biography and the companion article forthcoming in the *Journal of the Lancaster County Historical Society*, Benowitz produced, directed, wrote, edited, and designed the documentary film *The Prospect for Freedom: W. Miller Barbour's Human Rights Journey*, released in 2025. The film traces Barbour's life from his Middletown, Pennsylvania origins through his pioneering career as an Urban

League leader in Denver and Los Angeles, documenting his foundational contributions to the human rights movement in the decades preceding the canonical civil rights era. The documentary has been screened publicly at multiple venues throughout 2025 and 2026, with screenings sponsored and hosted by the Governor's Advisory Commission on African American Affairs in the Office of Governor Josh Shapiro, the Greater Harrisburg Area NAACP, the Popel Shaw Center for Race and Ethnicity at Dickinson College, and the Pennsylvania Chautauqua. The film has been named an official selection at the Hollywood International Indie Film Festival, scheduled for December 2026.

William Wilbur Miller Barbour: A Faith Full Witness for Human Rights is Benowitz's most sustained contribution to the scholarship of the American civil rights movement, and it represents the convergence of his scholarly interests in Anabaptist-Pietist history, the history of Elizabethtown College, and the history of American civil rights activism in the Long Civil Rights Movement period.

INDEX

www.ingramcontent.com/pod-product-compliance
Lightning Source LLC
Chambersburg PA
CBHW070851160726
48004CB00003B/1016